The Bible and the Ballot Box

The Bible and the Ballot Box

Religion and Politics in the 1988 Election

EDITED BY
James L. Guth
and John C. Green

BBfuL

Westview Press

BOULDER · SAN FRANCISCO · OXFORD

081417

0250194

Copyright © 1991 by Westview Press, Inc.

Published in 1991 in the United States of America by Westview Press, Inc., 5500 Central Avenue, Boulder, Colorado 80301, and in the United Kingdom by Westview Press, 36 Lonsdale Road, Summertown, Oxford OX2 7EW

The Bible and the ballot box : religion and politics in the 1988 election / edited by James L. Guth and John C. Green.
    p. cm.
  Includes bibliographical references and index.
  ISBN 0-8133-8183-5
  1. Religion and politics—United States. 2. Presidents—United States—Election—1988. 3. United States—Congress—Elections, 1988. 4. United States—Religion—1960–   . I. Guth, James L. II. Green, John Clifford, 1953–   .
  BL2525.B53   1991
  324.973′0927—dc20

91-21681
CIP

Printed and bound in the United States of America

∞ The paper used in this publication meets the requirements of the American National Standard for Permanence of Paper for Printed Library Materials Z39.48-1984.

10   9   8   7   6   5   4   3   2   1

Dedicated to

Cydelle Guth and Lynn Green

Contents

viii

Tables

Preface

Just three decades ago, the influence of religion in American politics seemed to be declining. After all, the first Roman Catholic had been elected to the White House, ecumenical unity was the watchword of the religious establishment, and science and technology dominated national thinking. Indeed, few observers in 1961 expected the dramatic events that were about to unfold: the involvement of black and white churches in the civil rights and anti-war movements, the Vatican II reforms in the Catholic Church, the rise of the Christian Right, and, eventually, a presidential campaign in which Baptist ministers mounted serious nomination campaigns in both major political parties.

Perhaps these events should not have been entirely unexpected. At a practical level, there was plenty of evidence that religious values, organizations, and identifications remained vital, despite conventional wisdom to the contrary. And at the level of theory, the secularizing tendencies of modern society were neither as strong nor as pervasive as generally assumed. Indeed, the connections between religion and politics were still important, although their character had changed along with American society. This lack of foresight prompts two related questions: first, what is the relationship between religion and politics at present, and second, how will this relationship develop in the future?

To answer these questions and many more besides, we have assembled this collection of original research on religion and politics in the 1988 campaign. These essays range from observations on the Jackson and Robertson campaigns (Part 1) and descriptions of the activities of American religious leaders (Part 2) to surveys of political activists (Part 3) and voters (Part 4). In Part 5 we attempt to outline the general relationship between religion and politics in America, drawing on the evidence presented in the previous chapters. We hope that these efforts, however limited, will help contemporary observers better anticipate the future.

A collection of this kind requires the assistance of many people. First, we would like to express our gratitude to all the contributing authors for their cooperation and good will. Much of the data presented here came from surveys undertaken by the authors themselves, and we are pleased they chose to present their work in this forum. Other data came from surveys made available through the Inter-University Consortium for Political and Social Research, including the 1988 American National Election Study and the Super Tuesday Survey, the ABC News 1988 General Election Exit Poll, the CBS/*New York Times* 1988 General Election Poll, and the *Times Mirror* 1987 Study of the American Electorate. We are pleased to acknowledge this assistance on behalf of the relevant authors. The American Political Science Association and the Lilly Endowment provided financial assistance for some of the research presented here. The Bliss Institute at the University of Akron and Furman University provided material assistance for the project itself.

Amy Eisenberg and the staff of Westview Press provided invaluable advice and assistance throughout the project, and Claude Stulting carefully edited the entire manuscript. We owe a very special thanks to Kimberly Haverkamp of the Bliss Institute, who mastered both the intricacies of word processors and the idiosyncrasies of college professors with great skill and good cheer. And to our spouses, to whom this volume is dedicated, we owe debts far too great for words.

James L. Guth
John C. Green

About the Contributors

Tod A. Baker, professor of political science at The Citadel, has written on state party activists, with an emphasis on the Christian Right. He is coeditor of *Political Parties in the Southern States* (1990).

Cleveland R. Fraser, associate professor of political science at Furman University, is interested in American foreign policy and comparative politics. He has written most recently on the foreign policy views of campaign contributors.

John C. Green, director of the Ray C. Bliss Institute of Applied Politics and associate professor of political science at the University of Akron, has written on campaign finance and religion and politics. Most recently he has studied the 1988 Robertson campaign.

James L. Guth, professor and chair of the political science department at Furman University, has published on interest groups, campaign finance, and religion and politics. He is best known for his research on the Southern Baptist clergy.

Anne M. Hallum, assistant professor of political science at Stetson University, has written on the politics of the Presbyterian Church and American religious groups in Central America.

Mary T. Hanna, the Miles C. Moore Professor of Politics at Whitman College, has published on ethnic and religious influences in American politics and is author of *Catholics and American Politics* (1979).

Allen D. Hertzke, assistant director of the Carl Albert Center and assistant professor of political science at the University of Oklahoma, is author of *Representing God in Washington* (1988) and is writing a book on the Jackson and Robertson campaigns.

Lyman A. Kellstedt, professor of political science at Wheaton College (Wheaton, IL), has written on evangelical Protestants in the mass public, including measurement issues and partisan realignment.

Paul M. Kellstedt is currently a Ph.D. student in political science at the University of Iowa. His research interests include the linkages between public opinion, government decisions, and social outcomes as well as religion and politics.

Henry C. Kenski, associate professor of political science and communication at the University of Arizona, has published on American Roman Catholic voters. He is the coauthor of *Attack Politics: Strategy and Defense* (1990).

Carl Lieberman, associate professor of political science at the University of Akron, has recently studied Jewish members of Congress and written on presidential programs and policy making.

William Lockwood holds a Ph.D. in sociology and is currently a computer analyst in the Department of Political Science at the University of Arizona. He is coauthor of several articles on Roman Catholics' political behavior.

Laurence W. Moreland, professor of political science at The Citadel, has participated in a long-term study of state party activists, with emphasis on the role of ideology in party coalitions. He is coeditor of *Political Parties in the Southern States* (1990).

Margaret M. Poloma, professor of sociology at the University of Akron, has done work on charismatic Christians and the Assemblies of God. Her most recent book is *Assemblies of God at the Crossroads* (1988).

Lee Sigelman, dean of the faculty of social and behavioral sciences and professor of political science at the University of Arizona, has published extensively on a wide variety of subjects in many different forums. He is coeditor of *Nominating the President* (1991).

Corwin E. Smidt, professor of political science at Calvin College, has published on the voting behavior of evangelical Protestants and is editor of *Contemporary Evangelical Political Involvement* (1989).

Robert P. Steed, professor of political science at The Citadel, has done research on state party activists, with an emphasis on change in party composition. He is coeditor of *Political Parties in the Southern States* (1990).

Clyde Wilcox, assistant professor of political science at Georgetown University, has published on religion and politics. He is the author of *God's Warriors: The Christian Right in Twentieth-Century America* (forthcoming).

PART ONE

Religion in the 1988 Presidential Campaign

Harvest of Discontent: Religion and Populism in the 1988 Presidential Campaign

Allen D. Hertzke

Nothing quite compares to the spectacle of an American presidential campaign. Marathon in length, appalling in expense, captivating in the drama of careers made or lost, the presidential quest is deeply embedded in our national psyche. Political lore is rich with stories of missteps and comebacks, turning points and defining moments. The glamour and excitement, moreover, unleash pent-up energies and channel the frustrations of constituencies galvanized by particular candidates. Stung by the political bug, novices mobilized in one presidential campaign often remain to form the party cadre in the future: nomination and battles often open cleavages within party coalitions that affect future campaigns (Kessel 1988).

Add a generous dose of religion to this already heady mixture and you have a potent blend indeed, as American history shows. From William Jennings Bryan's evangelical crusade in 1896 to Catholic John Kennedy's quest in 1960, religious cross-currents have profoundly influenced past campaigns. But while the Protestant/Catholic divide shaped the contours of past episodes, new forces were afoot in 1988. The Reverend Jesse Jackson, mobilizing a network of black congregations and ministers, and capitalizing on black angst and pride, mounted a serious and ongoing challenge to the Democratic establishment. Pat Robertson, exploiting the parachurch network of religious broadcasting and galvanizing charismatic evangelicals, brought moral conservatives into a direct clash with Republican regulars in a battle that continues. These forces seem, at first glance, confusing and contradictory. How can one make sense of the fact that the two ministers were on extreme ends of the political spectrum, Jackson far left, Robertson far right? What general conclusions can be drawn about religious political mobilization in such different contexts as black churches and white charismatic congregations?

I suggest that the radical nature of the Jackson and Robertson campaigns provides the very clue to understanding them. Radical ideas imply that problems are fundamental and thus unsolvable through mere incremental tinkering. Drawing upon the prophetic biblical tradition, Jackson and Robertson argued that the nation was faced with fundamental problems requiring a profound reordering of thinking and action. Their messages resonated with followers who experienced deep discontent with the state of things. Moreover, there was a common, "populist" analysis of the origin of those problems; both Jackson and Robertson viewed elites as hostile to or oppressive of their "people" (Hertzke 1990c). Thus, not only did these campaigns exemplify the scope and limits of religious political mobilization, but they also served as a barometer of increasing populist pressures in American society that had simmered for a decade or more.[1]

The Seeds of Discontent

Race and religion have helped to define party politics in much of American history. Prior to 1960, for example, white southerners voted solidly Democratic, a legacy of reaction against the party of Lincoln, while northerners commonly split along Protestant (Republican) versus Catholic (Democratic) lines. Those blacks in the North who could vote tended to be Democrats because of Franklin Roosevelt. The Kennedy-Johnson era altered these relationships and thus stands as a major hinge of change in American politics (Ladd and Hadley 1975). First, Kennedy's adroit handling of the religious issue in the 1960 campaign, along with the modernization of the Catholic Church through Vatican II, put to rest the deep Protestant/Catholic divide and muted its effect on partisan loyalties. Second, the civil rights revolution, supported by Kennedy and embraced by Lyndon Johnson, introduced new, race-based partisan cleavages. Newly enfranchised southern blacks joined northern black voters in becoming the most loyal constituency in the Democratic party. Republicans, meanwhile, were able to make inroads among southern white Democrats disaffected by their party's increasing tie to black aspirations. So central is race, indeed, that some scholars have attributed southern voting realignment almost exclusively to it (Black and Black 1987).

But race is not the whole story. The association of the Democrats with the counter-culture of the 1960s also created a Republican opportunity to appeal to evangelical Protestants and culturally-conservative Catholics throughout the nation. At the height of the counter-culture, while the mass media highlighted the sexual revolution, women's liberation, and gay liberation, a largely unnoticed religious movement was gaining strength. Evangelical churches were growing, and a charismatic movement blossomed across the religious landscape. A new cultural divide was emerging, at least in white America, between moral and religious traditionalists and those turned off by pietist faith (Wuthnow 1988). Thus, while one part of the nation rushed headlong into the modern age, the other part clung to the Rock of Ages. But most of the American public was then, as now, characterized by remarkably durable and orthodox religious values (Gallup 1985). As liberalism became associated with alternative lifestyles, loose morality, and hostility to religion, Republican campaign consultants made hay.

Thus were the seeds of Republican presidential hegemony planted in the soil of race and religion. By the time George Bush runs for re-election in 1992, Republicans will have controlled the White House for 20 out of 24 years, interrupted only by the Carter interregnum. In this light the election of Jimmy Carter, a "born-again" Christian, is of critical importance. Carter's nomination created an instant media fascination with his religion, and journalists made pilgrimages to Plains, Georgia, to discover what a "born-again" person was like. A highly-publicized Gallup survey revealed that Carter's born-again experience was shared by an astonishing 34% of the total adult population, and George Gallup, Jr. proclaimed 1976 the "year of the evangelical" (Gallup 1985). Thus, the last Democrat elected to the highest office did so by appealing to a greater number of theologically-traditional white Protestants than any national Democrat since. Notably, Carter was supported by *both* Jesse Jackson and Pat Robertson, a fact more startling now than it appeared then.

But many conservative evangelicals felt betrayed by Carter's too-liberal White House, and Ronald Reagan skillfully cast his rhetorical net for disaffected Democrats of all stripes -- "born-again" voters, conservative Catholics, pro-life activists -- by his appeal to "traditional values" in 1980 and 1984. Reagan's strategists also continued to promote racial polarization in the South, which, coupled with his supply-side attack on positive government, alienated many black voters.

The stage was being set for the church-based politics of discontent in 1988. Among Democratic groups, blacks suffered uniquely from economic and social tides of the 1980s. Blacks were particularly ill-positioned to benefit from Reagan's supply-side revolution, the rise of the service economy, and the transformation of the global marketplace. Many black workers, dependent upon inner-city industrial jobs and with little capital to cushion them, saw their economic position stagnate during the "go-go" years on Wall Street. This economic plight deepened the cultural crisis of out-of-wedlock pregnancies, inner-city violence, drug abuse, and lagging educational attainment, which left many young blacks especially vulnerable and alienated. Disturbing trends were noted. Nearly 60% of all black children were born out of wedlock, and 72% of them would live in a household that received welfare at some time before they were 18. College attendance by black students actually dropped in the 1980s, after peaking in 1975, and young black men were more likely to be incarcerated or on parole than in college. A sense of crisis grew in the black community, and intense debate occurred over the "black underclass," the "vanishing black male," and the weakening black family.[2] In response, the Reagan Administration attacked affirmative action. Thus, while many Democratic constituencies were unhappy with Reagan, blacks were by far the most deeply discontented.

On the Republican side, business interests got the most tangible policy benefits from the Reagan Revolution -- tax cuts and deregulation. Morally-conservative evangelicals got mostly rhetorical support and won few tangible victories: abortions continued, pornography survived, and public schools remained generally hostile to traditional faith (Hertzke 1990b). Ironically, the deregulatory emphasis in the 1980s may have even led to the kind of excesses in the marketplace that traditional Christians find so disturbing, such as increased violence and commercial exploitation on children's television (DeMoss 1990). Thus, while blacks expressed the greatest discontent in the Democratic coalition, white conservative Christians were the most angry among the Republicans. In a sense, then, while the soil was being prepared for decades, the seeds of the Jackson and Robertson crusades were planted in the Reagan era, one which represented a profound threat to blacks and a promise unfulfilled for white evangelicals. Jackson and Robertson harvested that discontent by leading church-based crusades infused with religious imagery (Hertzke 1990c).

What unites these two different movements is a populist critique of society. Populism is a term evocative of a rich legacy in nineteenth century America, but it enjoys currency in contemporary political parlance as well. In its broad, generic meaning, populism is comprised of the following characteristics: mass-movement politics based on the consciousness that elites are not responsive to the popular will, rhetorical celebration of the "people" whose virtues contrast with the exploitative greed or libertine immorality of the powerful, an embrace of politics as a means of asserting or recapturing a treasured way of life, and an emphasis on charismatic leadership. In a narrower sense, populism is used by political analysts to describe a distinct ideological position that combines economic progressivism and social conservatism. Both definitions are useful; the first describes a style of politics while the latter helps to illustrate the ideological strands that we see in the Robertson and Jackson campaigns. The elements of populist style can be found in each: the moralist challenge to smug complacency, the emphasis on crisis and charisma, the celebration of common people, the castigation of elites, and the polarized view of society. In Jackson, this populism takes the form of prophetic outrage at the economic exploitation of the poor by the rich; in Robertson, it is vented against cultural elites who undermine traditional moral values. A key difference between Jackson and Robertson lies in the perception of which elites are most responsible for the state of society. Jackson inveighs against the heirs of the robber barons: multinational corporations that export jobs, chic investment bankers, wealthy exploiters of laboring classes, and Republican plunderers of government. Robertson, in contrast, chastises the "new class" of secular leaders in education, entertainment, and the mass media, along with snooty artists, ACLU attorneys, government bureaucrats, and well-connected feminists bent on destroying the family. Each analysis was rooted in perceived sources of discontent among followers: an economic crisis in the black community, the cultural threat of secular domination for conservative Christians.

In 1988 two distinct "communities of discontent" were ripe for political mobilization. Jesse Jackson had already tested the waters in 1984 and was poised to strengthen his impact. And Pat Robertson, while politically untested, had cultivated a fervent following of viewers of his religious broadcasts. Thus each political party experienced the insurgency of a minister who exploited church networks and prophetic religious appeals for political gain. Though neither Jesse Jackson nor Pat Robertson won nomination, their crusades brought to the surface elements of discontent that will continue to influence party politics in the future. State by state battles continue between Robertson followers and Republican regulars, for example, while Jackson and his people remain players in Democratic politics. But an important, and largely unappreciated, part of the story is the role of churches in providing strategic resources for their campaigns.

Churches as Strategic Campaign Resources

The nature of party politics facilitated the infusion of church-based populism. American political parties, unlike others around the world, are unique in choosing presidential candidates through a relatively open process of electoral appeals to average citizens, not just party elites. Indeed, delegates to national nominating conventions function largely as bound agents of voters, and the convention itself resembles a coronation that ratifies the decisions of a mass electorate. Thus vast sums of money must be raised quickly, thousands of volunteers enlisted, and organizations built in 50 states -- all aimed at reaching millions of voters in a crazy quilt system of state primaries and caucuses. This "plebiscitary" system puts a premium on such strategic political resources as money and media exposure, especially since many voters get their cues from television rather than from the community contexts of family, village, and parish that operated in the past (Epstein 1986).

Moreover, the enormous resources it takes to mount a presidential campaign can evaporate quickly as donors and activists abandon perceived losers to board the front-runner's bandwagon. Strategic politicians -- big contributors, activists, interest group representatives, party leaders, and PAC directors -- do not back unconventional candidates who have little chance for electoral success (Jacobson and Kernell 1983). Jackson and Robertson were unique among the 1988 candidates because they could rely on sources of support, notably church networks and charismatic appeal, that were relatively independent of these strategic calculations.

More importantly, because American political parties are relatively porous, newcomers can potentially take over precincts, win delegates, bargain with old hands, and shape the party platform. That potential is often not realized because campaigning is hard and expensive without cohesive communities (Fenno 1978:234-235). Certain segments of religious America, however, run counter to depictions of America as a mass society of relatively unconnected individuals and thus offer collective bases for political mobilization. Different though they are in a number of respects, black congregations and charismatic churches share one thing in common: they are profoundly central to the life of their members. When ministers speak, parishioners listen; when the church makes demands, members respond. For the black church this centrality has roots in the legacy of slavery and segregation (Lincoln and Mamiya 1990). For the Pentecostal and charismatic churches, the commitment is often explained by psychological forces (Kelley 1972) and the dislocations of modernity (Poloma 1989). Add to these factors a sense of crisis and leaders who understand the potential, and populist mobilization is ripe.

What we learned in 1988 is that under certain circumstances churches are tempting sources of political resources -- money, forums, volunteer networks, a leadership cadre. This was certainly as true of tightly knit black congregations which served as the centerpiece of Jackson's daily appearances on the campaign trail as it was of the large charismatic congregations that Robertson forces captured through organizing efforts. But it was also true, perhaps in a less dramatic way, of Michael Dukakis' ethnic appeal to Greek-Americans, in which ties to Greek Orthodox churches and prelates proved valuable for fund raising and mobilization. Other candidates, too, sensed the possibilities of church networks and made attempts to capitalize on them. George Bush's organization employed a strategy of co-opting the evangelical vote with direct appeals to evangelical leaders and followers long before Robertson announced his bid. Jack Kemp aired ads on Christian radio stations, Paul Simon (an active Lutheran layman) spoke frequently at congregations, and Bob Dole's organization trumpeted Elizabeth Dole's evangelical roots. Strikingly, seasoned political operatives began speaking of churches in language reminiscent of the way their predecessors spoke of precincts. A Bush lieutenant referred to "Robertson churches," "Dole churches," and "Bush churches." A Dukakis aide lamented the way Jackson's churches effectively operated as precinct organizations in caucus states, "shutting us out" of the process.

Why this phenomenon? I suggest that candidates were responding to the exigencies of campaigning in a relatively individualistic cultural context, one bereft of the collective institutions that once brought people together. Churches, especially tightly knit ones, stand in marked and often lonely contrast to the atomizing tendencies in modern society. Thus, in spite of weighty church-state baggage, political mobilization through congregations is attractive. Still, most candidates are not very successful in such efforts. Jackson and Robertson harvested church-based resources, however, because they arose from, and made appeals to, distinctive religious communities where discontent was simmering.

The Reverend Jesse Jackson and the Black Church

Despite considerable social and religious diversity, blacks share a common defining experience in the legacies of slavery and discrimination. To be black in the United States was, and still largely is, to be different, "other," to live what Du Bois called the dual identity, black and American (Du Bois 1903). In this context one of the ironic legacies of slavery and Jim Crow is that black churches emerged in the nineteenth century as the primary institutions owned and operated by the blacks themselves. Churches became the haven where black folk could "be themselves," and the congregation served numerous community functions -- a place to socialize, celebrate, mourn, and later to plan political marches and boycotts. Significantly, the black minister was the one community leader independent of the white power structure.

Thus, political mobilization through black churches does not carry the divisive baggage it does in other, predominately white congregations. To be sure, prior to the civil rights revolution the black churches were cautious, even conservative, as ministers sought to protect and steward the unique position of the church in the community (Fowler 1985). But once the potential for political mobilization was realized in the 1960s -- through such organizations as the Southern Christian Leadership Conference -- there was no turning back. Gifted and ambitious young men like Jesse Jackson would seek the ministry knowing it offered enormous influence in the black community, both spiritually and politically. And in spite of dramatic social and political changes in the past three decades, the church retains its distinctive role. Even with the rise in numbers of black elected officials and professionals, black ministers are still enormously influential; they are real leaders with loyal followers. As one upscale, Vassar-educated, black state Senator put it, "When the preacher says give, I open up my purse."

Although there is disagreement about the relative importance of religion versus racial solidarity in the Jackson campaign (Colton 1989), the strategic value of the black church should not be questioned. Reverend Jackson himself has written and spoken extensively about the central link between his religious heritage and political philosophy (Jackson 1987), and he freely acknowledges that the black churches and ministers served as the key strategic resources in his presidential campaigns. Indeed, when Jackson ran in 1984 he quipped that while Mondale might have big labor, he had "Big Church" (Faw and Skelton 1986:35). Journalists and scholars who followed the campaign document the accuracy of that perception (Reed 1986; Barker 1988; Manning 1985).

To understand the role of churches in the Jackson movement, it is necessary to trace the evolution of Reverend Jackson's leadership among African-Americans. Born to an unwed teenage mother in 1941, Jackson struggled with a combination of extraordinary gifts and lack of recognition; erstwhile psycho-biographers have a field day writing of this "bastard son" whose inspirational refrain "I am somebody" speaks volumes (Sheehy 1988). Whatever its psychological sources, Jackson's burning ambition and brashness are legend (Reynolds 1985). As a college student in the early 1960s he was an effective and audacious organizer, but confidants of Martin Luther King saw Jackson as self-serving, and King himself chided the young upstart more than once (Garrow 1986).

Jackson chose the path of his hero and entered the ministry, striving to become one of the inner circle around King. But his behavior immediately following King's assassination led to deep enmity for him among other civil rights leaders. The infamous incidents are well known. Shortly after King was shot, Jackson was on the networks claiming to have cradled the dying man in his arms, though it was Abernathy who held King. Jackson also appeared at a Chicago city council meeting wearing a turtleneck sweater said to be smeared with King's blood. Jackson's exhibition of raw ambition, plus the desire of the press to anoint a successor, made him an instant celebrity at age 27. He graced the cover of *Time*, was proclaimed King's heir apparent by *Playboy*, and appeared frequently on network television. With a certain biblical logic, the press repeated the story that Jackson was the last man to speak to King before he died.

This notoriety only served to deepen the antipathy toward Jackson among King's inner circle. But if Jackson was suspect among some veterans of the civil rights struggle, he was also held in contempt by some leftist black scholars as the reincarnation of Booker T. Washington, selling self-help and bourgeois values to young blacks in his Operation Push, or worse, as a huckster for black capitalists (Manning 1985). That Jackson would ultimately mount a credible presidential campaign was laughable to some and disturbing to others. But Jackson understood, perhaps better than some black leaders and scholars, the potent force that the black church continued to represent. He exploited that force to the fullest, speaking to the black masses with a prophetic biblical imagery that resonates with the experience and heritage of African-Americans.

Thus, when Jackson began seriously contemplating a run for the presidency in 1983, the black church figured heavily in his ultimate decision to run, his early strategy, and his ongoing campaign operation. "The word went out . . . that 40,000 black churches could raise $250 each for what some Jackson aides insisted could be a campaign war chest of $10 million" (Faw and Skelton 1986:30). Jackson spoke in churches daily, raised money in them, and developed a cadre of local and state leaders among the activist clergy. But because Jackson was still suspect, and because his campaign was viewed as quixotic and possibly hurtful for Democratic chances against Reagan, a number of prominent blacks did not endorse his bid in 1984. Jackson, in response, used church networks to circumvent established black elected leaders, many of whom supported Mondale (Reed 1986). His charismatic campaign eventually captured the fascination of the media and sparked a growing popularity among the black masses.

This background is crucial for understanding the role of churches in 1988. Between his dramatic speech at the 1984 Democratic convention and the 1988 presidential race, Jackson ran what was effectively a perpetual campaign. The peripatetic minister seemed to show up everywhere and keep in the news. But most important, he solidified his black support. And he did so not just through political efforts, but in his ministerial role as well. He was there in 1986 to deliver the eulogies for athletes Len Bias and Don Rogers, vintage Jackson in their biblical cadences of solace for the family and prophetic call for a war on the scourge of drugs that killed them. We hear the minister in his solace for the family:

> I know that your hearts are heavy today. But I want to share with you this afternoon, as a friend and minister of the Gospel, to remind you that if you will but put your trust in God, even in your darkest hour, he is able to sustain you. . . . Even in the midst of tragedy, I am sharing with you in the spirit of Christian joy and celebration to remind you that for the Christian the tragedy of death has already been conquered by Christ's triumph over death. We serve a mighty, merciful, and loving God, and I know today that Don is at peace, having worked and served his purpose here on earth (Jackson 1987:174).

But we also hear the prophet:

> The KKK . . . and the rope have never killed as many of our young people as the pusher of dope. Pushers are terrorists and death messengers. . . . Drugs are the hound of hell for this generation. . . . When drugs attack, our minds go, our morals go, our morale goes, and pretty soon the hound of hell takes our liberties and our life. . . . The transmitters of our culture -- our artists, athletes, television, radio, video, and music are glorifying and adding glitter to the poison, which is making it socially acceptable as entertainment, a personal right and privilege. . . . Today we declare a state of emergency. . . . The living of our generation have been summoned to declare a war on a plague (Jackson 1987:175-176).

By 1988 Jackson was the undisputed leader of black America. As one scholar and activist put it, "He just dominates black politics now."

Thus, the black elite flocked to Jackson's second presidential bid, if not out of love for Jesse, then out of necessity to support the most popular figure in black America. The consequence: his monolithic support among black voters in 1988, combined with a respectable 12% of the white vote, brought him nearly seven million votes, victories in 13 primaries or first round caucuses, 1,200 delegates to the Democratic Convention, and a negotiating position within the Democratic Party (Nelson 1989).

The racial solidarity manifest in 1988 led some to conclude that religion or churches played no independent role in the Jackson campaign (*New York Times* 1988). But it is a mistake to separate the religious from the political in the black community, because such a separation discounts the unique historic role of the black minister as both spiritual and political leader (see Chapter 9). In interviews with campaign staff and delegates, it became clear that, as one person put it, "the ministers were in charge." White secular supporters of Jackson, in fact, remarked frequently about this religious character. Said a white liberal mayor in California, "I wasn't used to starting meetings with a prayer, but all the Jackson strategy meetings were like that." Similarly, a white advance man for Jackson quipped that if asked what church he belonged to he would say "AME [African Methodist Episcopal] because that's the church I've been in the most this past year." He also argued that churches were the critical component of advance planning for Jackson's visits. "There would be competition between ministers as to who would have his church featured by the Jackson visit, and then the pressure was on to generate the crowd." Given the network of black churches and ministers, there was "no problem in advance work getting a crowd . . . The minister is out to prove himself as an organizer." National convention delegates also confirmed the centrality of the black churches as strategic resources. They noted speeches by Jackson in their churches, solicitation of volunteers and funds, regional ministerial alliance strategy meetings, and the like.

Racial pride may have been Jackson's primary appeal, but the churches were his organization base and biblical cadences his rhetorical tool in galvanizing supporters. Jerry Austin, Jackson's campaign manager, noted that because of Jackson's magnetism and the natural organizational network of churches, the critical campaign need was money for air fare. "I concluded that the most important thing the campaign had to do was raise enough money to keep Jesse in the air." And the campaign raised money in churches, a strategy which was probably illegal under IRS rules, but was also terribly effective. As one reporter observed, an appeal would go out during the church service, and the plate would be passed or members would come forward with their contributions -- often to provide Jackson's fare to the next stop (Sheehy 1988). As Jackson's campaign progressed, money began to flow in from more conventional, liberal direct mail sources, but the early church-based resources were critical.

A fascinating pattern emerged: the "church as precinct." As one exasperated Dukakis organizer put it, "The parish is an ideal unit for organization, it's the same as a precinct. They [the Jackson organizers] would have a pre-caucus coffee at the neighborhood church . . . Then they would bring a bus and the Shepherd [the minister] would lead his flock to vote." This organizational structure was particularly effective in the Michigan caucuses because the confusing process put a premium on organization -- getting one's supporters to the right caucus site. But the power of the church networks was also seen elsewhere. "In Ohio we wanted to do outreach [for Dukakis] but the churches endorsed Jackson early. They shut us out."

Perhaps the unique feature of Jackson's campaign was the forums, which were like nothing we have seen in the contemporary era. They were filled with music, amens, and talk of Jesus. The gospel choirs, as one insider put it, "were a must." Indeed, the fact that Jackson was notoriously and egregiously late on campaign stops necessitated a means to keep exasperated followers from going home. That was no problem, since the campaign stops resembled extended church services, with the best music of the 1988 season, fiery sermons, and strategy planning all in one.

Some black scholars viewed the religious dimension of Jackson's crusades positively, arguing that the black church, as an authentic community institution, embodied the progressive and prophetic tradition among African-Americans (West 1982). The Jackson campaign was also analyzed as a means of increasing the leverage of blacks in the Democratic party (Walters 1988), and some suggested favorably that Jackson was adopted by the left and transformed by it (Manning 1985). He grew in this analysis because he shed his previous baggage to rally disparate progressive forces -- minorities, feminists, gays, socialists -- to make a forceful attack on Reaganism. Other scholars, however, criticized the reintroduction of religious charisma as retrogressive, drawing black politics away from more tangible gains won by the mundane but effective power of black elected officials. Indeed, Adolph Reed (1986) argued that Jackson wrapped himself in the mantle of civil rights and religion as a way to stifle dissent. Religious charisma, Reed argued, is anti-democratic and mirrors the authoritarian nature of many black churches. Jackson's evangelical style of campaigning, Reed contended, celebrated form without substance, protest without strategic gains, a vent for discontent without a means of ameliorating that discontent.

Jackson did champion the agenda of the left -- feminism, gay rights, the environment, third world advocacy, and the like. But his embrace of the Palestinian cause in 1988 fostered a particularly fascinating new political dynamic. Jackson was the choice of the growing Arab-American community in such strategic cities as Detroit, where an estimated 250,000 Americans of Arab descent reside. Preliminary evidence suggests that his smashing victory in Michigan reflected a growing alliance between blacks and Arab-Americans -- an alliance of black church and mosque. Jackson was free to develop this relationship because he had written off the Jewish vote, a fact that clearly hurt him later in the New York primary, when Mayor Koch said Jews would be "crazy" to vote for him. The solidifying alliance between blacks and Arab-Americans was evident at the Democratic National Convention. For the first time in American politics, Arab-Americans were given a highly visible national forum to air their concerns. Dr. James Zogby, close adviser to Jackson, orchestrated the debate over a proposed Palestinian plank at the convention, an unprecedented effort that disturbed Jewish leaders. While Zogby and Jackson ultimately agreed not to bring the issue to a vote, the development spotlighted the heightening tensions between blacks and Jews.

The Jackson campaign illustrates how important the black constituency, and by extension the black church, is to the American left. But there are inherent tensions. Many black ministers are socially conservative, and the message in black churches is not always sympathetic to the left's agenda on the family, gay rights, abortion, and art. As one black Democratic National Committee woman put it, "You won't find a more conservative lot on social issues than black ministers. They want me home making babies." Jackson was able to negotiate this delicate problem by a combination of racial pride, religious identification, and retention of some social conservatism (his anti-drug message). But it is one of the ironies of the presidential campaign that both Jackson and Robertson, at times, sounded remarkably similar in their calls for sexual responsibility, discipline and hard work in the schools, and temperance on drugs and alcohol. Indeed, Jackson insiders recounted how the puritanical Jackson did not like to see booze on the press bus. For the left, however, such oddities were irrelevant because Jackson alone championed their broader agenda.

Jackson clearly kept Dukakis off balance with implied threats to disrupt the convention, and he was thus able to extract concessions. The maladroit handling of Jackson by Dukakis is, of course, part of a larger pattern of what is now a legendary case of poor campaign planning. State Democratic pros spoke contemptuously of "the amateur hour" in the Dukakis general election operation. But the case of Jackson and Dukakis also illustrates the cultural gulf that separated the two politicians and many of their followers. Because Jackson monopolized the black vote, Dukakis did not have to make more than token appeals in the black community during the primaries. Conceding the black vote to Jackson was a pragmatic move, but it left Dukakis without a means of appealing to blacks independent of Jackson. Whereas Bush could appeal to evangelicals independent of Robertson, Dukakis had to deal with Jesse, something he was uniquely ill-equipped to do. Jackson was insulted not to have received the courtesy of learning from Dukakis of the selection of Lloyd Bentsen as his running mate. Then in tense negotiations at the Democratic convention, Dukakis, trying to be conciliatory, used the metaphor of the nominee as "quarterback," unaware that one of Jackson's formative experiences in college was learning that "blacks can't be quarterbacks" (Reynolds 1985). Dukakis finally agreed to provide Jackson a campaign plane to support the ticket, but disputes soon erupted over which states Jackson would campaign in. The perception that Jackson was not given due "respect" apparently hurt black turnout. Moreover, Dukakis learned too late that some of the populist economic themes in Jackson's message indeed energized Democratic voters (Wills 1988). This story contrasts dramatically with the experience on the Republican side, as we see below.

Pat Robertson and the Parachurch Network

The quixotic presidential campaign of Pat Robertson, a faith-healing charismatic televangelist with no prior elective experience, offers a fascinating example of the scope and limits of evangelical politics. While Jackson could rely on overt political support from ministers and church organizations, Pat Robertson had to approach his church base more delicately, owing to a long-standing suspicion of politics among theological conservatives. Thus, Robertson relied upon a parachurch network -- viewers of religious broadcasting, mailing lists of religious activists, and the like. But if his career as a religious broadcaster was a resource, it was also a potential handicap. Robertson had to overcome the deep skepticism of journalists and GOP regulars as well as the suspicion of many evangelical voters for televangelists.

Robertson's unique appeal was to the distinctive group of evangelical Protestants, charismatics and Pentecostals, who emphasize gifts of the Holy Spirit, speaking in tongues, and faith healing (Smidt 1988), all characteristics that separate them from the broader culture but enhance social bonds among themselves. Like Jackson, Robertson's experience mirrors that of many of his followers in key respects. Son of a prominent U.S. Senator from Virginia, his religious conversion not only changed the direction of his life but also brought him into the culturally distinct world of charismatic Christianity. Robertson confesses to have lived, as did St. Augustine, a life of "wine, women, and song" before his born-again experience, and thus he can argue persuasively about the need for, and the power of, the religious revival he trumpets. Moreover, his years as a minister have enabled him to hone his message -- a withering critique of the chaos of a modern culture cut adrift from its moral and religious moorings (Robertson 1986).

As founder of the Christian Broadcasting Network (CBN) and host of a popular religious program, the *700 Club*, Pat Robertson cultivated a religious constituency for years, and his campaign staff capitalized on that constituency in their attempt to penetrate the Republican Party. The early organization effort to secure names on endorsing petitions was largely church-based. In addition, a highly successful fund-raising effort was conducted through lists that included many ministers, evangelical associations, and contributors to CBN. A formidable political organization of local and state leaders was built through a network of local pastors, pro-life activists, and viewers of Christian broadcasting. Robertson strategists capitalized on the fervent support he enjoyed in "super churches," large charismatic congregations, many of which were affiliated with the Assemblies of God. Organizing would start quietly with the identification of key leaders and volunteers, then would grow with tacit acquiescence by the minister, and finally would mushroom as the congregation was effectively "captured" -- with Robertson organizers able to use the church facilities to pass out literature and sign up supporters. In caucus states this strategy was highly effective because it was so difficult to detect by opponents. Indeed, Robertson's support on election day in Iowa was double the projections by polls.

Robertson's political accomplishments deserve note. He raised nearly $30 million in contributions and federal matching funds, second only to George Bush, and received slightly over a million votes in GOP primaries and caucuses, some 9% of the total. His campaign, far more successful in caucuses than primaries, scored victories in Hawaii, Alaska, Nevada, and Washington, and made respectable showings in Iowa, Michigan, and Minnesota, primarily by enlisting new participants into Republican politics (Nelson 1989). Moreover, even in primary states where Robertson was defeated by Bush, his supporters packed party caucuses to elect actual delegates, draft platform statements, and control party machinery. Thus, a number of national convention delegates pledged to Bush in such states as Oklahoma, Georgia, Virginia, and South Carolina, were, in fact, Robertson newcomers (Hertzke 1989).

On the other hand, the campaign fell far short of either the fears of opponents or the expectations of supporters. Indeed, Robertson's million votes pale in comparison with the total evangelical vote (perhaps one-third of the electorate), and are dwarfed even by the petitions of three million supporters he purportedly secured prior to announcing his candidacy. Moreover, Robertson failed to move beyond the charismatic "super churches" that constituted his base (Wead 1988), and he remained a highly divisive figure among Republicans (Green and Guth 1988). Indeed, his own campaign manager, Marc Nuttle, referred to him as "a little radioactive," and his state coordinator in Hawaii, who ran unsuccessfully for the legislature, complained that his association with Robertson put the label "far right" on him (Reid 1988).

As to campaign strategy, the Robertson staff had two broad goals, one of which involved the close marriage with churches and the other which did not. The first goal was to mobilize followers from the church networks to pack party meetings and caucuses, an effort that was successful enough to cause apoplexy among Republican Party regulars. Robertson supporters were likened to "cockroaches from the floorboards of the South," "Nazis," or "freaks from outer space" by fellow Republicans (Edsall 1987)!

A big part of the story of the Robertson campaign, consequently, was not his own personal rise and fall, but the infusion of his fervent followers into the Republican Party (Oldfield 1988). The Robertson newcomers who stormed party caucuses demanded a place at the GOP table, and some got themselves elected to state party slots or even ran for local offices. The results were contentious and unpredictable. Robertson's early success in the first stage of delegate selection in Michigan stunned the party veterans and sent the party into a year-long struggle complete with rump conventions, court challenges, and ripe examples of hardball politics. In Georgia, "country club" regulars were offended that Robertson supporters, many of them former Democrats, expected to share power with long-time activists. In North Carolina, fist fights erupted when two Robertson-dominated delegations were disqualified at the 4th District Convention. In Oklahoma and Nevada, Robertson forces elected the state chairs, a mixed blessing in both cases because of later embarrassing charges that the chairs were incompetent in fund raising and party building. In Arizona, Robertson backers joined forces with hard-core supporters of former Governor Evan Mecham to write a state platform declaring the United States "a Christian nation" and asserting that the U.S. Constitution created "a republic based upon the absolute laws of the Bible, not a democracy." The national publicity that ensued -- including a remark by Barry Goldwater that the party had been taken over by a "bunch of kooks" -- delighted Democrats. State platforms also featured the concerns of the Christian Right. In Oklahoma, for example, the platform read like a catalogue of Robertson's critique of modern society -- opposition to homosexual marriage, New Age influence in education, abortion, surrogate motherhood, sex education, school-based health clinics, and the like (Hertzke 1990a).

Robertson supporters did indeed view themselves as distinct. As one prominent state leader put it, "There is something special about us. I never thought I'd say this, but we do resemble the Jackson people, we are different." But several of the key state leaders and delegates were quick to add that their involvement was not solely tied to Robertson. Said one, "We are bigger than Robertson though . . . we have issues versus just party loyalty." Another supporter observed, "I notice that everyone tries to make the movement very personal to Mr. Robertson, but I think that's a mistake. The issues will remain long after the candidate has stepped away from politics entirely" (*Atlanta Journal and Constitution* 1988). To a number of Robertson's supporters he was the vehicle this time, but perhaps not the next.

If the first major objective of the Robertson campaign, packing caucuses, was reasonably successful, the second goal, broadening the Robertson appeal to compete in primary states, was not. To appreciate this failure one must understand the strategic analysis of the Robertson campaign officials, particularly that of campaign manager Marc Nuttle. As a campaign professional, Nuttle had served as chief consultant in over 150 federal campaigns in all 48 continental states, and had worked as well with the Republican National Committee and as Field Counsel for the Reagan campaign. He was described as "extraordinarily good, meticulous" by columnist Jack Germond, who noted that at the time of the Iowa caucuses Nuttle had delivered consistently what he said he was going to do.

According to Nuttle, the transforming potential of the Robertson campaign was rooted in the awakening of culturally-conservative religious Americans over the past 25 years. In his analysis those who felt strongly about traditional religion were "left out of things in the 1960s -- whether in politics or in the broader culture." But then the national control of schools accelerated, and the government intruded into areas once the domain of families. "In 1968 Reagan burst on the scene and this group emerged out of primordial ooze as a distinct entity, concerned about divorce, taxes on families." In Nuttle's analysis this broad trend had not peaked yet:

> Approximately 35% of the population is at least partly motivated in terms of how to vote, what to buy, what to watch on TV, by conservative moral values . . . . These people are desperately seeking guidelines that will help them decide how to act. They are tired of drugs, the failure of schools, value-relativity. They will act on those values. As Madison Avenue begins to appeal to this group, as they did with blacks and Hispanics, they will become socially acceptable and more powerful. . . . Power sources, like the press, will have to pay attention.

Nuttle argued that Robertson's cultural message was potentially cross-cutting and could uniquely appeal to Democrats, including Catholics and possibly even blacks, who were fed up with collapsing moral codes. The cultural conservatism and religiosity of many blacks suggests that this analysis is at least plausible. Moreover, a remarkably large number of blacks apparently watched Robertson's religious broadcasts in the 1980s and viewed him more favorably than whites as a group (see Chapter 9). With respect to Catholics, Robertson spoke often of the need to build alliances with them, but he achieved limited success on that front.

The theme of social acceptability was central to the Robertson campaign strategy. The candidate's strengths -- his mastery of telecommunication, his exuberant leadership, his cross-cutting message about moral drift -- were evident. But the staff had no illusions about the "negatives" attached to Robertson, and, indeed, they employed expensive and sophisticated market research to design a strategy to overcome them. They distributed thousands of video and audio cassette tapes that stressed his leadership and business capabilities. Robertson began speaking of himself as a businessman and broadcaster, and he claimed that when journalists used the term "televangelist" they were engaging in religious slurs. There were brilliant newspaper ads comparing prejudice against John Kennedy's religion with prejudice against Robertson's religion -- ads that featured full-page photographs of Kennedy side by side with Robertson. All strategies were designed to make Robertson more socially acceptable. As Nuttle put it during Iowa caucus night:

> Robertson is the best speaker, captivating on video, exudes leadership, holds them spellbound . . . There are a lot of closet Robertson supporters out there, but it is not socially acceptable to be for him . . . The problem is religion. When it is socially acceptable to be for him, then watch out.

Two major factors undercut the Robertson strategy. First, the Bush organization proved tremendously effective. As Nuttle put it, "All the other candidates could not cut into Bush's base [which included many evangelicals]. His campaign was imaginative, creative, kept everyone at bay. They had awesome resources; it felt like running against the entire party." But more important still were particular circumstances attached to the Robertson campaign itself. In Nuttle's post-mortem analysis, a sequence of events conspired to undo the efforts to make Robertson socially acceptable, and they happened at the most critical juncture of the campaign:

> A campaign is like a spring; you stretch it and stretch it until it finally catapults you into credibility. We were just about there, had gotten the negatives down from 45% to 32% with the general population, and down to just 15 to 20% with our [evangelical] base.

Then, in what must be some of the worst timing in recent campaign history, Jimmy Swaggart fell from grace just two weeks before the Super Tuesday primaries, raising again public doubts about the seamy world of televangelism. Robertson himself got mired in "slippery lips and misstatements." Among the staff there were grumblings that Robertson did not read his briefing books carefully, and that he would not otherwise submit to the rigorous discipline of a campaign, resulting in "funny facts" that dogged his campaign. The worst episode was Robertson's assertion that the Bush organization might have been behind the Swaggart downfall. "It was obvious Swaggart did it [employed a prostitute], so it was silly to claim Bush was behind it" concluded Nuttle. This event, of course, happened at just the time when the campaign strategy called for distance from the world of televangelism. As Nuttle put it:

> Jim and Tammy Faye and Oral Roberts had happened within fourteen months. People were wary, but took a 'let's see' attitude. Then, at the time when Robertson's credibility was in question, we had about four funny facts and Swaggart and we lost 20 points in negatives overnight; the spring sprung back.

But there is a dimension that probably transcends campaign strategy and even disastrous events. Robertson's affiliation with the charismatic branch of evangelical Christianity did not sit well with many Southern Baptists, who might have agreed with him on political and social issues but found his religious practices unsavory. Robertson was never popular with members of the Southern Baptist Convention, a critical constituency in southern Republican politics (see Chapter 5 and 8). The theological diversity of the evangelical world, then, remained an impediment to Robertson's attempt to broaden his base. Indeed, some of Robertson's top lieutenants admitted privately that Robertson may not have been the best vehicle for their movement. Particularly disappointing was the fact that Robertson split the evangelical vote with Bush on Super Tuesday. Using a narrow definition of "evangelical," the *New York Times* reported that Robertson got only 45% of the evangelical vote, compared to Bush's 30%. Using a looser and more encompassing definition of evangelical, Bush adviser Doug Wead found that Bush got fully half of the born-again vote (see Chapter 8). Thus, while Robertson galvanized a particular segment of evangelicals, he may not have been the best vehicle for mobilizing a broad coalition of cultural conservatives, whose theological squabbles make an overtly religious appeal problematic.

The Robertson mobilization created a problem for George Bush, but one he handled rather adroitly. As an incumbent vice-president, Bush had valuable resources available to him. As early as 1985 Bush lieutenant Doug Wead began to arrange appearances for Bush on Christian media, stories in religious publications, and meetings with key evangelical leaders (Wead 1988). By 1988 Bush had been photographed with hundreds of leaders, and a biography stressing his faith appeared in Christian book stores. This effort, coupled with Reagan's popularity among evangelicals, paid off handsomely in goodwill. Moreover, Bush campaign staff monitored the Robertson effort and identified those counties where a Robertson takeover was possible. Survey research, spies in the Robertson camp, and other devices were also employed to track the potential of the insurgency. By 1987 it was clear to some in the Bush organization that Robertson had to be checked. Still, it took Bush's poor third-place showing in the Iowa caucuses behind Dole and Robertson to shock the full campaign staff into a major effort aimed at blunting Robertson. Wead designed a strategy of neutralizing the charismatic "super churches" that constituted Robertson's base, largely by identifying Bush operatives who would prevent overt capture of the church by Robertson supporters.

Illustrative of the sophistication of national GOP strategists is the case of how the Bush campaign handled workers and campaign staff for the rival Republican candidates after Bush won the nomination: they hired them. According to one state director for Robertson, this process accelerated when James Baker took over the Bush organization. Virtually all top lieutenants for Robertson were employed and then effectively shut up; once hired, campaign workers were instructed to clear any statement to the press. Moreover, Robertson himself was recruited as a surrogate speaker for Bush and campaigned obediently for the ticket. In some cases Robertson state organizations were placed at the disposal of the national campaign to staff phone banks. What the Bush people discovered, thanks in part to Robertson, was that they could court the evangelical vote in ways that did not undercut their support among other key voting blocs, an approach the national Democratic ticket never mastered. Moreover, Republican operatives learned that themes articulated by Robertson in the primaries -- ACLU's hostility to religion, opposition to the pledge of allegiance, and alleged support for child porn -- were devastating when aimed at Dukakis, who was an ACLU member (Taylor and Broder 1988). Thus, Bush not only blunted Robertson by courting the born-again vote in the primaries, but he also benefitted tremendously from his cultivation of that constituency in the general election.

Religion, Populism, and the General Election

In trying to discern the deeper meaning of the fascinating events of 1988, one is struck with the explicit blend of religious imagery and populist themes in the two, minister-led campaigns. Championing the "disinherited, disrespected, and the despised," Jackson offered a religious justification: "Jesus was rejected from the inn and born in a slum." He compared the onset of the Reagan administration to the Good Friday crucifixion, and then promised an Easter resurrection for the nation's downtrodden. Robertson, too, adopted prophetic imagery: "It looks like the bad guys are winning in this country, but so did it look that way on Good Friday" (*Denver Post* 1988a, 1988b). What links the admittedly different movements led by Jackson and Robertson is a religiously-inspired populist critique of elites whose greed or immorality exploits common folk, a theme that echoes throughout American history. Each party had to channel these populist energies, and the outcome reflects their structural strengths and weakness.

Democrats at the state level skillfully incorporated the Jackson forces into their coalitions, while Dukakis and the national party faltered. The reverse is true for the Robertson supporters, who caused all sorts of fissures in state-level politics, but were co-opted nationally by skilled campaign pros in the Bush organization.

The dynamics of the nomination struggle, coupled with broad economic and political forces, resulted in the election of George Bush. Notably, Democrats once again found themselves positioned "left of center" of the prevailing religious sentiments of the majority public. A breakdown of the national vote in 1988 reveals key religious cleavages in the American electorate. In addition to commanding support among white evangelicals, Bush also received strong support from other white Protestants, and split the Catholic vote with Dukakis. The majority of Jews voted for Dukakis, and black support for the Democrats was still commanding (see Chapters 8 through 11).

It is possible that the Republicans may have squeezed all they could out of the religious and cultural divide. By midterm in the Bush presidency, evangelical leaders found themselves complaining again about being used by the party with little to show for their support. Some worried that they would be betrayed again, as with Carter, or disappointed, as with Reagan. Robertson was miffed that Bush appointed so few evangelicals, and Wead left after Bush twice hosted gay groups at White House ceremonies (*Christianity Today* 1990). In addition, the Republicans were fractured over abortion and taxes, and the Democrats were rediscovering their own brand of "soak the rich" populism. A faltering economy could reduce the salience of social issues and heighten money concerns, and the unpredictable consequences of the Persian Gulf War might create a new yeasty political dough. Perhaps with the right candidate and the right circumstances by 1992 Democrats might be poised to shed "liberal" baggage and mount a serious challenge to Republican presidential hegemony.

But the danger remains for Democrats. Americans hold traditional values, even if they violate them in practice. Republicans have been able to capitalize on this dynamic to paint national Democrats as hostile to the religious and moral values of the majority. This suggests to some scholars that a European kind of party divide may be emerging -- a secular "left" party against a Christian "right" party. Voting patterns in 1988 suggest that *among whites* such a division may be occurring. Moreover, there is some evidence that among white voters frequent churchgoers are likely to be Republicans, a new and ominous pattern for Democrats (see Chapter 8).

But what do the populist currents of 1988 portend? I am led to believe that profound expressions of discontent will endure, even if temporary events occasionally submerge them, because powerful modern forces appear simultaneously disruptive to the economically vulnerable and the morally traditional (Hertzke 1990c). What the 1988 campaign tells us, then, is that even if religiously-harvested discontent is sparse in one year, it will likely return again, like grass sprouting through concrete, unpredictable but no less dramatic.

Notes

1. This analysis is based upon three years of research into the movements represented by the two reverends. The research involved attendance at the Iowa caucuses and both national political conventions in 1988, along with subsequent state and national party meetings in 1989 and 1990. During this research I interviewed Jerry Austin, campaign manager for Jesse Jackson, and Marc Nuttle, campaign director for Pat Robertson, along with convention delegates, caucus attenders, party officials, campaign lieutenants, and national journalists. Quotations in the text are from these interviews unless otherwise cited.

2. See Squires (1990) and Gibbs (1988) on industrial flight from the inner city; Wilson (1987) on related measures of cultural crisis and lagging economic attainment; Nichols-Casebolt (1988) and Dash (1989) on out-of-wedlock births; DeParle (1991) on welfare rates among children; McAllister (1990) on college attendance; *The Daily Oklahoman* (1990) on black incarceration rates.

References

Atlanta Journal and Constitution. 1988. "Pat Robertson's Follower's Persevering After Presidential Campaign." December 25:12A.

Barker, Lucius. 1988. *Our Time Has Come: A Delegate's Diary of Jesse Jackson's 1984 Presidential Campaign*. Urbana, IL: University of Illinois Press.

Black, Earl, and Merle Black. 1987. *Politics and Society in the South*. Cambridge: Harvard University Press.

Christianity Today. 1990. "It's Dog Days in D.C." September 10:60-62.

Colton, Elizabeth. 1989. *The Jackson Phenomenon: The Man, the Power, the Message*. New York: Doubleday.

Daily Oklahoman 1990. "One Out of Four Young Black Men in Justice System." February 27.

Dash, Leon. 1989. *When Children Want Children: The Urban Crisis of Teenage Childrearing*. New York: William Morrow.

DeMoss, Bob. 1990. "Help Your Kids Learn to Discern." *Focus on the Family Citizen*, August 20.

Denver Post. 1988a. "Wide Spectrum Crams to Hear Jackson." April 4:1A.

Denver Post. 1988b. "Robertson Vows to Push Quest Until He Wins." April 4:1A.

DeParle, Jason. 1991. "Suffering in the Cities Persists as U.S. Fights Other Battles." *New York Times*, January 27:1.

Du Bois, W.E.B. 1903. *The Souls of Black Folk*. Chicago: A.C. McClung.

Edsall. Thomas. 1987. "Will Feud Sink the GOP?" *Washington Post Weekly Edition*, June 15:29.

Epstein, Leon D. 1986. *Political Parties in the American Mold*. Madison, WI: University of Wisconsin Press.

Faw, Bob, and Nancy Skelton. 1986. *Thunder in America: The Improbable Presidential Campaign of Jesse Jackson*. Austin, TX: Texas Monthly Press.

Fenno, Richard. 1978. *Home Style*. Boston: Little Brown.

Fowler, Robert Booth. 1985. *Religion and Politics in America*. Metuchen, NJ: Scarecrow.

Gallup, George, Jr. 1985. "Religion in America 50 Years: 1935-1985." *The Gallup Report*, No. 236.

Garrow, David J. 1986. *Bearing the Cross: Martin Luther King, Jr. and the Southern Christian Leadership Conference*. New York: Vintage.

Gibbs, Jewelle Taylor, ed. 1988. *Young, Black and Male in America: An Endangered Species*. Dover, MA: Auburn House Publishing Company.

Green, John C., and James L. Guth. 1988. "The Christian Right in the Republican Party: The Case of Pat Robertson's Supporters." *Journal of Politics*, 50:150-165.

Hertzke, Allen D. 1990a. "The Role of Churches in Political Mobilization: A Look at the Presidential Campaigns of Jesse Jackson and Pat Robertson," in Allan T. Cigler and Burdett A. Loomis, eds., *Interest Group Politics*. Pp. 177-178. 3rd Edition. Washington, DC: Congressional Quarterly.

_____. 1990b. "Christian Fundamentalists and the Imperatives of American Politics," in Emile Sahilyeh, ed., *Religious Resurgence and Politics in the Contemporary World*. Pp. 67-80. Albany, NY: State University of New York Press.

_____. 1990c. "Populist Echoes of Discontent: Jesse Jackson, Pat Robertson, and the Crucible of Liberal Culture." Presented at the annual meeting of the American Political Science Association, San Francisco.

_____. 1989. "American Political Parties and Strategic Assimilation: The Lessons of Jackson and Robertson." Presented at the annual meeting of the Western Political Science Association, Salt Lake City, Utah.

Jackson, Jesse L. 1987. *Straight From the Heart*. Edited by Roger D. Hatch and Frank E. Watkins. Philadelphia: Fortress Press.

Jacobson, Gary. and Samuel Kernell. 1983. *Strategy and Choice in Congressional Elections*. New Haven: Yale.

Kelley, Dean M. 1972. *Why Conservative Churches are Growing*. New York: Harper and Row.

Kessel, John H. 1988. *Presidential Campaign Politics*. 3rd Edition. Chicago: The Dorsey Press.

Ladd, Everett C., with Charles Hadley. 1975. *Transformations of the American Party System*. New York: Norton.

Lincoln, C. Eric, and Lawrence T. Mamiya. 1990. *The Black Church in the African American Experience*. Durham NC: Duke.

Manning, Marable. 1985. *Black American Politics: From the Washington Marches to Jesse Jackson*. London: Verso.

McAllister, Bill. 1990. "The Plight of Young Black Men in America." *Washington Post Weekly Edition*, February 12:18.

Nelson, Michael, ed. 1989. *The Election of 1988*. Washington DC: CQ Press.

New York Times. 1988. "The Preachers and the Bully Pulpit." March 8:24.

Nichols-Casebolt, Ann M. 1988. "Black Families Headed by Single Mothers: Growing Numbers and Increasing Poverty." *Social Work*, July/August:306-313.

Oldfield, Duane. 1988. "Pat Crashes the Party: Reform, Republicans, and Robertson." Presented at the annual meeting of the American Political Science Association, Washington, DC

Poloma, Margaret M. 1989. *The Assemblies of God at the Crossroads: Charisma and Institutional Dilemmas.* Knoxville, TN: University of Tennessee Press.

Reed, Adolph L. Jr. 1986. *The Jesse Jackson Phenomenon.* New Haven: Yale University Press.

Reid, T.R. 1988. "Invisible Army Won Few Battles." *Washington Post*, December 26:3A.

Reynolds, Barbara A. 1985. *Jesse Jackson: America's David.* Washington DC: JFJ Associates.

Robertson, Pat. 1986. *America's Dates With Destiny.* Nashville, TN: Thomas Nelson.

Sheehy, Gail. 1988. "Power or Glory?" *Vanity Fair*, January 1988.

Smidt, Corwin. 1988. "Praise the Lord Politics: A Comparative Analysis of the Social Characteristics and Political Views of American Evangelical and Charismatic Christians." *Sociological Analysis*, 50:53-72.

Squires, Gregory D. 1990. "Economic Restructuring, Urban Development, and Race: The Political Economy of Civil Rights in 'Post Industrial' America." *Western Political Quarterly*, 43:201-217.

Taylor, Paul and David Broder. 1988. "Early Volley of Bush's Exceeds Expectations." *Washington Post*, October 28:1.

Walters, Ronald. 1988. *Black Presidential Politics in America.* Albany, NY: State University of New York Press.

Wead, Doug, 1988. "The Vice President and Evangelicals in the General Election" (Twice Abridged). April 15. Internal campaign document.

West, Cornell. 1982. *Prophesy Deliverance! An Afro-American Revolutionary Christianity.* Philadelphia: Westminster John Knox.

Wills, Garry, 1988. "The Power Populist." *Time*, November 21.

Wilson, William Julius. 1987. *The Truly Disadvantaged: The Inner City, the Underclass and Public Policy.* Chicago: University of Chicago Press.

Wuthnow, Robert. 1988. *The Restructuring of American Religion.* Princeton, NJ: Princeton University Press.

PART TWO

Religious Leaders and the 1988 Presidential Campaign

2

From Candidates to Agenda Setters: Protestant Leaders and the 1988 Presidential Campaign

Anne M. Hallum

Political commentator Garry Wills has asserted that "religion and electoral politics tend to be mutually debasing" (Wills 1988:14). In 1988, Protestant leaders struggled against that tendency in an intense effort to influence politics without selling their souls. Some emerged from the struggle more scarred than others, as it was an election that was both inspiring and humbling for the leaders involved. It is important to examine the interplay of religion and politics in 1988 because the role of religion was particularly overt, and the mixed results of religious activism have implications for 1992 and beyond.

It is possible to identify four major patterns of political activism that religious leaders have undertaken in recent elections: as direct campaigners, selective agenda-setters, broad agenda-setters, and candidate advisers. This essay will examine each of these patterns as they appeared in the 1988 presidential campaign, and then it will draw some conclusions regarding the impact of Protestant leaders in 1988 and their possible role in the future.

The Protestant leaders under discussion here are not so much the individual preachers in local churches as the group and denominational leaders, several of whom were interviewed for this essay.[1] These leaders come in two major types. First are the Protestant denominational leaders who are full-time professionals salaried by the denomination to advise and serve the hierarchy. For example, the Presbyterian General Assembly is the official denominational governing body made up of elected, temporary members, but advised by permanent professional staff. As is common in governmental settings, the staff advisers often are de facto leaders. The second category of leaders is officials from the extra-denominational agencies such as the National Council of Churches (NCC) and the National Association of Evangelicals (NAE), which serve a variety of member churches and denominations. Both types of religious professionals do similar work of preparing publications and resolutions, arranging conferences, and to some degree, engaging in politics.

Direct Campaigners

Religious leaders may become deeply and directly involved in a specific campaign, as many did for Pat Robertson and Jesse Jackson in 1988. Both campaigns provide some interesting lessons on the limitations and successes of voter mobilization by religious leaders. The evangelical leaders who endorsed Robertson were generally ineffective, whereas the black church leaders who backed Jackson were highly successful.

Television evangelist Pat Robertson decided to run for president based in part on the enthusiastic advice of Christian Right leaders whom he consulted at meetings held around the country in 1986. These leaders included Southern Baptist Convention president Charles Stanley; Campus Crusade for Christ president Bill Bright; Jerry Falwell, president of the now disbanded Moral Majority; Tim LaHaye, head of the American Coalition for Traditional Values, among others (Lawton 1986:34). Although some of these leaders eventually backed other Republican candidates (Beverly and Tim LaHaye supported Jack Kemp, and Jerry Falwell backed George Bush), a large number of evangelical church and parachurch leaders signed on to his campaign, and some 350 supported him openly.

At the March 1988 convention of the National Religious Broadcasters, Robertson clearly was the favorite among the four Republican candidates invited to speak (no Democrats were invited). However, even with the backing of this influential group of leaders, many of them fellow televangelists, Robertson made a dismal showing in the southern primaries. He had invested more time and money in the March 5th South Carolina primary than any other candidate, yet he finished third with only 19% of the vote to Bush's 48% and Dole's 21% (Kemper 1988:24). In the Super Tuesday primaries three days later, Robertson trailed Bush by an average of 27% to 49% *among born-again Christians* in seven southern states according to exit polls (Ladd 1988:5). Thus, even in the Bible Belt, after intensive efforts by many evangelical leaders, a majority of conservative Christians failed to fall in line. Indeed, only a fraction of Robertson's 10 million television viewers supported him (see Chapter 8). The fact is that the Christian Right leaders were simply unable to mobilize their followers on Robertson's behalf. The intensity of their support, as well as his own self-confidence, caused him to overestimate the number of committed voters he had in his corner. This does not mean that evangelical leaders were not a factor in the race--after all, Robertson did amass extensive resources (see Chapter 1). But the results probably indicate that conservative Christian voters are becoming political "professionals," strategically voting for candidates who can win rather than for candidates who best articulate their political and religious beliefs. Some observers, including Robertson, blamed his poor showing on hostile media and on political misstatements he made late in the campaign. However, evidence that he would not do well was apparent early in the race. He had difficulty in recruiting three million volunteers at the outset (Lawton 1987:34-35), and in 1987 surveys, opponents of Robertson's candidacy outnumbered supporters by large margins even among born-again Christian Republicans (Ladd 1988:5). In the end, Bush's sizeable victory demonstrated that the voters in the pews and in the television audiences were more politically sophisticated than some of the uncompromising leaders of the Christian Right.

In the general election most of the evangelical leaders supported Bush, but with palpable reluctance. For instance, David W. Balsiger published a booklet entitled the "Biblical Scoreboard" which endorsed Bush but also complained that in the Republican administration "there was plenty of traditional values and religious rhetoric" but "no real action!" (Steinfels 1988:44). Still, it is significant that Balsiger and others encouraged conservative Christians to vote against Dukakis rather than to withdraw from the political scene. While Christian voters did not follow leaders en masse to vote for Robertson, they were mobilized to vote overwhelmingly for Bush in the general election (see Chapter 8). These voters will be an important political force in 1992, but not a monolithic bloc in the primaries.

The solidarity of the black Protestant leadership and their members is an instructive contrast to the Robertson campaign. The black clergy's support for Jesse Jackson's candidacy was almost unanimous, and from the beginning black voters voted as a bloc. Of course, many blacks probably would have voted for Jackson even without urging from their pastor, but black congregations not only voted for Jackson, they worked for him as well. They distributed literature, ran telephone banks, organized voter registration drives, and provided speaking platforms. Church-based fund-raising was more difficult given changes in the tax code, but even here, pastors did encourage members to give on their own. Indeed, the black churches provided Jackson's major support network which allowed him to win 13 states in the primary season. And in the fall campaign, blacks were again the strongest supporters of the Democratic ticket (see Chapter 9).

The reasons behind this black solidarity are the obvious common social and cultural experiences of blacks in America. Both the root causes of black church activism and the methods for mobilizing political involvement differ fundamentally from white churches. The black churches do not rely on denominational hierarchies and staff to articulate their political positions as the mainline white Protestants do. Nor do they depend on television evangelists to rally the troops from the television studio. Their mobilizing tactics are at the level of the individual church and pulpit. In contrast, many white pastors, (although certainly not all) are reluctant to use the pulpit in overtly political ways. But this is probably the most effective mobilizing tactic. A recent study of individual congregations concluded that the theological climate in congregations contributes

> strongly to the members' political attitudes over and above the personal commitment of respondents to traditional Christian values and a variety of social and attitudinal variables. As churches constitute the single most widespread form of voluntary organizational affiliation in the United States, their potential political impact appears to be considerable (Wald et al. 1988:531).

Church members were found to conform to the dominant political attitudes of their congregation and to be politically active in a consistent way. Thus, it would appear that the most effective method for translating religious resources into political activism is at the level of the congregational community. Denominational resolutions and television exhortations simply do not have a comparable impact.

Jackson and Robertson: Shaping the Agenda

Beyond their electoral impact, both Robertson and Jackson helped shape the agenda for the 1988 election. In general, religious leaders interviewed expressed a positive attitude toward the candidacies of both ordained ministers. Even when they disagreed with their stance on the issues or did not want either candidate to win, they believed that Jackson and Robertson brought a needed moral dimension to the campaign. Both candidacies tapped political movements from outside the mainstream, and both were backed by constituencies who felt left behind by the 1980s: blacks, who were not part of Reagan's economic expansion, and conservative Christians, who were deeply concerned about the continued decline of traditional family values (see Chapter 1). As one *Christian Century* editorial noted, "many Jackson supporters resemble Robertson's followers--church going citizens of moderate means who long for the triumph of good over evil and for the realization of justice in our time" (Lynch 1987:908). Thus, both the Jackson and Robertson candidacies appealed to alienated segments of society on moral grounds. It was on specific issues, of course, that the differences between them emerged.

The impact of both candidacies in shaping the policy agenda was evident at the national nominating conventions. Jackson urged the Democratic nominee to end aid to Nicaraguan Contras, use comprehensive sanctions against South Africa, support a nuclear freeze, and propose strong child-care legislation. Jackson also gave a featured speech to the convention that focused on government responsibility to the poor in Gospel terms. A black state senator from Mississippi at the convention echoed the speech and testified to Jackson's influence:

> Jesse once told me, 'you can do anything, but don't forget, only what's done for Christ will last.' . . . My mission is to be an advocate for the poor, disenfranchised, damned, doomed, and locked out. I was ordained to the mission by Jesse--to keep hope alive (Wallis 1988:17).

It would be difficult to find a clearer statement expressing religious motivation for political activism. The Republican convention acknowledged the religious element of the campaign as well. Religious performers and orators were on the program, and the lengthy Republican platform supported much of the agenda of the Christian Right: voluntary prayer in the schools, opposition to abortion funding, and pro-family policies. As for Pat Robertson, he delivered a prominent, inspiring speech at the national convention, and his strongest supporters pledged to remain active in Republican politics (Lawton 1988:38).

Selective Agenda Setters

A contrast to direct religious involvement in campaigns is to focus on a few political issues. This model is best exemplified by the leaders of the National Association of Evangelicals (NAE). This extra-denominational organization was formed in 1942 as an educational and lobbying organization made up of an evangelical coalition of 47 denominations representing approximately 10 million members. Most of its membership is theologically and politically conservative, but the NAE eschews direct involvement in campaigns. When interviewed, Richard Cizik, NAE's Policy Analyst, repeatedly referred to the concept of "using Scriptures wisely," namely, becoming involved only in issues where scriptural guidelines were clear. Cizik explained: "We are in contradistinction to [liberal] mainliners who took a stand in 1988 on 58 distinct issues, and also in contradistinction to the New Religious Right knee-jerk stands on issues." He also voiced opposition to the candidacies of ordained ministers in 1988, noting that NAE polls consistently had shown how divided the evangelical vote was among the Republican candidates. Cizik asserted: "We don't need an evangelical in the White House." He stressed that the NAE never considered endorsing a candidate, not only because of the possibility of losing tax-exempt status, but because "we don't think we should. [Endorsement] violates our standards of prudence and wisdom. It's divisive to the body of Christ."

Cizik's views echo Garry Wills' opinion that "religion and electoral politics tend to be mutually debasing." Undoubtedly, direct campaign involvement by religious leaders carries certain risks for the church. The obvious possibility of losing tax-exempt status due to direct political engagement is only one of the risks. In addition, if religious leaders as candidates intend to win the election rather than serve as prophetic critics of government, they will be forced to moderate their religious convictions. Pat Robertson, for example, was campaigning to win, if not in 1988, then in 1992, so he began to tone down his religious beliefs in order to broaden his appeal. His beliefs were also subject to ridicule by the media, and both responses were painful to his core followers. The point is clear: electoral politics influence religious leaders almost as much as religious leaders influence electoral politics. It is very difficult for a ministerial candidate not to be drawn into the compromising, secular positions of professional politics.

The NAE and similar organizations avoid this problem of "debasement" not by withdrawing from the public arena, but by using different tactics. They have formed a religious coalition that targets its resources on a few issues such as the right of free exercise of religion in public schools, and the need to restrict gambling, pornography, drugs, and alcohol. One sophisticated method of political mobilization is the distribution to churches of a bulletin insert called "Washington

Insight" that offers a summary of selected political decisions from a "Christian perspective" and asks readers to contact government officials. The expectation is that the impact will be felt eventually because efforts are concentrated on a few items on the political agenda. Cizik and others interpret the right-ward move of the Republican Party in the 1980s as an indication of evangelical influence. Although nonpartisan in approach, these efforts may have on balance benefitted the Republican party, and judging from the election results, evangelical voters seem to have shared this bias.

Broad Agenda Setters

Rather than focusing on particular political candidates or targeting a few specific issues, religious leaders may use a shotgun approach of political involvement that addresses a broad range of issues. Thus, the mainline Protestant churches (Episcopal, Presbyterian, Methodist, Lutheran, United Church of Christ) and the National Council of Churches prepared official resolutions on dozens of specific issues in 1988, taking positions that often coincided with the Democratic party platform. For instance, the Washington office of the United Methodist Church (UMC) publishes an official magazine called *Christian Social Action*. In the midst of the 1988 election, a special article used three parallel columns for easy comparison of the Republican and Democratic platforms and the official statements passed by the UMC General Conference. The overall agreement with the Democratic Party on such issues as abortion, homelessness, Central America, South Africa, and gun control was clear. Similarly, Eleanor Ivory, Director of the Washington Office of the Presbyterian Church USA, explained, "we never endorse candidates; we compare church positions and candidate positions on the issues. . . . It's not deliberate [that the comparison favors the Democratic party]. We explain that the Democratic Party is the party of the people and the church is of the people." However, she went on to make the revealing point that the lay membership of the Presbyterian Church USA was roughly 35% Democrat and 65% Republican.

The disparity between the opinions of mainline leadership and lay members on many political questions has been widely noted by scholars (Hallum 1989; Hertzke 1988; Reichley 1985:267-81). Sometimes the theological and political polarization along liberal and conservative lines leads to structural changes. The Presbyterian Church USA (PCUSA) is a product of the union of the northern and southern Presbyterian churches in 1983, but this reunion was preceded by a breaking away of the conservative branch of the church, the Presbyterian Church in America (PCA). The Lutheran, Methodist, and Episcopal churches are also enduring the development of splinter groups that are either becoming separate organizations or seeking influence within the parent denomination.

Further evidence of polarization is provided by the variety of mainline church periodicals. *Christian Social Action* is an official publication of the United Methodist Church, but an unofficial magazine entitled *Good News: The Bimonthly Magazine for United Methodists* has a much larger number of subscribers. *Good News*, published by the Forum for Scriptural Christianity, Inc., not the UMC, is theologically and politically conservative. A group of Presbyterians calling themselves Presbyterians for Democracy and Religious Freedom (PDRF) publish a newsletter called *Mainstream: Report and Commentary on Presbyterians and Politics.* The newsletter provides strident denominational opposition to such General Assembly stances as ending military aid to El Salvador and Guatemala, advocating a Palestinian state in the Middle East, and urging the withdrawal of military bases in the Philippines. The PDRF is closely aligned with the conservative Institute on Religion and Democracy, and both organizations are a thorn in the side of the PCUSA leadership. The other mainline churches have maverick publications similar to PDRF's *Mainstream,* tolerated but not sanctioned by the denominational hierarchy.

The various mainline leaders are beginning to respond to the schisms within their denominations as it becomes evident that dissenters sometimes make up a majority of the laity. The General Conference of the UMC and the General Assembly of the Presbyterian Church USA, for instance, are using more scriptural references to support their social stances. Eleanor Ivory of the PCUSA insisted that the denomination was not compromising on its controversial social positions, but was simply becoming more sensitive to the conservatives by "avoiding 'red flag' terms; using honey rather than vinegar to get the point across." For the 1988 elections, the approach of these denominational leaders was simply to provide comparisons of candidate/party and church positions, and to support nonpartisan voter registration drives. The predictable result in the vote was division (see Chapter 8). One survey of Methodist pastors found an almost even split in votes between Bush and Dukakis (see Chapter 5). Thus, even half of the *pastors* refused to follow the advice of denominational leaders and their staffs to vote Democrat.

The risk in this issue-oriented political involvement is the alienation of some church members, a risk most church leaders are willing to accept. In fact, the staffs of these denominations have become almost complacent about their small number of followers. For instance, the editor of *Christian Social Action*, Lee Rack, admitted that in a denomination of over nine million Methodists, only 4,000 subscribed to the periodical. But he insisted that the publication's impact was magnified because the readers formed an active core group of "social action types." The social/political stances taken by these denominational leaders are often ignored or opposed by many of their own members, leaving them to "preach to the choir" of those who already agree. However, these religious leaders are motivated to be involved in social and political issues by their beliefs, not by the number of supporters they can or cannot recruit. The politically liberal hierarchy in these churches has grown accustomed to having little visible influence in presidential politics during the Republican 1980s.

A final option for political involvement by religious leaders is serving as advisers and confidants of presidential candidates. For example, it is well-known that Richard Nixon consulted Billy Graham for a biblical perspective on policy, and Jerry Falwell reportedly met with President Reagan at the White House. While there was not much evidence of this kind of influence in 1988, George Bush, himself an Episcopalian, has invited Reverend Brooks of the Washington office of the Episcopal Church to the White House to discuss various issues. Bush also consulted with mainline and evangelical leaders during the Persion Gulf crisis. This type of face-to-face contact is influential only if a persuasive rapport exists between the political and religious leaders. For religious leaders to obtain this enviable kind of access, however, is entirely at the discretion of the political leader.

The Religious Elites and Presidential Politics

What is an appropriate role for religious leaders in presidential politics? Let us recap some of the options discussed in this essay. First, religious leaders can become deeply and directly involved in a specific campaign, as the black church did for Jesse Jackson, and as many evangelical leaders did for Pat Robertson. The black church operating at the level of the local congregation was most successful in this regard. Evangelicals and especially liberal mainliners were unable to emulate their solidarity.

The level of political discourse benefitted, overall, from the presence of the preacher candidates. In fact, after Jackson and

Robertson left the presidential race to the party nominees, most observers agree that the campaign degenerated to self-serving, negative television imagery. But the risk of such a close connection between religion and politics is that if the candidates sense victory, they will subdue their religious message and no longer offer a special contribution to the political debate.

The presence of Jesse Jackson and Pat Robertson as candidates in 1988 was the logical extension of Jimmy Carter's "born-again Baptist" pronouncements and Reagan's close ties with the Christian Right. Ordained ministers as candidates can direct presidential politics to the heart of moral issues like poverty, peace, and abortion. They can also galvanize political outsiders to become involved in party politics and thereby have a lasting impact on the process. But can they win an election? Probably not, given our pluralistic society. According to historian Richard G. Hutcheson, "it is doubtful that any clergyperson, of necessity committed to one denomination or faith, officially as well as personally, could successfully serve as a symbol of unity for all the people" (Conn 1988:12). As candidates, clergy can bring a prophetic critique to our political system as did Jesse Jackson and Pat Robertson, but they would probably be a divisive presence in the White House.

Second, the approach toward politics taken by the National Association of Evangelicals offers another alternative to church leaders. They target a few moral and First Amendment issues, capitalize on the consensus of evangelicals on these topics, and avoid the divisive tactic of endorsing presidential candidates. In the future, they will continue to mobilize voters around narrow issues, thus having more of an impact on the general election than in the fragmented primary stage.

Third, religious leaders may choose instead to focus on a broad range of issues. Thus, the mainline Protestant churches prepare official resolutions on dozens of specific issues such as American policy in Central America, South Africa, Cuba, the Middle East; domestic concerns such as homelessness, gun control, opposition to the death penalty; and most recently, environmental protection. We have seen, however, that these resolutions are prepared by the official hierarchy and the professional staff; the people in the pews and the pulpits often disagree. The mainline leaders largely educate the few politically attentive members. They publicize church rulings on many issues, but they know that their impact on their diverse congregations is limited.

Finally, the possibility often exists for person-to-person religious influence on presidential office-seekers. This impact can be considerable, but it is individualistic and unpredictable.

Religious leadership in presidential campaigns can be as direct as running for office, or as tangential as expressing opinions on political issues. In 1988, we probably witnessed as close a linkage between religion and politics as the general American public will allow in the candidacies of Jackson and Robertson. In the role of providing a sense of prophetic conscience and idealism to the campaign, the presence of religious leaders was not only acceptable, but welcome.

Notes

1. This research is based in part on interviews with prominent Protestant leaders during the spring and summer of 1990, including Richard Cizik, National Association of Evangelicals; Eleanor Ivory, Washington Office of the Presbyterian Church USA; Lee Rack, Washington Office of the United Methodist Church, and Clint Shaw, Washington Office of the Episcopal Church.

References

Conn, Joseph L. 1988. "Campaign Conflict." *Church and State*, 41:12.

Hallum, Anne Motley. 1989. "Presbyterians as Political Amateurs," in Charles Dunn, ed., *Religion in American Politics*. Pp. 63-73. Washington, DC: CQ Press.

Hertzke, Allen D. 1988. *Representing God in Washington: The Role of Religious Lobbies in the American Polity*. Knoxville, TN: University of Tennessee Press.

Kemper, Vicki. 1988. "Looking for a Promised Land." *Sojourners*, June:24.

Ladd, Everett C. 1988. *The Ladd 1988 Election Update*. New York: Norton. 1:5.

Lawton, Kim. 1986. "One Step closer to a Bid for the Oval Office." *Christianity Today*, October 17:34.

_____. 1987. "Will Pat Run?" *Christianity Today*, August 7:34-35.

_____. 1988. "Republicans or Reaganites." *Christianity Today*, September 16:38-39.

Lynch, Timothy B. 1987. "Pat Robertson's Bid: Good for Democracy." *Christian Century*, October 21:908.

Reichley, A. James. 1985. *Religion in American Public Life*. Washington, DC: Brookings Institution.

Steinfels, Peter. 1988. "Biblical Scorecard Chooses Bush, but with Reluctance." *New York Times*, October 16:44.

Wald, Kenneth D., Dennis E. Owen, and Samuel S. Hill, Jr. 1988. "Churches as Political Communities." *American Political Science Review*, 82:531-548.

Wallis, James. 1988. *Sojourners*, "Signs of the Times." November:15-21.

Wills, Garry. 1988. "Faith and the Hopefuls: The Race for God and Country." *Sojourners*, March:14.

3

Divided, Distracted, and Disengaged: Catholic Leaders and the 1988 Presidential Campaign

Mary T. Hanna

The fascinating thing about the Catholic bishops' participation in the 1988 elections was how little of it there was. For more than a dozen years, Catholic bishops had played a major role in American politics. They had, in part, helped to set the nation's political agenda. In 1976 a committee of bishops, after interviewing presidential candidates Jimmy Carter and Gerald Ford, stirred public debate by seeming to indicate church support for Ford. This event was overshadowed by the controversy that arose in the 1984 elections over the abortion issue, which eventually involved a number of prelates, including Cardinal John O'Connor of New York, on one side, and such prominent Catholic politicians as vice-presidential candidate Geraldine Ferraro and Governor Mario Cuomo on the other. During the 1980s, the bishops also issued the two most widely publicized and most controversial pastoral letters in American history -- their letter on war and peace in 1983, which strongly criticized American nuclear strategy, and their equally critical letter on the U.S. economy in 1986.

One of the other contributors to this book has suggested that religious leaders can play four different roles in politics: actively campaign for candidates, pursue a few special issues, pursue a broad range of issues, or serve as advisers to politicians (see Chapter 2). Catholic bishops have played all of these roles in the past. If there are few examples of them campaigning *for* candidates, there are certainly examples of bishops campaigning *against* candidates, mainly on moral issues. In 1984, for example, Cardinal O'Connor's warning that Catholics could not in good conscience vote for a politician who favored abortion was widely interpreted as being directed against

42

Democrat Ferraro. In both 1976 and 1984 many bishops strenuously argued the central importance of the abortion issue in elections. In 1984, too, the National Conference of Catholic Bishops and its President, Bishop James Malone, tried to focus attention on a wide range of issues from the threat of nuclear war and the suffering of the Third World to domestic concerns, such as health care and the plight of minorities. In an earlier era, Cardinals Francis Spellman of New York and Richard Cushing of Boston served almost as house chaplains of the Kennedy family.

But there was very little activity of any of these kinds in the 1988 elections; instead, the bishops were almost entirely silent. Newspapers record no comments from them even on the two religious leaders, Pat Robertson and Jesse Jackson, running in the primaries that year. We see the bishops neither in the partisan role several seemed to play in earlier elections nor in the prophetic role they assumed in their pathbreaking pastoral letters. The few public statements they issued were remarkably low-keyed and cautious. In 1988, the bishops seemed almost to emulate the League of Women Voters, restricting themselves to reminding citizens of their civic responsibilities to educate themselves and to vote and to unimpassioned evaluations of candidates and issues. If there was anything to be gleaned from them regarding church preference between presidential candidates George Bush and Michael Dukakis, it seemed to be "neither of the above."

Three factors seem to me to account for the bishops' sudden quiescence. First, and probably most important, by 1988 the Catholic bishops were divided among themselves and involved in a series of conflicts with the Vatican. Their own internal church concerns were so serious that they apparently had little energy or time to involve themselves in national politics. Second, changes in our laws and, perhaps, public criticism of their earlier, more active role seem to have made them much more cautious of even the appearance of involvement in partisan politics. And, finally, the bishops tried to apply Cardinal Joseph Bernardin's theory of a consistent ethic of life to the candidates' stands and found little to support and much to dislike in both candidates' positions.

The Bishops Divided

After the Vatican Council of 1962-1965, which brought about so many reforms in the Catholic church, the American bishops, like those of many other countries, set up a national organization for themselves. Through this organization they came into frequent contact with one another and found a unified voice in speaking out on both church and political matters. This unity began unravelling in the months just prior to the 1988 election.

The American Catholic church is actually composed at the national level of two, closely intertwined organizations: The National Conference of Catholic Bishops (NCCB) and the United States Catholic Conference (USCC). The NCCB is the national organization of all the bishops in the United States. Under its aegis, the bishops meet annually in November (and often a second time in June) to discuss and decide upon political, social, theological, and pastoral issues. Between meetings the NCCB continues operations through a series of bishops' committees (much like congressional committees) and through the interim leadership of its Administrative Committee, composed of a number of NCCB officials, all bishops elected to their positions, and several other bishops chosen to provide regional representation. The second national organization, the USCC, is under the direction of the NCCB and serves as its bureaucratic arm. It provides research, communications, public relations, and other services for the bishops. These national organizations give the bishops a meeting place to iron out differences, specialists to help with advice and administration, and a forum from which they can issue formal church statements and opinions. During the late 1970s and the first half of the 1980s, the bishops became more unified and with that more active and influential on political issues.

The bishops' committee charged by the NCCB with writing the 1983 letter on war and peace carefully negotiated between the hawks and the doves in the episcopate to develop a letter which broke new ground for its boldness in criticizing American foreign policy, but which also gained the overwhelming support of American bishops. The bishops' letter on the U.S. economy was, if anything, even more controversial than the war and peace letter. It went through four drafts over a six-year period. The bishops' committee charged with writing it held hearings with experts; they sent drafts out to the dioceses for lay and clerical comment; they discussed the letter at length at several national conferences of Catholic bishops; and in the end that letter, too, was accepted by an overwhelming majority of the assembled bishops.

This hard-won unity among American bishops began coming apart in the middle 1980s as the important religious and political issues became, not defense or the economy, but sexual, moral, and gender problems. The abortion issue never lost the tone of anger and conflict it acquired during the 1984 elections when Cuomo, Ferraro and Cardinal O'Connor engaged in their long, heated debate over it. By

1986 and 1987, birth control, which many Catholics believed had been given a quiet burial as an issue by the laity, priests and bishops alike, suddenly re-emerged because of strong Vatican reiteration of its banning (*Catholic Almanac 1989* 1988:232-233). These two issues were joined by controversies over homosexuality, by the emergence of AIDS, by the spotlighting of such medical-religious issues as *in vitro* fertilization, surrogate motherhood, and euthanasia, and by the bishops' own attempts to follow up on their nuclear war and economics letters with a pastoral letter on the role of women in the church and society. In 1987 and 1988, American bishops seemed confused and divided among themselves on these issues, and they were responding to them in very different ways.

Bishops across the country tried to reconcile pastoral care for homosexuals and AIDS victims with a Vatican directive which reinforced the notion of homosexuality as sin and which expressed reservations about the widespread American church practice of holding special masses for homosexuals (Congregation for the Doctrine of the Faith 1986b:377-382). In New York City, Cardinal O'Connor terminated those special masses. In Chicago, Cardinal Bernardin removed the Catholic homosexual organization, Dignity, as the sponsor of the masses, but he continued them under archdiocesan sponsorship, saying, "To cancel the Mass would be a serious pastoral mistake" (Bernardin 1988a:49). The Administrative Board of the United States Catholic Conference, composed of bishops, issued a statement on AIDS and its prevention which suggested that school children might be taught about condoms: "We are not promoting the use of prophylactics, but merely providing information that is part of the factual picture" (U.S. Catholic Conference Administrative Board 1987b:486). The statement was supported by many bishops, but it was also strongly denounced by several influential American prelates and by the Vatican. Bishops in various dioceses also rendered different decisions on the conditions under which life support systems could be cut off to comatose patients (*Catholic Almanac 1989* 1988:65,76; *Catholic Almanac 1990* 1989:56-58). Approval of the bishops' letter on women was postponed by the National Conference of Catholic Bishops meeting of 1986 and then was postponed again in 1988 because of controversy over it. In 1990, under conflicting pressure from women in religious orders and the Vatican, and divided among themselves, the bishops decided again to postpone it, agreeing that it was better to issue no letter at all than one so controversial. Sexual and moral issues, birth control, divorce, pornography, and now abortion and homosexuality, have long tended to divide Catholics from many other Americans and to cause dissension in the American Catholic church itself. The sudden emergence into the religious and political arenas of a complex host of sexually related issues in the late 1980s left the bishops in disarray.

In his history of American Catholicism, Andrew Greeley wrote of the nineteenth-century American bishops and their troubles: "And at all times there was Rome, usually (though not always) trying to be sympathetic, but almost never able to achieve understanding" (Greeley 1977:34). The Vatican and the American bishops saw this situation re-emerge in the mid-1980s. At the 1986 NCCB meeting, papal representative Pio Laghi remarked, "We have not yet reached the 'magic number' of 100 but we are not very far from it" (Laghi 1986:398). He meant that almost 100 bishops had been appointed since he had come to serve as the Pope's envoy in America in 1980. What he didn't say, -- but what the bishops listening to him knew full well -- was that those men were largely conservatives, much in the image of Pope John Paul himself and decidedly different from the religiously and politically liberal bishops appointed during the decade of the 1970s.

Through such appointments, the Pope was weakening and dividing the NCCB from within. He and his *curia* began weakening it from without as well. In 1986, in a very unusual action, the Vatican intervened in the internal governance of the Seattle, Washington Archdiocese. Liberal Archbishop Raymond Hunthausen was stripped of power over such important areas of diocesan life as marriage annulments, the training of new priests, and relations with married former priests. This power was then put in the hands of a conservative bishop recently appointed by Rome to serve with Hunthausen. A bishop or archbishop presiding over a diocese is never shorn of his authority, or any part of it, unless he is physically or mentally unable to exercise it effectively. Concerned over this perceived threat to episcopal power, in 1987 a committee of American bishops, appointed by the NCCB, managed to negotiate a kind of compromise which effectively reversed the Vatican's decision to limit Archbishop Hunthausen's control over his own diocese (*Origins* 1987:37-43). Thus, the bishops began negotiating among themselves and with the Vatican to try to redefine the relationship between the ecelesiastical roles of hierarchy and theologians in a way that would somehow steer between the shoals of church obedience and American pluralism.

In 1987 Father Charles Curran was removed from his post as professor of moral theology at Catholic University by papal order because of his questioning of certain church teachings on contraception, masturbation, homosexuality, and other family and sexual issues (Congregation for the Doctrine of the Faith 1986a:201-

203). This led to a rancorous situation which plagued the bishops on many fronts. Bitter debates broke out among moral theologians and other Catholic academics and between them and the church hierarchy. Many non-Catholics concluded that the church was retreating from the liberal approaches it had taken over the past two decades and, further, that it was violating American principles of academic freedom. Arguments were raised again over church positions on birth control, abortion, premarital sex and homosexuality. The bishops found themselves in what, over the past few years, has become for them an ongoing situation -- attempting to negotiate with the Vatican.

In 1987 and 1988, American bishops would come under an even greater threat as the Vatican began to question the legitimacy of the national bishops' conferences themselves. In 1986, Cardinal Joseph Ratzinger, the powerful director of the Congregation for the Doctrine of the Faith, the Vatican office with responsibility for church orthodoxy, fired the first shot. He suggested that the Vatican Council, which had in effect sanctioned the formation of such national bishops' organizations, had never intended them to have anything but advisory authority. Then in 1987, the Vatican sent out a draft statement on national conferences to the world's bishops, asking for their comments. The proposed document would have substantially limited the powers of the bishops' conferences. The fact that they could come together and act as a group empowered bishops. A collective body of almost 300 bishops announcing collective decisions and acting as a unit is a much more potent, influential force than is a single bishop answerable alone to Rome. So in November, 1988, the American bishops strongly criticized the Vatican draft (as did the bishops of many other nations) and appointed a committee composed of all the past presidents of the NCCB to respond to it (Dulles 1990:7-9). They were fighting for their organizational church life in 1988. No wonder they had little energy or time for what was after all a lackluster election.

The Bishops Distracted

In 1987 and 1988, the bishops were confronted by a series of court cases, new laws and regulations which distracted their energy and attention from political concerns and made them extremely cautious of political involvement. The American Catholic church and many of its component organizations were spending a good deal of time in court during these years. Georgetown University had been sued for discrimination by student homosexual groups because they were not permitted, as organizations, to use campus facilities. The suit was only resolved by mutual agreement in March 1988. In addition, that same year, Father Curran sued to retain his teaching post. Most important, however, the NCCB was fighting a suit brought by Abortion Rights Mobilization. ARM was trying to force the Internal Revenue Service to revoke the tax-exempt status of virtually every Catholic church entity in the country for alleged violations of laws forbidding political activity by tax-exempt groups. ARM charged that church anti-abortion activities were political in nature and therefore in violation of IRS law. For most of 1988 the church was threatened by fines of $100,000 a day for refusing subpoenas for its records (*Origins* 1988a:98). These cases again mired the church in contentious battles over sexual and moral issues and, in the minds of many non-Catholics and some Catholics, raised questions about the Catholic church's role in a pluralistic society.

These cases undoubtedly caused the church to react with extreme caution when the IRS established new rules in 1987 which limited the role tax-exempt institutions could play in elections and which added significantly greater penalties for violations. The United States Catholic Conference's general counsel, Mark Chopko, issued a detailed memorandum on July 14, 1988, spelling out what could and could not be done politically by church organizations:

> Exempt organizations may not make statements . . . supporting or opposing any candidate for public office. . . . may not provide financial support to any candidate. . . . may not provide support to any individuals or organizations *opposing* a particular candidate. . . . may not distribute campaign literature that supports or opposes a particular candidate or political party . . . . (Chopko 1988:181-185).

Chopko also pointed out that what is permitted to tax-exempt organizations lies with what we might call "civic duty" kinds of activities: non-partisan voter registration drives; encouraging citizens to exercise their voting rights "provided no bias for or against any candidate or political party is evidenced"; sponsoring "unbiased public forums, debates or lectures" in which candidates explain their views to the public, as long as the sponsoring organization does not indicate its own views on the candidates or their stands on issues. Chopko finished with a warning that "unfortunately, what constitutes prohibited political campaign activity can be a close question that requires consultation with legal counsel." The church and the bishops heeded these cautions.

The Bishops Disengaged

A divided body of bishops, distracted by legal issues and new federal rules, took a far more low-keyed, neutral, less partisan but also more detached and disengaged role in the 1988 elections than they had in the past twelve years. To be sure, since 1976, prior to each presidential election, the USCC's Administrative Board *has* issued a statement setting forth church views on the major political issues of the day. But when in October 1987 the Administrative Board announced church views on the major issues involved in the 1988 campaign, it carefully declared that the bishops "do not seek the formation of a religious voting bloc; nor do we wish to instruct persons on how they should vote by endorsing or opposing candidates" (U.S. Catholic Conference Administrative Board 1987a:372). The phrase renouncing any desire to *oppose candidates* was a new one. It meant that the fierce battles that erupted in 1984 when several bishops questioned the right of Catholic politicians to make a distinction between their personal views on abortion and the role they felt they were obliged to play on the issue as elected officials would not re-emerge in 1988.

The church's participation in the 1984 campaign had centered almost entirely around the abortion issue. The Democratic party nominated Catholic Geraldine Ferraro for the vice-presidency. When she supported the party's pro-choice stance on abortion, many of the bishops felt they had to react to her and to other prominent Catholic politicians who were taking the same position. Even in this situation, though, as the campaign went on, a number of bishops worried publicly that abortion was overshadowing equally important church concerns over the threat of war and the poor.

So in the 1988 elections, the bishops attempted to enlarge public awareness of the many issues with which they were concerned by adopting Cardinal Bernardin's "consistent ethic of life" as the measuring stick for evaluating candidates and their stances. Throughout the 1980s, Bernardin had argued for a religious and philosophical schema by which Catholics and others could make moral and political decisions: does a proposed solution or an action protect human life and promote human dignity?

> As a guide to moral truth a consistent ethic of life can help us clarify our priorities and assess the moral coherence of various proposals for social advancement. . . . [A] consistent ethic demands protection of life as a basic human good that is the condition for all others. It also supports efforts to enhance life by providing the material and spiritual assistance others may need to appreciate and enjoy life, and to live it with dignity" (Bernardin 1988b:187).

As they had in earlier elections, the bishops argued that voters should examine the positions of candidates on a full range of issues. In their 1988 statement, however, they urged that these positions be examined under the "consistent ethic of life scheme:"

> We are convinced that a consistent ethic of life should be the moral framework from which we address all issues in the political arena. In this consistent ethic we address a spectrum of issues, seeking to protect human life and promote human dignity from the inception of life to its final moment" (U.S. Catholic Conference Administrative Board 1987a:372).

The bishops proceeded to examine issues, using the consistent ethic formula. Although they implied that all these issues were equally important, by deciding to list them alphabetically, abortion became the first issue addressed. The bishops, however, then did go on to discuss a wide range of issues. They voiced their support for arms control and repeated their limited, conditioned acceptance of nuclear deterrence policy; they voiced their opposition to capital punishment; they opposed racial, ethnic, age and gender discrimination; they argued that the nation must accept the concept of economic rights -- that everyone has a right to life, food, clothing, shelter, rest, medical care, education and employment; they supported governmental responsibility for protection of the environment; they urged the American government to avoid military involvement in Central America and to support political and social reform there and, together with private organizations, to press the South African government to end apartheid.

In the spring of 1988, Frank Monahan, director of the USCC's Government Liaison Office, spoke for the USCC at the Democratic and Republican National Campaign Platform Committees. He insisted, too, that all of the positions which the USCC urged the parties to adopt were in accordance with the consistent ethic of life philosophy. Quoting the bishops to the Democratic and Republican party leaders, he said, "'We urge you to measure every policy and proposal before you for how it touches the human person and whether it enhances or diminishes human life, human dignity and human rights'" (Monahan 1988:76).

The USCC in its testimony stressed the same issues discussed by the Administrative Board, although the testimony did deal more concretely with specific proposals before the Congress and the candidates. When in July 1988 the USCC sent questionnaires to candidates George Bush and Michael Dukakis, asking for their written opinions on a variety of issues, those issues again reflected the Administrative Board's statement and their demand that political issues be judged by adherence to a "consistent ethic of life." The responses Bush and Dukakis gave illustrate the difficulties of applying the consistent ethic of life to political issues.

But their responses, more importantly, also help explain the bishops' relative inaction and silence during the 1988 elections. Cardinal Bernardin's consistent ethic of life philosophy is one of the few attempts in modern American political life to develop a complex, coherent system of thought by which we can frame, discuss and judge political issues. It is a million miles away from the TV "soundbite," which, unfortunately, has both diluted and poisoned political discussion in this country. The problem with the consistent ethic of life is that it *is* complex. The traditional American categorization of issue positions and leaders as liberal, moderate or conservative cannot readily be applied using consistent ethic of life principles.

The argument that one must always act to protect human life, for example, requires opposition to both abortion *and* capital punishment. The argument that one must oppose anything that demeans or degrades human life argues support for bilingual education to "ensure every limited-English child's right to an equal education" *and* regulation to restrict the use of the telephone to make indecent or pornographic materials available. The consistent ethic of life envisions a politician's opposition to the MX missile *and* his support for handgun control (U.S. Catholic Conference Administrative Board 1987a:369-375). The bishops did not expect that any candidate would embrace all of the consistent ethic of life positions they advocated. In fact, they specifically urged voters to "examine the positions of candidates on the full range of issues as well as their personal integrity, philosophy and performance." However, an examination of Bush's and Dukakis' responses to their questionnaire show the bishops' difficulties in deciding which party or candidate best fulfilled the consistent ethic of life standard. It shows why, perhaps, the bishops were so silent.

In examining Democratic Michael Dukakis' responses to issues, the bishops must have been pleased to see that he supported a comprehensive test ban treaty and a substantial increase in the federal minimum wage, and that he opposed the death penalty. But Dukakis also opposed a constitutional amendment to overturn *Roe vs Wade* and strongly supported federal funding for abortions for poor women. In examining George Bush's responses, they must have been pleased at his strong opposition to abortion and to government funding of abortions. On the other hand, Bush opposed a test ban treaty; he opposed ending capital punishment; and he opposed an increase in the federal minimum wage. Furthermore, Dukakis' and Bush's positions on many issues could not be discerned because they both reinterpreted the bishops' questions to allow them to repeat standard, vague campaign speeches and pledges (*Origins* 1988b:311-315). In the end, most prelates probably came to agree with Alaskan Bishop Michael H. Kenny. On November 4, just before the election, he described both the Democratic and Republican parties as having "horrendous blind spots" when it came to a consistent ethic of life. "What seems to be lacking in both parties is an all-out, across-the-board commitment to human life and dignity" (*Catholic Almanac 1990* 1989:67).

Conclusions

"Horrendous blind spots," understood in a variety of ways, probably explains the bishops' unusual quiescence in the 1988 presidential elections. The bishops themselves were trying to find their way out of the confusion and disunity that the rise of a new set of issues had brought to their own ranks. They were forced to try to negotiate and mediate with a Vatican and a Pope with little understanding of cherished American church and societal values. In a period when American politics was least given to complex, programmatic thought, they were trying to move political debate into a philosophical framework.

In another essay in this collection, Catholic voters are described as a "swing vote" in the 1988 elections (see Chapter 10). If Catholics did indeed provide the "swing vote" in 1988, they could hardly have been influenced by their bishops. The bishops' role in the 1988 elections was far too negligible to be influential. It produced almost no media coverage. There were none of the dramatic, even if divisive, statements on political races we saw both in 1976 from the bishops meeting with Carter and Ford and in 1984 from prominent prelates such as Cardinal O'Connor and Bishop Malone. There was an attempt to promulgate the consistent ethic of life as a set of principles to judge candidates' stands, but this received almost no coverage in the secular media. And even the National Catholic News Service simply reported Dukakis' and Bush's responses, without any interpretations or certainly recommendations from the NCCB or any individual prelate. If you are barely visible on the national radar, you can scarcely wield influence.

How large a role the Catholic church and its bishops will play in future elections is hard to determine. Certainly the bishops remain intensely divided, and their difficulties with Rome continue. They are still embroiled in disputes with Rome over their own conference; over who, the bishops or the Vatican, should control teaching, especially by theologians, in Catholic universities and colleges; and over their proposed letter on the role of women in church and society. More recently, a new dispute has broken out over a universal catechism proposed by the Vatican as a guide for church teaching world wide (Steinfels 1990:A7).

If, however, as it appears more likely with each new appointment to the American hierarchy, conservative bishops sympathetic to the Vatican's views come to dominate the American hierarchy, we may see a rebirth of church political activism. This activism, if it comes, will be far more conservative in nature than has been true in the recent past. Rather than the letters on war and peace and on economic justice, moral issues will be central. Lost will be the willingness to listen to all sides of an issue, as Archbishop Rembert Weakland, for example, has demonstrated in regard to abortion, or the eagerness shown by Cardinal Bernardin and Bishop Malone to weigh *all* factors that diminish life. The possible emergence of this kind of rigidly conservative, single-minded position-taking by the hierarchy has already been signaled in the off-year elections that have taken place since 1988. A Catholic candidate for state office in California was denied Holy Communion by her bishop because she advocated a pro-choice position on abortion. Cardinal O'Connor in June 1990 raised the specter of excommunication for Catholic politicians persisting in their support for abortion. At the behest of their bishops, many Catholic parish organizations and even some Catholic colleges and universities have refused to allow Catholic and non-Catholic pro-choice politicians to speak on *any* subject before them. If these trends continue, we may view the bishops' disengagement in 1988 as an aberration. Their revitalized political engagement, however, may well resemble more that of the Moral Majority than the generally liberal, open Catholic presence felt in politics in the first half of the 1980s.

References

Bernardin, Joseph. 1988a. "Chicago Archdiocese Assumes Sponsorship of Mass." *Origins: NC Documentary Service*, July 9:49-51.
_____. 1988b. "The Consistent Ethic of Life and Individual Voters." *Origins*, September 1:186-189.
Catholic Almanac 1989. 1988. Huntington, Indiana: Our Sunday Visitor, Inc.
Catholic Almanac 1990. 1989. Huntington, Indiana: Our Sunday Visitor, Inc.
Chopko, Mark. 1988. "Political Campaign Activities and Tax-Exempt Groups." *Origins*, September 1:181-185.

54

Congregation for the Doctrine of the Faith. 1986a. "Letter Informing Father Curran He Cannot Teach Catholic Theology." *Origins*, August 28:201-203.
_____. 1986b. "The Pastoral Care of Homosexual Persons." *Origins*, November 13:377-382.
Dulles, Avery. 1990. "Episcopal Conferences: Their Teaching Authority." *America*, January 13:7-9.
Greeley, Andrew. 1977. *The American Catholic*. New York: Basic Books.
Laghi, Pio. 1986. "Pope's Message to U.S. Bishops' Meeting." *Origins*, November 20:398-399.
Monahan, Frank J. 1988. "USCC Platform Testimony to Democratic and Republican National Convention Platform Committees." *Origins*, June 16:76-79.
Origins. 1987. "Resolution of the Situation in Seattle." June 4:37-43.
Origins. 1988a. "On File." June 30:98.
Origins. 1988b. "Presidential Candidates: Responses to USCC Questionnaire." October 20:311-315.
Steinfels, Peter. 1990. "U.S. Bishops Fault Guide on Teaching." *New York Times*, April 10:A7.
U.S. Catholic Conference Administrative Board. 1987a. "Political Responsibility: Choices for the Future." *Origins*, November 5:369-375.
_____. 1987b. "The Many Faces of AIDS: A Gospel Response." *Origins*, December 24:481-489.

4

Jewish Community Leaders
and the 1988 Presidential Campaign

Carl Lieberman

Every election involves interactions between the mass public and political elites, represented by the candidates and various kinds of activists who seek to mobilize support on their behalf. Some of these elites are readily identifiable -- party leaders and campaign managers -- while others, including campaign contributors, interest group and community leaders, are less visible and not as well known. Leaders of religious groups, such as the Jewish community, by and large fall into the latter category. The influence of these kinds of leaders on a campaign can take several forms. First, they can endorse candidates or directly participate in their campaigns. Second, they can advocate a set of issues, narrowly or broadly defined. And finally, they can serve as advisers to particular candidates or campaigns (see Chapter 2).

The leaders of major national Jewish organizations were not particularly active in the 1988 presidential campaign. Organizations did not endorse candidates, although there was some evidence of direct involvement in the campaigns, including giving and raising funds, and providing political information to the Jewish community. Some organizations raised issues in the campaign, but most of these were long-standing concerns and not specifically tied to the election. All told, the Jewish leadership was far more diverse than commonly understood, and this diversity helps account for their political quiescence.

The Nature of the American Jewish Community

Investigating the political activity of American Jewish leaders involves a number of difficulties, some of which are peculiar to the Jewish community. To be Jewish means not simply sharing certain religious beliefs, but often sharing an ethnic identification as well. In fact, some Jews who have no formal religious affiliation nevertheless identify with the Jewish people as a result of family background, a common sense of history, or a set of customs and outlooks that set them apart from the general population. Despite broad agreement that Israel must be defended and a tendency to favor the Democratic Party and liberal causes, the American Jewish community is by no means monolithic (Selzer 1970).

The United States has never seen the development of a *kehillah* or self-governing community of the type found in many European countries until the eighteenth or nineteenth centuries (Cohen 1972). The European *kehillah* was usually a local body, but it could also be a national entity bound together by self-governing institutions (e.g. the Jewish population of Poland, which was held together for about two centuries by local communities organized into a national body -- the Council of the Four Lands). Although truly autonomous Jewish communities never existed in the United States, there were attempts to revive on a limited basis the idea of the *kehillah* in New York and other cities in the early years in the twentieth century. By the end of World War I, however, the *kehillah* movement had declined.

The lack of a centrally organized community has meant that there is no religious authority accepted by all observant Jews and no single body or council that speaks for the almost six million Jews in America. Rather, one finds a myriad of charitable, fraternal, religious, and political groups organized nationally and locally, including the lay and religious leaders of largely autonomous congregations scattered throughout the country, and the officers and directors of the local branches of national organizations.

Despite the absence of officially recognized leaders of the Jewish community, there is at the national level a Conference of Presidents of Major American Jewish Organizations, and in many cities Jewish federations and community relations councils. The Conference of Presidents of Major American Jewish Organizations, which has forty-nine members, was formed in the 1950s in response to complaints from Abba Eban, then Israeli ambassador to the United Nations, and Secretary of State John Foster Dulles that they had to meet with many Zionist and Jewish organizations on every issue (Spero 1990). Groups that are part of the Conference of Presidents vary widely in size and importance; some are divisions of larger organizations and have no members (e.g. the World Zionist Organization-American Section), while others are umbrella groups (e.g. the Council of Jewish Federations and the National Jewish Community Advisory Council) whose components belong to this body. Because many organizations are members of the Conference in their own right as well as members of umbrella groups, they may be represented two or more times (Spero 1990).

The existence of a national body designed to coordinate the responses of organizations to issues of concern has not eliminated the rivalries between groups nor ensured a unanimity of opinion. Thus, the American Israel Public Affairs Committee (AIPAC), an organization that lobbies for Israel in the United States and is perhaps the chief rival of the Conference of Presidents, is nevertheless a member of that body. There are also groups that vie with one another in speaking for Soviet Jews -- the National Conference on Soviet Jewry, the National Jewish Community Relations Advisory Council, and the Union of Councils for Soviet Jews. Three prominent groups that make statements or take policy positions when the Conference fails to speak -- the Anti-Defamation League of B'nai B'rith, the American Jewish Congress, and the American Jewish Committee -- may or may not represent the opinions of other elements of the Jewish community. Although such women's groups as Hadassah and Na'amat have large memberships, it is doubtful that they are looked upon as major spokespersons or power brokers (Spero 1990).

Divisions between organized groups reflect the fissures that exist among American Jews. Not only are there differences between religiously observant and secular members of the community, but there are also disagreements among those who belong to synagogues about matters of ritual and belief. Of the three major movements within American Judaism, the Conservative and Reform bodies have the most adherents, and both deviate in some measure from their more traditional Orthodox coreligionists in their devotion to *Halakhah* or Jewish religious law (Trepp 1980). There are disputes as well over support for Israeli policy. Although concern for the security of Israel is commonplace, there are many Jews in the United States who favor territorial compromise as a means of resolving the Israeli-Palestinian conflict (Goldberg 1990; Novik 1986). And although many Jewish leaders are known for their liberal stands on social and economic issues, there is a vocal group of more conservative dissenters, including prominent "neo-conservative" intellectuals (Reichley 1982).

A combination of religious beliefs, historical circumstances, and high socio-economic status have lead American Jews to be more active in politics than most other religious or ethnic groups. Jews generally vote more frequently than the population at large, and they are sufficiently numerous in such states as New York, California, and Florida to influence the outcomes of closely contested presidential elections. In addition, Jews have been an important component of the Democratic coalition for better than fifty years. Jews also form a large part of the politically active population, serving disproportionately as political "gladiators," and they often participate as financial contributors, campaign advisers, and opinion leaders even when they were not themselves candidates for office (Levy and Kramer 1972; Silberman 1985; Milbrath 1965).

Given the prominence of Jews in American politics, it is hardly surprising that Jewish leaders would be looked upon as an important and influential elite. Of course, there are also conspiracy theories that have historically linked Jewish power to political change, claiming that a small group of prominent Jews has conspired to control events in the United States and, indeed, throughout the world. Even some of those who might categorically reject such theories as naive or pernicious nevertheless have argued that organized Jewish groups play an important part in national politics, influencing electoral outcomes and foreign policy in the United States (Curtiss 1990; Tivnan 1987).

What follows is an assessment of the activities of Jewish leaders in the 1988 campaign, drawing on journalistic sources and interviews with a select number of leaders and executives of national Jewish organizations.[1]

The 1988 Presidential Campaign and the Jewish Community

In some respects the 1988 presidential campaign was a repetition of the 1984 Reagan-Mondale race which preceded it. Concerns about the influence of Jesse Jackson in the Democratic Party and the association of national Republican leaders with the Christian Right were issues that mattered to Jews in both elections. The outcome -- about two-thirds of the Jewish electorate voting for the Democratic candidate -- was also similar (see Chapter 11). There were, of course, some important differences as well. Jesse Jackson played a more prominent role in the 1988 campaign, and the Democratic nominee, Michael Dukakis, was less tied to traditional liberal politics than Walter Mondale. The Christian Right, in the form of Pat Robertson, was much more active in the Republican party, and while there was no incumbent president, the Republican nominee, George Bush, was closely associated with the Reagan administration, although not with all of Reagan's conservative allies.

As in 1984, both parties and many candidates made direct appeals to the Jewish community. Not surprisingly, these appeals were most prominent in the Democratic party, where all candidates expressed support for Israel and sought endorsements from prominent Jewish activists. In the crucial New York primary, Michael Dukakis, Albert Gore, and Jesse Jackson courted Jewish religious and political leaders. New York City Mayor Ed Koch openly endorsed Gore and suggested that "Jews would be crazy to vote for Jesse Jackson." Despite Koch's endorsement, Dukakis won most of the Jewish vote and the primary, while Jackson secured widespread support among black and Hispanic voters and finished second (Dowd 1988a; Weinraub 1988; Lynn 1988; Cook 1988).

Jesse Jackson was the focus of great concern in the Jewish community and surely had the most difficult time convincing Jewish voters and activists to support him. Although he may have suffered from the general disaffection between blacks and Jews in recent times, his specific difficulties resulted from a perception that he was insensitive to Jews, if not anti-Semitic. His "Hymietown" reference to New York in 1984; his friendship with Louis Farrakhan, who had referred to Judaism as "a gutter religion"; and his closeness to foreign leaders opposed to Israel all served to create substantial opposition within the Jewish community (King 1987; Dionne 1988; Cook 1988).

Indeed, Jackson was perceived by many Jews as being habitually antagonistic to Israel. Given their concern for Israel -- a concern resulting from a history of persecution capped by the Holocaust, pride that Jews had reestablished a state after almost 1900 years of dispersion, and, for some, a strongly held religious belief that God intended the Land of Israel to be the homeland and patrimony of the Jewish people -- this perception was likely to be especially salient. The centrality of Israel to American Jewish life is also reflected in the fact that for persons who do not have strong religious ties to the community, to make contributions to and do fund-raising for the state of Israel and its charitable institutions is a way of achieving prominence (Cohen 1983; Fein 1988).

Thus, Jackson's foreign policy positions, which never questioned Israel's right to exist, but which seemed tilted toward 'Arafat, the PLO, and the Palestinians, were seen as a complex threat. If Jackson won the presidency or even became a powerful force in a new Democratic administration, it was feared that he would work against the interests of Israel. But at another level, it may be that Jackson's coalition of poor and black voters was feared because of what they might demand. As Lorenzo Morris (1990:8) noted in reference to Jackson's 1984 campaign:

> . . . [T]here was a clear presumption that black and poor sentiments of anti-semitism and 'anti-other things' had emerged with an electoral bent . . . these new voters would have to demand something that would subsequently deprive some other members of the old coalition. Because Jackson's formal campaign positions never sought to discredit the other liberal agendas, other Democrat leaders were inclined to suspect that the real agenda was hidden.

Although his campaign manager, Gerald Austin, and one of his more important advisers, Ann Lewis, were Jewish, Jackson failed to develop close contracts with the heads of major Jewish organizations. For example, he refused to speak at a public forum proposed by Jewish community leaders in New York which he perceived as being biased against him (A. M. Rosenthal 1988), and he met privately only with a limited number of religious and lay leaders in Southern California prior to the primary in that state. The latter meeting was boycotted by several organizations, including the Anti-Defamation League of B'nai B'rith, the Los Angeles Jewish Federation Council, and the Simon Wiesenthal Center. David Lehrer, regional director of the Anti-Defamation League, said, "There was an invitation from the organized Jewish community for an open public meeting. That was the appropriate forum" (Obeskes 1988).

If Jesse Jackson's candidacy was of great concern to Jewish voters and activists, the role of the Christian Right was a more subtle issue and one that did not gain salience. The attempt by Pat Robertson to secure the Republican presidential nomination was the culmination of a movement by evangelical Christians to influence public policy. Although most Jews probably opposed key Christian Right issues, such as school prayer and restrictions on abortions, concern with the potential power of the Christian Right may have been as much symbolic as substantive.

The growing tendency of politicians, most them Republican, to seek the support of well-known conservative Protestant ministers has made many Jews uneasy. Suggestions that the United States is a Christian nation or that only Christians should be elected to positions of public trust tend to reinforce the marginal position of Jews in a society where they constitute only a small minority of the population. Despite the relative affluence and high level of education of American Jews today, they have suffered discrimination in the past and have achieved most of their success only in the postwar period. There is a continued fear that anti-Semitism might be revived if the political or social environment were to change. For the most part, Jews have fared better in the United States when tolerance and pluralism have flourished; they could not achieve equality if they were confronted with a relatively solid or monolithic majority arrayed against them (Bole et al. 1985; Castelli 1986; Neuhaus 1985; Hertzberg 1989). The failure of Robertson's campaign to attract much support and his early withdrawal from the Republican race, therefore, was likely viewed with relief by many Jews.

George Bush and Michael Dukakis sought to develop effective appeals to Jewish voters even before they officially became their respective party's nominees. Their strategy during the campaign attempted to reinforce positive images in the Jewish community, but it also sought to arouse apprehension, particularly on the issue of Israel. Dukakis was a potentially attractive candidate to Jewish voters. His ethnic background and his Jewish wife, Kitty, probably helped him to secure support among Jews, and his liberal stands on domestic policy may have helped as well. However, his views on Israel were open to question, and after winning the Democratic presidential nomination, he had to decide how to deal with Jesse Jackson and his supporters (Germond and Witcover 1989:28,312).

Early in the campaign, Dukakis had endorsed a letter sent by thirty senators to Israeli Prime Minister Yitzhak Shamir, criticizing his quick rejection of Secretary of State George Shultz's attempts to open negotiations. Shortly before the New York primary, his aides were asked by Andrew Cuomo, the governor's son and chief political adviser, to soften his support for that letter. At the same time, Cuomo suggested that Dukakis might want to announce publicly that he would consider Jesse Jackson for the vice-presidential nomination. Dukakis hesitated to follow Cuomo's advice. A weakening of his position on the senatorial letter might lead to the perception that he was pandering to Jewish voters. On the other hand, announcing a willingness to consider Jackson for the vice-presidential nomination could lead to defections among Jews and other white ethnics (Germond and Witcover 1989:316-317).

During the general election campaign, Dukakis continued to keep Jackson at arm's length for fear of a backlash from white voters. Dukakis hoped to win back "Reagan Democrats," so he did not include two key Jackson advisers, Mayor Richard Hatcher of Gary, Indiana, and former Governor Tony Anaya of New Mexico, in the upper levels of his operation, though Jackson campaigned for him both in the North and the South (Drew 1989:337-338). Realizing his vulnerability on the question of American policy toward Israel, Dukakis tried to reassure Jewish voters and activists of his sensitivity to that country's interests. In California, for example, he reversed a position taken in New York and said that Jerusalem should be the capital of Israel; he had previously maintained that this was a negotiable matter. Before securing the Democratic nomination, Dukakis told AIPAC that he was not advocating an independent Palestinian state and would not support a resolution of the Israeli-Palestinian conflict that was unacceptable to Israel or Jordan (Andrew Rosenthal 1988).

George Bush was part of an administration that was widely seen as favorably disposed toward Israel. Nevertheless, the increased association of the Republican party with conservative religious forces and Ronald Reagan's blunder in 1985 in visiting a German military cemetery at Bitburg, Germany (where members of the Waffen SS were buried) served to reduce somewhat the luster of that relationship (Germond and Witcover 1989:28-29,151). Moreover, Bush's own positions on policy issues were somewhat muddied. He was opposed to abortion, but he said that he favored more federal support for child care and equal pay for women workers. He placed emphasis on improving schools, calling for more money for Head Start, support for Pell grants to low-income college students (which the Reagan administration tried to cut) and tax-free college savings bonds; during the campaign, however, he pledged that he would oppose higher taxes. Clearly, his proposals would raise some doubts among more liberal voters (*Congressional Quarterly* 1988:51-65).

Both campaigns skirmished over the Jewish vote throughout the fall. The Dukakis forces accused some of the leaders of ethnic committees in the Republican campaign of pro-Nazi and anti-Semitic tendencies (Edsall and Petersen 1988; Berke 1988). They attacked one Bush operative, Fred Malek, who had been involved in gaining information about Jewish employees in the Bureau of Labor Statistics during the Nixon administration in order to purge them from positions of influence in that agency. Malek had been proposed by Bush as a person who could run the daily operations of the Republican National Committee (Dowd 1988b). The Republicans countered by pointing to the adoption of pro-Palestinian resolutions in nine Democratic state parties and the appointment of three controversial Jackson allies to the Democratic National Committee (Edsall and Petersen 1988). Bush supporters also raised the specter of Jesse Jackson. How influential would he be within the Democratic Party and in a Democratic administration? Would his views on foreign policy, particularly as they related to Israel, be reflected in a Dukakis White House? (Fiedler 1988). Whether the concerns raised about Israel actually influenced many voters is difficult to say. As one Jewish member of Congress remarked, "You hear a lot of talk among elites, but most Jewish voters are not members of Israeli PACs preoccupied with the intricacies of Middle East policy" (Edsall and Petersen 1988). In all probability deeper partisan and ideological commitments had more significant impact on the Jewish community.

Activities of Jewish Community Leaders

Given the political background and social status of American Jews and the events of the 1988 election, one might have expected Jewish leaders to have been actively involved in the campaign. In fact, however, their involvement appears to have been fairly limited. Few leaders or organizations endorsed candidates in the primaries or the general election, although the level of direct campaign activity was more impressive. Advocacy of issues was somewhat more common, usually on narrow issues of long-standing concern to the proponents, and only a few leaders served as advisers to candidates.

The presidents or executives of national Jewish organizations interviewed indicated a general lack of partisan political activity. I was told repeatedly in interviews that most organizations are tax-exempt and "nonpolitical" in nature. Only one of the organizations contacted testified before a platform committee of the major political parties and only a few leaders mentioned taking part in the campaign, such as speaking out for a candidate or debating other leaders in Jewish community forums. Although many Jewish organizations tended to lean towards the Democratic party, at least one, the National Jewish Coalition, promoted Jewish involvement in Republican politics. In addition, AIPAC did not confine its help to Democratic candidates; indeed, as a director of another group suggested, it actively aided Republicans in 1988, to the consternation of many Jewish Democrats.

There were more reports of informal campaign activity on the part of individual leaders or members of their organizations. Many leaders reported contributing to presidential campaigns, and a few served as fund raisers, most in support of Dukakis or another Democratic candidate. Jews had been deeply involved in campaign finance for many years, particularly in the Democratic party (Domhoff 1972), and they remained active in 1988 (see Chapter 5). In addition to individual donors, a host of "pro-Israel" political action committees were active in the 1988 primary campaign, particularly on the Democratic side. Collectively these PACs gave Michael Dukakis $24,713; Albert Gore, $18,250; Richard Gephardt, $16,750; and Paul Simon, $12,694. However, donations also went to Republicans, including $13,250 to Jack Kemp, and $5,000 each to George Bush and Alexander Haig. These PACs were also quite active in congressional campaign finance, with some forty-two organizations giving some $3.8 million to House and Senate candidates in 1986, and the 10 largest providing $519,000 to congressional candidates in 1987 (Tivnan 1987; Curtiss 1990; Babcock 1990; Berezansky and Cohen 1990). The distribution of such contributions has tended to favor Democratic candidates, but it has hardly been one-sided. While these sums are large, they are comparable to the resources provided by other interest groups, such as labor unions and sectors of the business community.

Another activity mentioned was providing information to the Jewish community. One executive director sought policy statements from all candidates and participated in preparing documents "for several key groups." A Jewish community relations executive prepared speeches to the Jewish community on the importance of the election. A few organizational executives said that they encouraged members to vote or write letters to the editor and to public officials, but none of them urged persons within their group to support particular candidates.

A number of organizations took stands on issues in the campaign and provided advice to candidates. Not surprisingly, the bulk of these activities concerned American policy toward Israel or the Middle East. However, some organizations had broader agendas, including church-state relations, peace issues (disarmament, the nuclear test ban), and the plight of Soviet Jews. A group with an ongoing interest in public policy mentioned its concern with women's and family issues -- day care, family leave legislation, abortion, and the like. Several leaders mentioned preparing position papers for both parties and providing advice to both nominees. Some Jewish leaders were particularly close to the Republican and Democratic candidates, with the leadership of AIPAC working with the Bush campaign, and Hyman Bookbinder, former Washington representative of the American Jewish Committee, advising Dukakis (Greenberger 1988).

It could be, of course, that the real political strength of the Jewish community lies in its local organizations and synagogues. American Judaism is not a highly structured or hierarchical faith, thus creating opportunities for local initiative. One leader, for example, volunteered that some of the local chapters of his organization actively opposed the nomination of Jesse Jackson. However, there is little evidence that the many unaffiliated or nominally observant Jews were easily mobilized by local groups. And rabbis of local congregations probably were wary about "instructing" their members how to vote. They would have risked being ineffective at best, and, at worst, they could easily have offended those persons who would consider such instruction inappropriate.

The leaders interviewed were asked to assess the importance to them and their members of Jackson and Robertson. Although a few of the leaders and executives said that there was concern about Pat Robertson seeking the Republican nomination, most did not perceive this to be an issue of crucial importance. As one person noted, "'Interest' probably; but no evident concern because candidacy was not considered serious."

Concern about the candidacy of Jesse Jackson was much more frequently cited. Over half of the respondents referred to Jackson's seeking the Democratic nomination. The explanations of concern and interest were more complex than one might expect. Some mentioned Jackson's position on Israel and his perceived anti-Semitism as the cause of the concern, while others said that his potential influence on foreign policy and the Democratic Party was the major reason for consternation. The strongest reaction to Jackson came from a leader of a small organization (less than 10,000 members) who wrote, "Our membership was alarmed and was active in respective chapters in defeating his candidacy. Our membership viewed Jackson as an anti-Semitic, black racist, and dangerous to America." A leader of a pro-Israeli organization said that he opposed any clergyman running for public office.

However, some remarks indicated ambivalence about Jackson or even support for his candidacy. One person noted that, "Some members felt support because of his disarmament positions; others feared what they saw as his blindness to Jewish religious, cultural, and political interests." Another stated that, "Jackson provided the most thoughtful human rights/Soviet Jewry statement of all candidates. However, we had widespread concern for his anti-Semitism/pro-Farrakhan history." Leaders of smaller organizations that have a left-wing or pacifist orientation noted that a number of their members supported Jackson's candidacy partly because of the positions he took in regard to Israeli-Palestinian relations (e.g., a two state solution, Palestinian rights) or in regard to domestic issues such as social welfare and economic regulation.

Clearly, then, the Jewish leadership is not monolithic. Even in regard to Jesse Jackson, there were a variety of responses by members and officers of national groups. Indeed, the recently elected Democratic senator from Minnesota, Paul Wellstone, is Jewish and co-chaired Jackson's 1988 campaign committee in that state. On the other hand, one Republican Jewish leader expressed a minority opinion among those interviewed. He favored the Republican candidate for president because he thought Bush was more experienced and competent than Dukakis and because Bush would probably continue the policies of the Reagan administration toward Israel. Unlike the 1930s, he suggested, present-day liberals are likely to be isolationists and supporters of the enemies of Israel. Whether his point of view is growing among Jewish voters and organizational leaders is difficult to say. Surely, there are Republican officeholders such as Warren Rudman and Rudy Boschwitz who are relatively conservative. However, there is no evidence that conservative Republican viewpoints were more common in 1988 than in years past (Fisher 1989; Solomon 1988).

Many voices are heard in the Jewish community, and there are sometimes bitter divisions over religion, ideology, and policy regarding Israel. As Letty Cottin Pogrebin (1990:15) warned recently:

> Although an ardent fan of Jewish disputation, I believe our rancor has gone too far--so far, in fact, that intra-communal hostility seems as urgent a threat to Jewish survival today as the external peril of antisemitism.

Conclusions

Jews are among the most affluent and politically active groups in American society, and their high rates of turnout and campaign activity were once again evident in 1988. However, the leaders of national Jewish organizations were not particularly active in the 1988 presidential campaign, and when they were involved, their activities tended to focus on less visible, "insider" activities, such as contributing to campaigns, informing the Jewish community on political matters, and giving advice on Jewish concerns to candidates. While still largely within the orbit of the Democratic party, Jewish leaders and activists are far more diverse than commonly understood. Thus, the perception of extraordinary cohesion and power on the part of the Jewish community needs to be reexamined.

The reasons for the lack of participation among Jewish organizations in 1988 are varied. First, it is possible that the fear of an anti-Semitic backlash may serve as a constraint on the leadership style of American Jews. Highly visible partisan political activity could be seen as threatening to the Jewish community. For a candidate to be viewed as either supported or opposed by organized groups could resuscitate the belief among some segments of the population that there is a Jewish cabal seeking to control the government. If there was a perception that such political activity was motivated largely by a concern for Israel, the charge of dual loyalty might be raised. Contributions to candidates, even when orchestrated by political action committees, would probably be more acceptable, because fund-raising and campaign donations are largely insider activities, mainly of interest to better-informed, more highly committed individuals. Likewise, speaking to and on behalf of Jewish concerns is less likely to attract unwanted attention.

On the other hand, the tax-exempt status of most organizations obviously makes their officers wary about taking overtly partisan stands or pursuing policy positions too vigorously. And one suspects that some executives are reluctant even to divulge their own political affiliation as a result of an atmosphere of nonpartisanship that permeates many of these groups. Indeed, many groups have diverse memberships, and endorsing particular candidates or highly controversial policies would risk alienating those who hold contrary positions. The Jewish community is far from monolithic, and there are forces at work that will probably increase its diversity in the future: the assimilation of many Jews into the broader American culture, their dispersion throughout the country, and the long-term effects of high levels of education and income may all contribute to the development of greater Republican and conservative support in the future.

Finally, the absence of highly politicized Jewish organizations and a group of militant, partisan leaders intent on mobilizing the Jewish community on behalf of a particular cause reveals much about the diversity of Jewish voters. It suggests that the Jews probably do not look to a leadership class for clear cues on how to vote. If they usually support the Democratic party, its candidates, and liberal causes, this may have more to do with patterns of political socialization and historical factors -- for example, the New Deal and the tendency for national Democratic politicians to be more friendly toward minority groups than their Republican counterparts -- than with organizational activity or efforts of leaders to mobilize their constituents. Barring a dramatic change in the issue agenda, there is no reason to believe that Jewish leaders will be more active or effective in national campaigns in the near future.

68

Notes

1. Forty-two presidents or executive directors of national Jewish organizations were chosen from a list of groups classified under the headings of "community relations" or "Zionist and pro-Israel" bodies by *The American Jewish Year Book 1989* (Philadelphia: American Jewish Committee). Twenty-one persons responded in the summer and fall of 1989.

References

Babcock, Charles. 1990. "Ruling: Pro-Israel Lobby Does Not Control PACs." *Philadelphia Inquirer*, December 22:6-A.

Berenzansky, Williams, and Richard E. Cohen, 1990. "Do Pro-Israel PACs Work in Concert?" *National Journal*, March 19:746.

Berke, Richard L. 1988. "Bush Panelist Out After Reports of Anti-Jewish Ties." *New York Times*, September 9:15.

Bole, William, Larry Cohler, David Anderson, A. James Rudin, and Adam Simms. 1985. "The New Christian Right." *Present Tense*, Winter:22-39.

Castelli, Jim. 1986. "What Makes Pat Run?" *Present Tense*, Autumn:25-29.

Cohen, Naomi. 1972. *Not Free to Desist: The American Jewish Committee 1906-1966.* Philadelphia: The Jewish Publication Society of America.

Cohen, Steven M. 1983. *American Modernity and Jewish Identity.* New York: Tavistock Publications.

Congressional Quarterly, 1988. *Candidates '88.* Washington, DC: Congressional Quarterly, Inc.

Cook, Rhodes. 1988. "The Door Opens for a Dukakis Run to Daylight." *Congressional Quarterly Weekly Report*, April 25:1086.

Curtiss, Richard H. 1990. *Stealth PACs: How Israel's American Lobby Took Control of U.S. Middle East Policy.* Washington, DC: The American Education Trust.

Dionne, E.J. Jr. 1988. "Jackson's Burden Among Jews." *New York Times*, April 14:D27.

Domhoff, G. William. 1972. *Fatcats and Democrats.* Englewood Cliffs, NJ: Prentice-Hall.

Dowd, Maureen. 1988a. "Jesse Jackson: A Jewish Leader Provides a Forum for the Candidate." *New York Times*, April 18:A16.

_____. 1988b. "Adviser to Bush Quits GOP Post Amid Anti-Semitism Allegations." *New York Times*, September 12:A1,16.

Drew, Elizabeth, 1989. *Election Journal: Political Events of 1987-1988.* New York: William Morrow and Company, Inc.

Edsall, Thomas, and Bill Peterson, 1988. "Emerging Fears Threaten Jewish Ties to Democrats." *Washington Post*, October 17:A1b.

Fein, Leonard. 1988. *Where Are We? The Inner Life of America's Jews.* New York: Harper and Row.

Fiedler, Tom. 1988. "Bitter Fight for Their Support Has Angered Jewish Voters." *Miami Herald*, October 21:A1.

Fisher, Alan M. 1989. "Where the Jewish Vote is Going." *Moment*, March:41-43.

Germond, Jack W., and Jules Witcover, 1989. *Whose Broad Stripes and Bright Stars?*

The Trivial Pursuit of the Presidency 1988. New York: Warner Books, Inc.

Goldberg, David Howard. 1990. *Foreign Policy and Ethnic Interest Groups.* Westport, CT: Greenwood Press, Inc.

Greenberger, Robert S. 1988. "Pro-Israel Lobby Faces Political Tug of War: Conservative Leadership vs. Liberal Constituents." *The Wall Street Journal,* December 20:A16.

Hertzberg, Arthur. 1989. *The Jews in America, Four Centuries of An Uneasy Encounter.* New York: Simon and Schuster.

Levy, Mark R. and Michael S. Kramer, 1972. *The Ethnic Factor: How America's Minorities Decide Elections.* New York: Simon and Shuster.

Lynn, Frank. 1988. "Ethnic Coalitions Mark the Voting." *New York Times,* April 20:B7.

King, Wayne. 1987. "Three Years Later, Jackson is Haunted by Anti-Semitism of Farrakhan." *New York Times,* June 13:6.

Milbrath, Lester. 1965. *Political Participation: How and Why Do People Get Involved in Politics.* Chicago: Rand McNally and Co.

Morris, Lorenzo. 1990. "The Range and Limits of Campaign Politics," in Lorenzo Morris, ed., *The Social and Political Implications of the 1984 Jesse Jackson Presidential Campaign.* Pp. 3-13. New York: Praeger.

Neuhaus, Richard. 1985. "What the Fundamentalists Want." *Commentary,* May:41-46.

Novik, Nimrod. 1986. *The United States and Israel: Domestic Determinants of a Changing U.S. Commitment.* Boulder: Westview Press.

Obeskes, Michael. 1988. "Jackson in Bid to Heal Rift Meets with California Jews." *New York Times,* May 19:B12.

Pogrebin, Letty Cottin. 1990. (untitled). *Moment,* October:15.

Reichley, A. James. 1982. "The Reagan Coalition." *The Brookings Review,* 1:6-9.

Rosenthal, A.M. 1988. "A Call from Mr. Jackson." *New York Times,* July 26:A21.

Rosenthal, Andrew. 1988. "Bush and Dukakis Are Emerging in Early Battle Over the Jewish Vote." *New York Times,* May 29:A24.

Selzer, Michael, ed. 1970. *Zionism Reconsidered: The Rejection of Jewish Normalcy.* New York: Macmillan.

Silberman, Charles E. 1985. *A Certain People: American Jews and Their Lives Today.* New York: Summit Books.

Solomon, Herbert L. 1988. "The Republican Party and the Jews." *Judaism,* 37:276-287.

Spero, Robert. 1990. "Speaking for the Jews: Who Does the Conference of Presidents of Major American Jewish Organizations Really Represent?" *Present Tense,* January-February:15-27.

Tivnan, Edward. 1987. *The Lobby: Jewish Political Power and American Foreign Policy.* New York: Simon and Schuster.

Trepp, Leo. 1980. *The Complete Book of Jewish Observance.* New York: Behrman House, Inc. and Summit Books.

Weinraub, Bernard. 1988. "Albert Gore, Jr.: Seeking Ethnic Votes." *New York Times,* April 18:A16.

PART THREE

Religion and Political Activists in the 1988 Campaign

5

Pulpits and Politics: The Protestant Clergy in the 1988 Presidential Election

James L. Guth
John C. Green
Corwin E. Smidt
Margaret M. Poloma

Ministers have long been an important force in American politics. From the Revolution to the Civil War to the early decades of the twentieth century, Protestant clergy were a crucial source of political activism, sometimes on both sides of major controversies. During the 1960s and 1970s, however, political participation by the clergy seemed the province of theological liberals from mainline churches (Hadden 1969; Quinley 1974) and black clergy in the civil rights movement (Morris 1984). In contrast, theologically conservative Protestants shunned social and political activity (Koller and Retzer 1980; Nelsen and Baxter 1981). Indeed, so rare was such involvement that Stark et al. (1971) heard only the "sound of silence" emanating from orthodox ministers and attributed it to their "otherworldly" theology.

During the late 1970s and 1980s, however, the balance shifted dramatically as conservative pastors went public, both in preaching from the pulpit and in weekday political action (Guth 1984; Beatty and Walter 1988, 1989). Of particular concern were issues related to traditional morality and "family values." So great was the increase in political activism among traditionalists that the gap between liberal and conservative ministers nearly disappeared (Guth 1989). And some analysts saw important political effects from this change, attributing part of Reagan's success as candidate and president to his support from conservative Protestants and their leaders. In this chapter, we will look at the outlines of the emerging "two-party" system among contemporary American Protestant clergy, based on conflicting religious worldviews and expressed in dramatically different political commitments.

Ministers and Politics

Ministers' impact on the political process has at least two sources. First, clergy have the potential to influence the political opinions and involvement of their congregations. As Welch et al. (1990:1-2) point out, in a church ministers play "perhaps the most important role" in the political communication process, being "in the best position to transmit political cues and mobilize their flocks to get political action." The evidence shows that many churchgoers expect ministers to speak out on political issues and that pastoral activities do influence attitudes of the laity, although there may be considerable disagreement on specific issues (Wilcox 1990). Secondly, even if clergy are unable to move most of their parishioners, they may often activate a core of sympathizers who can agitate on issues, raise money, and otherwise assist candidates. For that matter, ministers themselves possess skills and resources which are extremely valuable to parties and candidates.

Despite all this, our understanding of clerical politics is very limited. Much of our knowledge is based on data collected in the late 1960s, while more recent studies focus on only one or two denominations (Guth 1983; Hailey 1988) or on local samples from a specific religious tradition, such as "evangelicals" (Langenbach 1988; Harder 1988). A final difficulty is that most studies stress either the social movement tactics of the liberal "New Breed" clergy of the 1960s, such as protest marches and civil disobedience, or the church-related activities of the Christian Right, such as voter registration, petition drives, or pulpit endorsement of candidates. Relatively little attention has been paid to routine electoral efforts by mainstream religious liberals and conservatives.

The presidential campaign of 1988 provided an almost ideal opportunity to assess pastoral politics. A Southern Baptist minister turned religious broadcaster, Marion G. "Pat" Robertson, sought the GOP nomination, making religiously tinged appeals and inviting conservative pastors and laity to form an "invisible army." On the Democratic side, Reverend Jesse Jackson invoked religious imagery and built a political base in black congregations; but he also campaigned in many white churches and attracted religious liberals of all races. Both tapped deep veins of religious feeling and, perhaps in self-defense, other candidates adopted special strategies to win over the religious and mobilize their leaders. In the fall, Bush and the Republicans repeated, if more quietly, the same appeals to conservative Protestants that worked so well for Reagan in 1980 and 1984, while Dukakis and the Democrats embraced policies more congenial to religious and secular liberals (see Chapters 1 and 2).

How successful were all these efforts? To find out, we analyzed political attitudes and activities in 1988 among clergy from seven Protestant denominations: the pentecostal Assemblies of God, one of the most rapidly growing Protestant churches (Poloma 1989); the theologically conservative Southern Baptist Convention, the nation's largest Protestant denomination (Ammerman 1990); two Dutch Calvinist churches, the Christian Reformed Church and the Reformed Church in America (Bouma 1984; Luidens and Nemeth 1987)[1]; and three "mainline" churches, the United Methodist Church (UMC 1990), the Presbyterian Church in the U.S.A. (Hallum 1988), and the Christian Church (Disciples of Christ) (Friedly and Cummins 1987). Although these denominations hardly exhaust the diversity within American Protestantism, they claim a large portion of the nation's white Protestants and represent several distinct traditions. (For details, see the Appendix.)

After a look at ministers' theological beliefs, we will examine how denominational affiliation and theological orthodoxy influenced their political attitudes and behaviors during the 1988 election, including (1) social and political agendas; (2) views on political issues; (3) partisan orientations; (4) presidential candidate preferences; and (5) activism during the presidential campaign.

Theological Orientations

The impact of religious perspective on clerical politics has been repeatedly demonstrated: theology influences the political attitudes of clergy, their views about ministerial role, and the kinds of social and political activism in which they engage. To map the religious beliefs of ministers, scholars have used several strategies. The customary one is simply asking about adherence to traditional Christian orthodoxy or, on the other hand, to "liberal" or "modernist" versions of the faith (Hadden 1969; Quinley 1974). More recently, investigators have used theological self-identification as a preferable, or at least more succinct, measure (Guth 1983; Beatty and Walter 1988). Although we have

TABLE 5.1 Theological Orientations of Protestant Clergy

	AOG	SBC	REFORM	METH	PRES	DISC
(N)	(406)	(653)	(746)	(723)	(917)	(1289)
Doctrine						
Jesus only way to salvation	97%[a]	88%	65%	40%	30%	22%
Virgin birth of Jesus	--	82	58	--	22	17
Devil actually exists	95	79	60	32	18	15
Hell is real place	--	72	32	--	13	17
Adam and Eve historical	--	72	46	--	9	9
Scriptures inerrant	88	60	17	19	5	6
Believe in Church's "rapture"	83	54	--	18	5	8
Bible teaches premillennialism	50	27	2	6	1	3
Agree with "dispensationalism"	22	15	--	2	1	3
Orthodoxy Index						
Most Orthodox	96[b]	80	35	32	13	11
Orthodox	4	13	46	24	28	18
Modernist	0	6	15	20	34	29
Most Modernist	0	1	4	24	25	42
(Total)	100%	100%	100%	100%	100%	100%

[a] Entries are percentages "agreeing strongly" with each belief.
[b] Entries are percentages of ministers in each denomination within a category.

Source: Surveys conducted by authors.

both types of questions, here we rely primarily on specific doctrinal issues.[2] Based on earlier studies, we have clear expectations: Assemblies clergy should be the most orthodox, with Southern Baptists close behind, followed by Reformed ministers, Methodists, Presbyterians, and finally, on the theological left, the Disciples. Table 5.1 reports the proportion of clergy in each denomination giving the strongest "orthodox" response to questions on religious doctrine.

These ministers live in different theological worlds. The Assemblies of God are uniformly orthodox, while Southern Baptists are only slightly less traditionalist. Many in both denominations adhere to the cardinal points of dispensationalism and premillennialism (belief that the End Times are approaching, with the great final conflagration at Armageddon, the Second Coming of Jesus, and his thousand year reign on earth). This was once an anti-political, otherworldly perspective, but has more recently been linked to the Christian Right (Turner and Guth 1989). No doubt the Assemblies' clergy hold to a different version than their Baptist brethren: they consider "charismatic gifts," such as speaking in tongues, as evidence of the approaching Millennium, while Baptists see these behaviors as harbingers of the Antichrist.

The Reformed clergy are quite orthodox on traditional Christian doctrines, but differ with their Assemblies and Baptist brethren on nature of the Bible. Reformed ministers prefer the doctrine of "infallibility" (that the Scriptures are authoritative for Christian faith and practice, but not as instruction in science or history), while the Assemblies clergy and most Baptists believe in "inerrancy" (that the Scriptures are literally accurate in all things). Nor, given their Calvinist roots, are Reformed pastors much attached to premillennialism or dispensationalism (Smidt 1988).

The mainline clergy deviate more often from strict and unquestioning orthodoxy. Methodists are the most conservative and Presbyterians, as their recent national sessions attest, are quite divided over traditional formulations of Christian faith. The Disciples usually resemble Presbyterians, but they are slightly more liberal, doubting or denying the exclusive role of Jesus in salvation, the actual existence of a Devil, and the Virgin Birth. Neither Presbyterians nor Disciples are influenced by premillennial or dispensationalist views. All in all, both "modernist" and "traditionalist" clergy are well-represented in our sample.

We suspected that a general orthodoxy dimension underlies specific doctrinal questions. After confirming this by factor analysis, we used the questions on the exclusive role of Jesus in salvation, the existence of the Devil, and Biblical inerrancy to construct an orthodoxy index.[3] Although in subsequent statistical analysis we will use the index in its full thirteen-point range, for illustration we show a collapsed version in Table 5.1, roughly dividing the range into four parts.

Denominations differ dramatically on this summary measure, with the Assemblies having both the most orthodox ministers and the most uniformity of belief. Baptists are less concentrated in the most orthodox group, but they are virtually all on the traditionalist side. Reformed pastors are split between the two orthodox categories, with a small contingent of modernists, while Methodists are quite diverse, with many pastors in all categories. Presbyterians and, especially, Disciples, occupy distinctly liberal positions, but not without significant orthodox dissent. In the rest of the chapter, we focus on clergy in each denomination, but we will use the orthodoxy index to predict differences on political attitudes and choices, finding it a powerful indicator of factional alignments among ministers.

Political Agendas

According to previous research and conventional wisdom, orthodox and modernist clergy have differing political and social agendas. During the 1960s and 1970s liberal clergy battled for civil rights, protested against the Vietnam war, and participated in the War on Poverty, and by the 1980s, they had moved on to other fronts, fighting for nuclear disarmament, environmentalism, and equal rights for women. In the 1960s, orthodox clergy usually confined their attacks to personal and social vices such as pornography, sexual immorality and alcohol. Such questions were politicized during the 1970s and 1980s, as actions by the Supreme Court, Congress and other institutions affronted conservative sensibilities. During this period, however, both conservative and liberal leaders fought to broaden the limited agendas of their clerical supporters. Christian Right spokesmen such as Jerry Falwell and Pat Robertson tried to link social issues to conservative economic and foreign policy, while some liberals, such as Jesse Jackson, renewed their emphasis on personal and social morality in addition to preaching on social justice themes. Both of these efforts seemed to run against the grain of clerical concerns.

To determine ministers' policy priorities in 1988, we asked how frequently they addressed specific issues in sermons, public activities and private efforts. Table 5.2 reports both the responses by denomination and the correlations between the orthodoxy index and frequency of addressing each issue.

Theological conservatives still prefer traditional "sin" issues, albeit in contemporary political guise: pornography, abortion, school prayer, and gambling legislation top the list, followed by education, alcohol and drug abuse, homosexuality, and "family issues." (Interestingly, conservative dominance is reduced on a few of these by considerable liberal activity -- on the other side, of course.) Modernists, as expected, are more likely to work on apartheid in South Africa, civil rights, defense spending and arms control, feminism, and the environment. In addition, they more often raise "secular" issues such as relations with the USSR, American policy in Latin America, the economy and hunger (although there is a good bit of conservative attention here). Orthodoxy does not predict agenda preferences for capital punishment and the Middle East, which receive equal attention from orthodox and unorthodox (with the partial exception of the Assemblies' special interest in Israel). There are a few remnants of specific "denominational agendas," such as the Methodists' concern with substance abuse, Baptist preoccupation with gambling, the

TABLE 5.2 Issue Agenda of Protestant Clergy

(N)	AOG (406)	SBC (653)	REFORM (746)	METH (723)	PRES (917)	DISC (1289)	r =
Family Problems[a]	91%	92%	76%	82%	83%	84%	.09*
Alcohol/Drug Abuse	91	86	75	84	73	78	.14*
Abortion	89	72	65	54	37	29	.41*
Pornography	89	75	51	50	30	34	.46*
Gay Rights	67	47	19	35	19	19	.13*
Hunger and Poverty	61	69	81	89	87	91	-.24*
School Prayer	60	50	15	35	20	23	.23*
Education	57	48	48	37	34	36	.17*
Israel/Middle East	53	29	19	25	27	25	.02
Gambling laws	44	57	21	45	14	19	.21*
Death Penalty	38	36	19	35	22	26	.03
Civil Rights	33	35	52	65	65	71	-.34*
Budget Deficit	31	22	19	23	33	38	-.17*
Environment	29	26	52	67	61	64	-.32*
Unemployment/Economy	28	27	34	57	54	55	-.24*
Relations with USSR	22	15	18	32	40	39	-.24*
ERA/Women's Rights	22	22	28	44	42	50	-.33*
Defense Spending	17	23	33	44	50	67	-.33*
South Africa/Apartheid	12	9	37	41	40	42	-.34*
Latin America	11	8	17	26	29	26	-.24*

[a] After an inventory of political activity inside and outside the church, ministers were asked: "If you have made your views known in any of the ways listed above, how often have you addressed these issues?" Percentages are those answering "Very Often" or "Often."

*Pearson correlation with orthodoxy significant at .05 level. Positive correlations mark an issue on which conservatives are more active, negative ones identify issues on which liberals are more involved.

Source: Surveys conducted by authors.

Reformed disinterest in school prayer, and the Disciples' high score on civil rights. But the main divide is theological: orthodox and modernist clergy have distinct agendas and seldom address the same issues.[4]

The old patterns, then, persist. Christian Right pleas to broaden the orthodox agenda to include economic and foreign policy concerns have been ignored, as have comparable attempts to get liberals to cross the issue divide. In any case, traditionalist and modernist priorities show a remarkable correspondence with campaign themes of the Republican and Democratic parties, respectively, in the 1988 presidential race.

Political Attitudes

Every recent study of political attitudes among Protestant clergy reveals much diversity, with traditionalists holding conservative political views, and modernists more liberal ones. We have no reason to expect different findings, although some churches in the sample have not been surveyed extensively before. Table 5.3 reports on several measures: (1) mean scores for each denomination on various social, economic, and foreign policy questions; (2) denominational means for pastors' self-placement on a seven-point ideological scale; and (3) correlations between orthodoxy and conservatism on each item.

With few exceptions, ministers fall into the same ranks on political ideology as on theological orthodoxy. Assemblies pastors are most conservative, especially on social issues, sometimes making Southern Baptists seem liberal by comparison. The Baptists, in turn, are somewhat right of the Reformed ministers, both on individual issues and ideological self-identification. Methodists are the most diverse group politically, as they are theologically, and they truly constitute the political mainline, clinging to the liberal edge of the middle on most issues -- and almost on dead center by self-placement. Presbyterians and Disciples hold down the left flank, exhibiting solid political liberalism. Although there are a few obvious signs of denominational tradition, such as the Baptists' separationist skepticism about tuition tax credits and the Reformed enthusiasm for them, usually the patterns are familiar and predictable, strongly hinting the influence of theology on policy preferences. This inference is confirmed by the correlations of orthodoxy with both conservative attitudes and ideological self-placement, which range from the robust to the extraordinary.

The greatest differences deriving from theological perspective seem to occur on social issues, with smaller gaps on foreign policy and economic issues, where the orthodox are sometimes more moderate. For example, the Assemblies and Southern Baptist clergy actually take faintly liberal stances on the environment, social welfare programs, and strategic arms limitations. On some issues this modest liberalism probably reflects the needs of working- and lower-middle class congregations; on others, such as environmentalism, it may simply express the contemporary public mood. In either case, the evidence

TABLE 5.3 Ministers' Political Attitudes and Ideology

(N)	AOG (406)	SBC (653)	REFORM (746)	METH (723)	PRES (917)	DISC (1289)	r=
Social Issues							
Abortion amendment	1.50[a]	1.89	2.41	3.10	3.75	3.78	.75*
Death penalty	1.62	1.85	2.59	3.03	3.45	3.44	.61*
Gay rights	1.85	2.44	3.26	3.40	3.95	3.86	.63*
Equal Rights Amendment	1.87	2.28	----	3.30	3.47	3.51	.63*
Tuition tax credits	1.91	3.09	2.39	3.12	3.63	3.62	.51*
Prayer in schools	2.10	2.70	----	3.31	3.83	3.76	.65*
Affirmative action	2.78	2.85	3.82	3.64	3.80	3.64	.42*
Creationism	----	2.06	2.62	----	3.43	3.48	.64*
Sex education	----	2.76	3.57	----	4.06	4.08	.57*
Gun control	----	----	----	----	3.97	3.77	.25*
Economic Issues							
Environment	3.10	3.73	----	4.04	4.16	4.11	.40*
Poverty policy	3.35	3.39	3.73	4.08	4.03	3.95	.38*
Smaller government	----	2.51	----	----	3.50	3.42	.54*
National health plan	----	----	----	----	3.94	3.91	.28*
Foreign Policy							
Sanction South Africa	2.65	2.94	3.55	3.59	3.58	3.69	.39*
Defense spending	2.74	3.09	----	3.90	4.21	4.18	.57*
Israel make concession	2.77	3.29	----	3.89	4.20	4.06	.46*
Support "Contras"	2.83	2.77	----	3.67	4.11	4.04	.60*
Strategic arms limits	3.10	3.54	----	4.08	4.19	4.13	.42*
Back friendly dictator	----	3.21	3.29	----	3.69	3.69	.26*
Star Wars	----	----	----	----	4.00	3.95	.47*
Ideological Self-Identification	2.52[b]	2.61	3.71	4.02	4.40	4.51	.74*

[a] Entries are mean scores on five-point Likert items, recorded so that a score of 1 is the most conservative option and a score of 5 the most liberal.

[b] Mean scores on a scale ranging from 1 (extremely conservative) to 7 (extremely liberal).

*Pearson correlation with orthodoxy significant at .05 level.

Source: Surveys conducted by authors.

dashes Christian Right hopes for a systematic political conservatism incorporating traditionalist social policy, a laissez-faire economic system, and international militancy. Still, despite the occasional moderation of the traditionalist clergy, the relative order of both denominations and theological groups remains the same, providing powerful evidence of the potency of religious perspective.

Partisanship and Party Change

How are such contrasting theological attitudes, public agendas, and political attitudes manifested in partisanship? Here we have less to go on. Although some studies have noted ministers' partisan affiliations in passing, few have examined party attachments in detail (Hadden 1969:82-85; Quinley 1974:83-87). We asked not only about ministers' current party identification, but also about their loyalties at age 21.

Party identification among clergy varies markedly by denomination and theological bent (Johnson 1966). Table 5.4 shows that Assemblies pastors are overwhelmingly Republican, with Baptists -- from the formerly Solid Democratic South -- not far behind. The third "evangelical" group, Reformed ministers, are somewhat less strongly Republican. Methodists are evenly split, with almost identical numbers of Strong Republicans and Strong Democrats, Weak Republicans and Weak Democrats, and Independents leaning each way! The Presbyterians and Disciples have Democratic pluralities, reinforced by large contingents of Independent leaners. Republicans and their Independent allies constitute one-third or less of these mainline clergy. As expected, theology and party are closely linked: traditionalists are Republicans, modernists are Democrats. Indeed, over 80% of the most orthodox pastors identify or lean Republican. This drops steadily as orthodoxy declines: only 6% of the most modernist clergy identify at all with the GOP (data not shown).

The coincidence of theological and partisan lines may result, in part, from a recent realignment of some orthodox ministers toward the GOP (cf. Guth 1985-86). Correlations between ministers' partisanship now and at age 21 are remarkably similar for all denominations, ranging from .54 for the Reformed pastors to .47 for the Assemblies. These figures reveal some stability, but hardly stasis; ministers are obviously moving. That the realignment is theological (hence, ideological) is suggested by the higher correlation between theology and current partisanship (.57) than between theology and party identification at age 21 (.22). To investigate this movement, we calculated a "party change" score (Table 5.4).[5]

There has been a considerable migration toward the GOP among Assemblies pastors (already quite Republican) and Southern Baptist clergy, gravitating away from Democratic and independent identifications. Reformed ministers exhibit a slight weakening of their dominant Republicanism, while Methodists demonstrate equal and opposite reactions, some moving toward the Democrats and others toward the GOP. Democrats have enjoyed a net gain among

TABLE 5.4 Ministers' Party Identification and Party Change

(N)	AOG (406)	SBC (653)	REFORM (746)	METH (723)	PRES (917)	DISC (1289) r=
Party Identification						
Strong Republican	37	25	15	16	9	8
Weak Republican	21	12	15	8	9	7
Independent-Republican	31	31	29	20	15	16
Pure Independent	6	10	11	10	8	9
Independent-Democrat	1	8	17	19	20	20
Weak Democrat	2	8	6	9	14	13
Strong Democrat	2	6	7	18	25	27 .57*
(Total)	100%	100%	100%	100%	100%	100%
Party Change						
Strongly Republican	18	21	6	8	6	7
Weakly Republican	21	27	18	20	20	18
No change	55	43	42	44	40	40
Weakly Democratic	6	7	26	19	20	22
Strongly Democratic	0	2	8	9	14	13 .33*
(Total)	100%	100%	100%	100%	100%	100%

*Pearson correlation with orthodoxy significant at .05 level.

Source: Surveys conducted by authors.

Presbyterians and Disciples, with one-third moving toward the Democrats and smaller numbers away. And partisan change varies with theology -- the orthodox in all denominations have been drawn toward the GOP and modernists toward the Democrats.

We cannot completely untangle here the exact route of ministers' theological and political pilgrimages, but the pattern varies by denomination. Many Southern Baptists, for example, have always been orthodox and ideologically conservative, but they have recently switched allegiances as party identities changed, leaving the Democrats for the Republicans. Others, especially in mainline churches, have adopted a new partisanship as their theology evolved. For example, Presbyterians and Disciples who say that they are now more orthodox or modernist than they were at age 21 also claim to have swung toward the Republicans or Democrats, respectively. Whatever the individual case, there are systematic partisan changes. Thus, religious polarization has eroded the old partisan alignments of specific denominations -- once rooted in ethnicity, region, and class -- and created new, ideological allegiances.

Voting and Candidate Choice in 1988

How were these political preferences manifested in the 1988 election? Again, we have relatively little to go on from previous studies. Indeed, not until the Moral Majority's advent did social scientists systematically explore the influence of religion on voting and other electoral activities, but even then, primarily within the general public rather than among religious leaders. We asked ministers about both their candidate preferences for the Republican and Democratic presidential nominations and their choices between George Bush and Michael Dukakis. Table 5.5 reports on ministers' voting decisions in the primaries and general election.

First, note the high turnout. About two-thirds of the clergy in each denomination voted in the primaries or caucuses, with no difference between the "otherworldly" Assemblies and Southern Baptists, and the "thisworldly" mainline pastors. (The Reformed ministers' percentage may be depressed by their location in the early caucus states of Michigan and Iowa.) And virtually all clergy voted in November, bettering the typically high turnout of citizens with college and postgraduate educations, although many of the Assemblies and Baptist clergy still lack such degrees.

The choice of party primary is by now predictable. Virtually all Assemblies pastors and most Southern Baptist ministers voted in the GOP contests (despite the hopes of the Southern Democratic inventors of Super Tuesday!), as did Reformed pastors. Methodists marched in two equal-sized columns to Republican and Democratic polls, while Presbyterians and Disciples cast their votes with the Democrats. Having made their choice of primaries, Republicans from all denominations behaved quite similarly, while Democratic clergy diverged. In the GOP contest, Robertson, Bush and Kemp all made overt appeals to Christian conservatives, especially in the early caucuses and Super Tuesday primaries, but their rewards varied. Bush won a uniform two-thirds among Republicans in all churches, but the distant runner-ups differed. Robertson got one-quarter of the vote from fellow charismatics in the Assemblies of God, a crucial target of his campaign, but he failed badly in another target group, his fellow Southern Baptist ministers (in part because he was a charismatic). Surprisingly, Robertson also ran second among Methodist Republicans, but elsewhere Bob Dole was the alternative to Bush. Jack Kemp had appeal only to Baptists -- and not much there. Compared to the Republicans, Democratic ministers had diverse preferences. There were some clear denominational favorites. The Baptists wanted one

TABLE 5.5 Ministers' Presidential Choices

(N)	AOG (406)	SBC (653)	REFORM (746)	METH (723)	PRES (917)	DISC (1289) r =
Voting						
Voted in Primary	69%	64%	53%	69%	67%	72%
Voted in November	99	99	98	98	99	99
Primary Vote						
Republican Primary	98	70	66	49	27	29
Democratic Primary	2	30	34	51	73	71
(Total)	100%	100%	100%	100%	100%	100%
Republican Primary Vote						
George Bush	64	64	65	67	67	65
Pat Robertson	27	11	6	16	5	11
Jack Kemp	4	12	8	3	4	3
Robert Dole	5	13	21	13	22	19
Others	0	0	0	1	2	2
(Total)	100%	100%	100%	100%	100%	100%
(N)	(272)	(293)	(240)	(242)	(167)	(266)
Democratic Primary Vote						
Jesse Jackson	29	13	48	33	40	41
Michael Dukakis	29	20	32	40	38	34
Dick Gephardt	29	8	2	5	2	5
Albert Gore	14	50	0	11	10	7
Paul Simon	0	6	15	9	9	10
Others	0	3	3	2	1	3
(Total)	100%	100%	100%	100%	100%	100%
(N)	(7)	(127)	(124)	(256)	(449)	(668)
Presidential Vote						
George Bush	99	83	67	50	35	34 .63*
Michael Dukakis	1	17	33	50	65	66
(Total)	100%	100%	100%	100%	100%	100%

*Pearson correlation with orthodoxy significant at .05 level.

Source: Surveys conducted by authors.

of their own, Tennessee Senator Al Gore, and Methodists liked Dukakis. However, Jackson won a plurality of Reformed, Presbyterian and Disciples Democrats and finished second among Methodists and third among Baptists.

Although the pattern is somewhat complex, the influence of theology extends even to intra-party choices. Among Republicans in all denominations, Pat Robertson's supporters were most orthodox, followed by voters for Jack Kemp, George Bush, and Robert Dole, in that order. Although Democratic clergy, as we have seen, are much more modernist than Republicans, theology was still important: those preferring Richard Gephardt and Albert Gore were much more orthodox than those choosing Paul Simon or Michael Dukakis, who in turn were more traditionalist than Jackson voters (data not shown).

The November election elicited starkly differing choices. Assemblies pastors voted almost unanimously for Bush, joined by four-fifths of the Baptists and two-thirds of the Reformed. Methodists again split down the middle, while Presbyterians and Disciples gave overwhelming majorities to Dukakis -- voting in the opposite direction from those in the pews (see Chapter 8). Theology strongly influenced the vote: 94% of the most orthodox voted for Bush, while fewer than 5% of the most modernist ministers did. A comparison of Tables 5.4 and 5.5 shows that in conservative churches more ministers voted for Bush than identify with the GOP. Perhaps orthodoxy not only produces political conservatism and GOP loyalty, leading to Republican votes, but has an independent influence. A number of tests confirm that even when party and ideology are accounted for, orthodoxy boosts the Republican vote.[6]

Electoral Activism in 1988

Most previous studies of ministerial activism have focused either on social movement activities such as protest marches and civil disobedience or on church-related actions such as forming action groups or preaching on social issues. As we have shown elsewhere, few clergy in either camp engage in "disorderly" behavior, but traditionalists and modernists alike are active within the church (Guth 1989). And our surveys reveal that both traditionalists and modernists are involved citizens in other ways: they are very interested in politics, talk about issues and candidates frequently, sign and circulate petitions, join national political organizations, write letters to public officials and newspaper editors, and often give money to candidates. Here, however, we want to focus on one target of such involvement: supporting candidates for public office, in this case, the presidency. All but one of our surveys asked about ministers' activity in the 1988 presidential nominating and electoral process.

First, note that in Table 5.6 the proportion of ministers reporting campaign activity beyond voting varies considerably by denomination in both primaries and general election, with the latter predictably

TABLE 5.6 Ministers' Presidential Activism

(N)	AOG (406)	SBC (653)	REFORM (746)	METH (723)	PRES (917)	DISC (1289)	r=
Activity in Primary							
Very Active[a]	3	1	--	2	3	4	
Somewhat Active	7	11	--	6	11	14	
Slightly Active	4	5	--	3	8	8	
Inactive	86	83	--	89	78	74	-.10*
(Total)	100%	100%		100%	100%	100%	
Activity in Fall Election							
Very Active	2	6	--	2	3	4	
Somewhat Active	9	20	--	6	18	22	
Slightly Active	6	11	--	4	15	16	
Inactive	83	63	--	88	64	58	-.09*
(Total)	100%	100%		100%	100%	100%	
Beneficiary of Activism							
George Bush	99	86	--	49	26	31	
Michael Dukakis	1	14	--	51	74	69	.73*
(Total)	100%	100%	--	100%	100%	100%	
(N)	(66)	(241)	--	(84)	(329)	(602)	

[a] Entries are percentages of ministers responding to the following: "Many people also work for a candidate by wearing campaign buttons, putting a sign in the yard, attending speeches and rallies, etc. Beyond voting, did you *actively support* a candidate during the primaries and caucuses? If YES, which candidate? How actively?" The question was also asked for the general election.

*Pearson correlation with orthodoxy significant at .05 level.

Source: Surveys conducted by authors.

drawing more interest. In the primaries, Disciples and Presbyterians have a slight edge, although a few Baptist and Assemblies pastors also report activity. Somewhat surprisingly, Methodists are the least active. Assemblies and Methodist clergy are no more visible in the fall (and those involved are the same people), but the activist corps swells among Baptists, Presbyterians and Disciples. Using the four orthodoxy categories in Table 5.1 shows that liberals have a slight edge: in the primaries 17% of the most orthodox were active, compared to 29% of the most modernist; in the general election, 29% of the most orthodox were active, but 43% of the most modernist were.

Still, the Southern Baptists' campaign activism suggests that the global figures hide denominational differences. Among the Assemblies and Baptists, activism peaks on the right: 42% of the most orthodox Baptists report involvement in the general election. In all the mainline churches the most modernist group has the largest proportion of activists: 18% among the Methodists, 49% among the Presbyterians, and 54% among the Disciples. In the Disciples of Christ, however, there is a curvilinear relationship: the most orthodox lag slightly behind the most modernist, but they are much more active than theological centrists. Ministers' decisions to enter electoral politics may thus depend in part on denominational context. Among the overwhelmingly conservative Southern Baptists, a decision to work for the Republicans is appropriate, while in the liberal environment of mainline churches, modernist and Democratic ministers feel more comfortable becoming involved. And there must be constraints which preclude widespread activism among Assemblies and Methodist clergy, whether "otherworldly" theology among the former (cf. Poloma 1989:155-157) or precarious theological and ideological balance among the latter. By this point the beneficiaries of pastoral assistance should come as no surprise. During the primaries, the clerical activists were distributed among candidates in much the same fashion as ministerial votes. Bush was the favorite of Republicans in all denominations, even among the Assemblies of God and Southern Baptists, where Robertson failed to make the inroads he had hoped for. Among Democrats, Jesse Jackson and Michael Dukakis drew almost equal numbers (data not shown). In the fall, Bush was the favorite of virtually all Assemblies activists, the overwhelming majority of Baptists, and half the Methodists, while Dukakis secured an even higher proportion of work than votes from Presbyterians and Disciples. And the correlation of activists' orthodoxy with their choice of campaigns was an impressive .73.

Conclusions

We are now approaching a full "two party" mobilization in American Protestantism: on the one hand modernist liberals of the Protestant mainline are holding to their political commitments and activism, but on the other hand, they have been joined by their orthodox colleagues, who, though they may still resist full electoral involvement, have supported recent conservative presidential candidates in substantial numbers (see Chapter 2). Indeed, given membership trends in the (growing) evangelical and (declining) mainline denominations, the traditionalists may have achieved superiority in numbers -- plus the advantage of being on the winning side, at least in presidential contests.

There is also a considerable -- and perhaps growing -- attitudinal consistency between the theological and political beliefs of clergy. Perhaps this is not surprising. Two recent works on American Protestantism have argued that two "factions" or "clusters" constitute the new formations in American Protestantism (Roof and McKinney 1987; Wuthnow 1988). These factions disagree not only on theology but also on the role of the church, social issues, economic priorities, and foreign policy. And although some denominations are dominated by one faction and some by the other (and a few like the Methodists may be split down the middle), the bipolar struggle has largely displaced ancient battles between denominations, with their historic creeds and traditions.

But we have also seen some important residues of denominational traditions, preoccupations, and leadership. Whether in the limited political involvement by the Assemblies of God, the Reformed preference for religious schools, the "peace and justice" liberalism of the Disciples, or the careful abstention of Methodists from campaigns, we see hints of resistance to the political changes unleashed by theological realignment. Denominations do have cultures of their own, whether regional, ethnic, or bureaucratic, which at least channel the tides of theological restructuring of political attitudes. But our results show that the theological battle lines being drawn today are indeed powerful organizing forces for both conservatives and liberals, breaking up smaller battalions and reforming them into larger armies.

Our findings provide further impetus for reassessment of earlier claims for the permanent advantage in activism of modernist, "thisworldly" clergy over their traditionalist, "otherworldly" rivals. Although liberals still possess a slight advantage in electoral activism, the orthodox are seldom far behind, especially in conventional electoral politics which, after all, may ultimately be the most effective kind (cf. Guth 1989). In fact, literature on clerical activism has centered too much on ministers' political roles as corporate leaders, and not enough on ministers' own definitions of the proper political avenues for clergy. Write-in comments, especially from conservatives, make it clear that the orthodox can simultaneously hold to old notions of the spiritual primacy of the church, and also adopt new, more aggressive ideas about the minister-as-citizen, as a recruit to the ranks of electoral activists.

Finally, this study raises some old and new questions about the impact of clerical involvement. In the 1960s and 1970s, New Breed liberal activism in mainline churches often set off resistance by traditionalist laity. We have shown elsewhere that there are still yawning chasms between liberal clergy and conservative laity among Methodists, Presbyterians, and Disciples (Smidt and Penning 1990). And these differences are intensified if one looks only at regular churchgoers. The overwhelming Republican vote for president among the mainline laity proves the limits of clerical influence over parishioners. But comparable, though smaller, differences have appeared on the right: Assemblies and Baptist clergy are more conservative and Republican than their flocks (see Poloma and Gallup in press), although in this case differences are reduced if the analysis is confined to active laity. Moreover, there are tantalizing hints that Democratic laity in these denominations are beginning to replicate, if not emulate, the exodus of their clergy to the GOP (Kellstedt and Noll 1990). As it is in "evangelical" churches that many laity -- though not all -- are most supportive of clerical activism, a convergence of pastoral and lay attitudes could have enormous impact in future presidential contests, consolidating and extending Republican gains among formerly Democratic constituencies in these churches.

Appendix:
The Denominational Surveys

The data are drawn from national mail surveys of almost 5,000 ministers, conducted with some coordination by six investigators in three separate studies. The first study focused on the Southern Baptist Convention, the Presbyterian Church in the U.S.A. and the Disciples of Christ, and was conducted by James Guth and Helen Lee Turner of Furman University, as part of a larger study of the Disciples of Christ, generously funded by a grant from the Lilly Endowment. These surveys were administered in the fall and winter of 1988-1989. The Assemblies of God and United Methodist Church surveys were conducted by John Green and Margaret Poloma of the University of Akron during the summer of 1989. The studies of the Christian Reformed Church and the Reformed Church in America were done by Corwin Smidt and James Penning of Calvin College during the summer of 1989.

The survey instruments varied somewhat, but they were designed to elicit pastors' views on theological, social and political issues. They included items on most issues considered by the denominations' recent national meetings and several questions which surfaced during the 1988 campaign. And they inquired about ministers' presidential votes and their involvement, if any, in the 1988 campaign. Response rates varied: Assemblies of God (52%), Southern Baptists (47%), Reformed (66%), Methodists (54%), and Presbyterians and Disciples (both 64%). Although the Assemblies survey had a high rate of undeliverable forms, there is little evidence of response bias.

Notes

1. As the Christian Reformed Church is reputed to be more conservative than the Reformed Church in America (the CRC belongs to the National Association of Evangelicals, whereas the RCA is in the National Council of Churches), we initially examined each separately. To our surprise, the CRC and RCA ministers proved remarkably similar, so we created a "Reformed" category to simplify analysis and presentation.

2. Because of limited survey space and the tailoring of questions to tap current denominational debates, we have only four common doctrinal items: the crucial role of Jesus in salvation, the existence of the Devil, belief in Biblical inerrancy, and premillennialism. Fortunately, as we shall see, each is an excellent indicator of theological alignments in most of these churches.

3. To construct an orthodoxy index, we subjected the four common items to a principal components factor analysis. All four items loaded heavily on a single factor, with premillennialism somewhat weaker. We decided to drop the premillennial item on both empirical and logical grounds. The relatively weak loading indicated that it was tapping another dimension, and the fact that pre-, post- and a- millennial stances have all been "orthodox" among Protestants made us reluctant to include it. A second principal components analysis of the other items revealed a single factor with an eigenvalue of 2.33, explaining 78% of the variance. All three items loaded strongly: the literal existence of the Devil (.90), the exclusive role of Jesus in salvation (.89), and the inerrancy of Scripture (.86). After confirming that the three items tapped a single factor, we constructed a simple additive index, ranging from three ("Strongly Agree" with all orthodox statements) to fifteen ("Strongly Disagree" with all). Reassuringly, the index correlates strongly across the sample with other items, such as the historicity of Adam and Eve ($r = .84$), the Virgin Birth (.77), the Second Coming (.69) and the reality of Hell (.54). And correlations between index scores and such items are almost as strong within each denomination. In addition, we found correlations of .62 to .70 with the various denominational self-identification scales. (Only among the monotonously uniform Assemblies' ministers was there no such association -- there was no variation in the orthodoxy index!)

4. These results strongly parallel another test of ministers' priorities, in which we asked about the "most important problem confronting the United States." Although clergy have an occupational propensity to perceive social and moral priorities (Quinley 1974:87-90), this tendency is strongest among conservatives. For example, 78% of Assemblies clergy mention such issues, compared to 43% of Disciples; conversely, only 17% of Assemblies ministers listed an economic or welfare issue, but 44% of the Disciples did. Mainline clergy were almost alone in putting priority on foreign policy issues (Green and Poloma 1990).

5. The party change score was calculated by subtracting a minister's identification score at age 21 from the current one. The results ranged from -6 (Strong Democrat at age 21 but Strong Republican today) to +6 (the opposite movement). We then recoded the scores: "strong" changes are those of three points or more on the seven-point scale; "weak" changes, of one or two points. Pastors not moving at all are put in the "no change" category.

6. For example, a Multiple Classification Analysis (MCA) of the 1988 presidential vote yields etas of .80 for party, .72 for ideology and .66 for orthodoxy and betas of .55 for party, .21 for ideology, and .18 for orthodoxy, explaining 71% of the variance.

References

Ammerman, Nancy. 1990. *Baptist Battles*. New Brunswick: Rutgers University Press.

Beatty, Kathleen, and Oliver Walter. 1988. "Fundamentalists, Evangelicals and Politics." *American Politics Quarterly*, 16:43-59.

_____. 1989. "A Group Theory of Religion and Politics: The Clergy as Group Leaders." *Western Political Quarterly*, 42:129-146.

Bouma, Gary. 1984. *How the Saints Persevere: Social Factors in the Vitality of the Christian Reformed Church*. Clayton, Australia: Monash University.

Friedly, Robert, and D. Duane Cummins. 1987. *The Search for Identity: The Disciples of Christ*. St. Louis: CBP Press.

Green, John, and Margaret Poloma. 1990. "The Issue Agenda of American Protestant Clergy: An Analysis of Ministers Across Six Denominations." Presented at the annual meeting of the Society for the Scientific Study of Religion, Virginia Beach.

Guth, James. 1983. "The Southern Baptist Clergy: Vanguard of the New Christian Right?" in Robert Liebman and Robert Wuthnow, eds., *The New Christian Right*. Pp. 118-130. New York: Aldine.

_____. 1984. "The Politics of Preachers: Southern Baptist Ministers and Christian Right Activism," in David Bromley and Anson Shupe, eds., *New Christian Politics*. Pp. 239-249. Macon, GA: Mercer University Press.

_____. 1985-86. "Political Converts: Partisan Realignment Among Southern Baptist Ministers." *Election Politics*, 3:2-6.

_____. 1989. "Pastoral Politics in the 1988 Elections." Presented at the annual meeting of the American Political Science Association, Atlanta.

Hadden, Jeffrey. 1969. *The Gathering Storm in the Churches*. Garden City, NY: Doubleday.

Hailey, Mel. 1988. "The Political and Social Attitudes of Church of Christ Ministers." Presented at the annual meeting of the American Political Science Association, Washington, DC

Hallum, Anne Motley. 1988. "Presbyterians as Political Amateurs," in Charles W. Dunn, ed., *Religion in American Politics*. Pp. 63-73. Washington, DC: CQ Press.

Harder, Kathleen. 1988. "Pastors and Political Mobilization: Preaching Politics." Presented at the annual meeting of the American Political Science Association, Washington, DC

Johnson, Benton. 1966. "Theology and Party Preference Among Protestant Clergymen." *American Sociological Review*, 31:200-208.

Kellstedt, Lyman, and Mark Noll. 1990. "Religion, Voting for President, and Party Identification, 1948-1984," in Mark A. Noll, ed., *Religion and American Politics*. Pp. 355-379. New York and Oxford: Oxford University Press.

Koller, Norman, and Joseph Retzer. 1980. "The Sounds of Silence Revisited." *Sociological Analysis*, 41:155-161.

Langenbach, Lisa. 1988. "Evangelical Elites and Political Action: The Pat Robertson Presidential Candidacy." Presented at the annual meeting of the American Political Science Association, Washington, DC

Luidens, Donald, and Roger Nemeth, 1987. "'Public' and 'Private'" Protestantism Reconsidered: Introducing the 'Loyalists'." *Journal for the Scientific Study of Religion*, 26:450-464.

Morris, Aldon. 1984. *The Origins of the Civil Rights Movement*. New York: The Free Press.

Nelsen, Hart, and Sandra Baxter. 1981. "Ministers Speak on Watergate: Effects on Clergy Role During Political Crisis." *Review of Religious Research*, 23:150-166.

Poloma, Margaret. 1989. *The Assemblies of God at the Crossroads*. Knoxville, TN: University of Tennessee Press.

Poloma, Margaret, and George Gallup. Jr. (in press). *Varieties of Prayer: A Survey Report*. Philadelphia: Trinity Press International.

Quinley, Harold. 1974. *The Prophetic Clergy*. New York: Wiley.

Roof, Wade Clark, and William McKinney. 1987. *American Mainline Religion: Its Changing Shape and Future*. New Brunswick: Rutgers University Press.

Smidt, Corwin. 1988. "Evangelicals Within Contemporary American Politics." *Western Political Quarterly*, 41:601-620.

Smidt, Corwin, and James Penning. 1990. "The Partisan and Ideological Orientations of American Protestant Clergy: An Analysis of Ministers Across Seven Denominations." Presented at the annual meeting of the Society for the Scientific Study of Religion, Virginia Beach.

Stark, Rodney, Bruce Foster, Charles Glock, and Harold Quinley. 1971. *Wayward Shepherds: Prejudice and the Protestant Clergy*. New York: Harper and Row.

Turner, Helen Lee, and James Guth. 1989. "The Politics of Armageddon: Dispensationalism Among Southern Baptist Ministers," in Ted G. Jelen, ed., *Religion and Political Behavior in the United States*. Pp. 187-208. New York: Praeger.

United Methodist Church, General Council on Ministries, 1990. "An Analysis of Major Issues Addressed by the 1988 General Conference and a Comparison With Beliefs and Attitudes of Local Church Members." Dayton, OH: General Council on Ministries, United Methodist Church.

Welch, Michael, Lyman Kellstedt, and Kenneth Wald. 1990. "Pastoral Cues and Congregational Responses: Evidence From the 1989 NES Pilot Study." Presented at the annual meeting of the American Political Science Association, San Francisco.

Wilcox, Clyde. 1990. "Religion and Politics Among White Evangelicals: The Impact of Religious Variables on Political Attitudes." *Review of Religious Research*, 32:27-42.

Wuthnow, Robert. 1988. *The Restructuring of American Religion*. Princeton: Princeton University Press.

6

Preachers and Politics: Jesse Jackson, Pat Robertson, and the 1988 Presidential Nomination Campaign in South Carolina

Tod A. Baker
Robert P. Steed
Laurence W. Moreland

The connections between religion and politics have long intrigued students of the American political system. The civil rights movement of the 1960s and the anti-Vietnam war protests of the 1960s and early 1970s, for example, contained religious elements. In the 1980s, the emergence of such organizations as Moral Majority and Christian Voice heightened the concern of many public officials about the electoral impact of religion (Plotkin 1981:51; Reichley 1985:311-331). A related development was the increased saliency of social issues -- abortion, pornography, family values, drug use, homosexuality, law and order -- which these organizations worked to bring to the center of the political arena.

Presidential nomination contests during the 1980s also blurred the lines between the religious and political spheres. This culminated in 1988, when two ministers -- Jesse Jackson and Pat Robertson -- made serious efforts to capture the nominations of the Democratic and Republican parties. Although neither effort was successful, each was an important part of the electoral process in 1988, and each had potentially significant consequences for its party.

John Kessel (1980) has argued convincingly that at least some people recruited into party activity during presidential campaigns remain active, even after the candidacies or issues which prompted their entry into the political arena have faded. They become part of the

94

organizational core and thus influence the future directions of their party. In turn, activists do much to define the internal operations and external perceptions of the party (Eldersveld 1964; Sorauf and Beck 1988). Certainly, both of the winning candidates, Bush and Dukakis, found that they had to accommodate at least some specific concerns of the losing preachers in their platforms and campaign strategies (Pomper 1989).

This chapter examines the Jackson and Robertson campaigns in one state, South Carolina, and analyzes the nature of their support at the parties' state conventions in 1988. Specifically, the analysis addresses two questions: (1) What effects did the Jackson and Robertson candidacies have on the composition of their respective parties, and (2) What impact did the two candidacies have on ideological and issue cleavages within each party? Clearly, if Jackson and Robertson activists differed sharply from other delegates in religious, socioeconomic, and political backgrounds, and in programmatic predispositions, the effects could extend beyond 1988. And given the religious character of these candidates and their campaigns, religion may emerge as an especially important factor among party activists.

Jackson, Robertson, and the 1988 Presidential Nomination Campaign in South Carolina

During the presidential nomination process, South Carolina was crucial to several candidacies, especially among the Republicans. The South Carolina Republican primary was held the Saturday preceding Super Tuesday and was widely seen as a significant harbinger of what was to come. Consequently, George Bush, Jack Kemp, Bob Dole, and Pat Robertson all campaigned in the state because they saw the South Carolina primary as a strategic necessity in winning the Republican nomination.

The Robertson Campaign. Pat Robertson, particularly, mounted a strong effort to carry South Carolina, and he expected to do well. In 1987, his success in South Carolina (and Michigan) stunned party regulars and resulted in national publicity suggesting that he would have to be taken seriously. In that year preceding the presidential race, Robertson supporters -- newcomers to the party organized as the Carolina Conservative Coalition (CCC) and consisting mostly of evangelical Christians -- turned out in large numbers at the Republican precinct reorganizations. They gained control of the Charleston County Republican Party, in one of the state's three largest urban areas, and did very well in Richland County, the site of Columbia, the state capital.

Considerable bitterness surrounded the Robertson effort. In Charleston County, party regulars, led by North Charleston Mayor John E. Bourne, Jr., sought to overturn their ouster from party positions by (unsuccessful) appeals to the party apparatus. In Richland County, party regulars maintained control by declaring ineligible most of the CCC delegates on the ground that they had not been registered to vote in their precincts at least 30 days prior to reorganization; these denied delegates filed suit in state court (later dropped) (*Charleston News and Courier* 1987). Inasmuch as South Carolina Republicans were utilizing a primary (delegates were bound to the winner for two ballots), these maneuverings made sense only if the balloting at the national convention went to three or more ballots, an eventuality expected by the Robertson camp; then the actual persons chosen by the state convention as national delegates would become important, and the Robertson forces hoped to have their own people in place. Thus, the Robertson camp took their participation in the state convention quite seriously.

For the Robertson campaign, South Carolina's primary was a do-or-die effort. If Robertson could not win in South Carolina, despite his success in the 1987 caucuses, it was doubtful he could win elsewhere. The Robertson campaign took out full-page advertisements in South Carolina newspapers attacking Bush. Titled "Who Hijacked the Reagan Revolution?" the ads singled out "Eastern Republicans," headed by Bush, who would not let "Reagan be Reagan." The solution, asserted the ads, was to elect "solid conservatives from the beginning," not "wimps" (*Charleston News and Courier* 1988a).

Despite the Robertson effort and Senator Strom Thurmond's endorsement of Bob Dole, George Bush easily won. With the help of Governor Carroll Campbell and campaign manager Lee Atwater (a South Carolina native), Bush carried all six congressional districts, and all the convention delegates, winning 48.6% of the vote; Robertson finished third with 19.2% behind Dole's 20.7% (*Charleston News and Courier* 1988b). This victory, coupled with his earlier success in New Hampshire, provided Bush the momentum to sweep through Super Tuesday three days later and on to the nomination; at the same time it ended Robertson's nomination prospects.

The Jackson Campaign. For the Democrats, South Carolina did not have the same strategic significance that it had for the Republicans. Not only did the Democrats use precinct caucuses, but their caucuses also came anticlimactically on the Saturday *after* Super Tuesday. Even so, Jackson's personal and political attachments made the state an integral part of his campaign. For one thing, Jackson is a native of Greenville, South Carolina, and he continues to visit often to see his mother. Indeed, in 1984 he was miffed at the state Democratic executive committee when it endorsed Senator Ernest F. Hollings as the "favorite son" of the state's delegation to the Democratic national convention, a designation that Jackson felt equally entitled to have. In 1988 Jackson moved his legal voting address to Greenville, amid considerable speculation that Jackson might return to lay groundwork for a run for the U.S. Senate. Finally, in 1988 Jackson expected to win as much support in South Carolina as he obtained anywhere; the state ranked behind only Mississippi in percentage of black population, and blacks often represent one-half or more of the Democratic caucus turnout, although only 27% of registered voters. About 45,000 Democrats participated in the caucuses and, as expected, Jackson easily won, emerging with 28 of the 44 national convention delegates; Albert Gore won nine and Michael Dukakis seven.

For both Robertson and Jackson, then, South Carolina represented an important step in their respective candidacies. Each mounted a strong campaign, and each had a sizeable presence at the state conventions held in April. Consequently, South Carolina is a useful research environment in which to test and clarify the nature of each candidate's support.

Data and Methods

This chapter utilizes data on party activists drawn from surveys of the Democratic and Republican state conventions held in Columbia, South Carolina in April 1988 (see Appendix for details). In this analysis, we group Democratic delegates into Dukakis, Gore, and Jackson supporters, and further divide Jackson supporters in two racial categories to assess his effort to broaden his coalition. We group Republicans into those who supported Bush, Dole, Robertson, and all other candidates, and further divide the "Other" category in two religious categories, "Evangelical" and "Non-Evangelical." The criterion for including a delegate in the Evangelical subgroup was self-identification as an evangelical and/or fundamentalist and/or charismatic Protestant. This categorization of Other delegates allows for a more refined analysis of religion in South Carolina presidential nominating politics.

Party Composition

The impact of the Jackson and Robertson candidacies on their respective parties' composition is examined by analyzing the religious beliefs, age, length of party activity, state of childhood, and strength of party attachment of the Jackson and Robertson delegates vis-a-vis other Democratic or Republican delegates.
Religion. We begin with data on religious beliefs and practices. Among Democrats, there are some clear religious differences. The Gore and black Jackson delegates were more likely than the other Democratic delegates to say that the Bible is God's word and that they had been "born again" (Table 6.1). Ten percent of the black Jackson delegates identified as charismatic, and 27% of the Gore delegates identified as religious conservatives. The Dukakis delegates and the white Jackson delegates, on the other hand, were more likely to say that their religion was liberal or to classify themselves as humanist, agnostic, or atheist. If the South is the Bible Belt, then, in cultural terms, the Gore and black Jackson supporters are the most "southern" and the Dukakis and white Jackson supporters, the least "southern."

The denominational affiliations of delegates are consistent with this picture. Among white Democrats the Gore delegates tended to be the most southern -- over half were Methodist or Baptist -- whereas churches not traditionally strong in the South -- Catholic, Lutheran, Unitarian, Quaker -- showed up among the Dukakis and white Jackson delegates (23% and 28%, respectively). Over 80% of the black Jackson delegates were Methodist or Baptist.

Data on church attendance also suggests that Gore and black Jackson delegates are more religious than other Democratic activists. Forty-six percent of the Gore delegates and 64% of the black Jackson delegates reported that they attend church every week, compared to 32% for Dukakis and 22% for white Jackson supporters. At the opposite extreme, 30% of the Dukakis delegates and 57% of the white Jackson delegates said they attend church only a few times a year or never, compared to only 19% of the Gore delegates and 15% of the black Jackson delegates.

These findings rather strongly suggest that Jackson's role as minister played little or no part in broadening his coalition. Rather, his efforts contributed, ironically, to the secularization of the South Carolina Democratic Party. Certainly, the Dukakis activists were a part of the secular wing of the party, and the Dukakis and white Jackson delegates were drawn from the same population; within this context, however,

TABLE 6.1 Religious Characteristics of Democratic Delegates

Beliefs and Identifications	Delegates			
	Dukakis	Gore	White Jackson	Black Jackson
Bible is God's Word	27%	58%	25%	82%
Born Again[a]	11%	19%	13%	35%
Charismatic	4	2	4	10
Fundamentalist	3	5	2	4
Evangelical	4	9	6	4
Conservative	8	27	4	8
Liberal	27	12	34	13
Humanist, Agnostic, or Atheist	29	9	43	8
Church Attendance				
Every Week	32	46	22	64
Almost Every Week	28	26	8	21
A Few Times a Month	10	9	14	11
A Few Times a Year	23	15	26	4
Never	7	4	31	0
(Total)	100%	100%	100%	100%
(N)	(90)	(131)	(51)	(276)

[a] Figures do not add up to 100% due to multiple classifications.

Source: Surveys by the authors.

white Jackson delegates constituted the leading edge of a movement toward a more secular Democratic Party.

On the other hand, Robertson drew highly religious people into the Republican Party (Table 6.2). On literal belief in the Bible, evangelicalism, and born-again status, Robertson supporters and Other Evangelical delegates ranked considerably higher than the other candidates' delegates. However, the two sets of evangelical delegates differed substantially in self-identification: 61% of the Robertson delegates were charismatic, while 82% of the Other Evangelical delegates were fundamentalist. Sharp denominational differences existed between the Robertson delegates and the Other Evangelical delegates as well. Thirty-five percent of Robertson delegates were members of non-denominational or community churches and 18% were members of Pentecostal churches; in contrast, 70% of the Other

100

TABLE 6.2 Religious Characteristics of Republican Delegates

Beliefs and Identifications	Delegates			Other	
	Bush	Dole	Robertson	Evan.	Non-Evan.
Bible is God's Word	68%	64%	99%	98%	51%
Born Again[a]	27%	32%	76%	69%	19%
Charismatic	6	4	61	15	0
Fundamentalist	11	22	36	82	0
Evangelical	12	14	50	43	0
Conservative	54	50	62	62	34
Liberal	1	4	1	0	8
Humanist, Agnostic, or Atheist	2	8	1	0	14
Church Attendance					
Every Week	55	53	95	92	44
Almost Every Week	20	16	4	7	15
A Few Times a Month	12	8	1	2	15
A Few Times a Year	13	14	1	0	16
Never	1	8	0	0	11
(Total)	100%	100%	100%	100%	100%
(N)	(257)	(49)	(192)	(60)	(62)

[a] Figures do not add up to 100% due to multiple classifications.

Source: Surveys by the authors.

Evangelicals were Baptists. Robertson thus drew a different wing of the evangelical movement into the GOP, thereby broadening the evangelical presence. The religiosity of the Robertson delegates is further confirmed by data on church attendance. Table 6.2 shows that over 90% of the Robertson and Other Evangelical activists attended church at least once a week, well above the comparable percentages for the other three groups. The Bush, Dole and Kemp delegates were much more conventionally Protestant in their beliefs, identifications, and behavior. Note, however, that as a group Republicans are much more religious than Democrats.

Age and Length of Party Service. In contrast to the data on religion, age differences among Dukakis, Gore, and black Jackson delegates were relatively slight; still, the black Jackson supporters were somewhat younger, indicating that Jackson did recruit a slightly higher

TABLE 6.3 Years Active in Democratic Party Politics

Years Active in Party Politics	Delegates			
	Dukakis	Gore	White Jackson	Black Jackson
One to Four	36	27	57	25
Five to Eight	14	10	8	15
Nine to Twelve	13	13	6	17
Thirteen and Above	37	50	29	44
(Total)	100%	100%	100%	100%
(N)	(86)	(131)	(49)	(262)

Source: Surveys by the authors.

proportion of young people. What is most startling is the age of the white Jackson delegates, 47% of whom were under 35 years of age, compared to 26% of the Dukakis delegates, 27% of the Gore delegates, and 31% of the black Jackson delegates. Thus, although Jackson's effort to broaden the Rainbow Coalition beyond his 1984 black base was partially successful (inasmuch as 84% of his 1988 delegates in South Carolina were black), what success he did have was disproportionately youthful (data not shown).

Among Republicans, the Robertson delegates were the youngest: 33% of the Robertson delegates were under 35 years old compared to 17% for Bush delegates, 16% for Dole, 23% for Other Evangelical delegates, and 23% for Other Non-Evangelical delegates. Conversely, almost one-half (48%) of the Bush delegates were fifty-five or older

TABLE 6.4 Years Active in Republican Party Politics

Years Active in Party Politics	Delegates				
	Bush	Dole	Robertson	Other Evan.	Other Non-Evan.
One to Four	19	21	74	31	27
Five to Eight	16	13	10	24	13
Nine to Twelve	17	21	6	24	20
Thirteen and Above	48	46	10	22	41
(Total)	100%	100%	100%	100%	100%
(N)	(266)	(48)	(197)	(59)	(64)

Source: Surveys by the authors.

compared to only 18% of the Robertson delegates. Assuming that a relatively high proportion of Robertson delegates remain active, Robertson's success in attracting younger people to the GOP could affect its makeup for decades to come (data not shown).

Among Democrats the white Jackson delegates and the Dukakis delegates clearly constituted the "new guard" while the black Jackson delegates and the Gore delegates made up the "old guard" (Table 6.3). Over one-half of the white Jackson delegates and slightly more than one-third of the Dukakis delegates said they had been active in party politics for four years or less, but only about one-fourth of the Gore and the black Jackson delegates gave this response. The pattern is reversed at the other end, as larger percentages of Gore and black Jackson delegates said they had been active thirteen or more years; not surprisingly, the white Jackson delegates constituted the smallest proportion in this category.

This finding suggests that Jackson was not very successful in recruiting blacks to the ranks of Democratic Party activists; rather, blacks already active in Democratic politics simply shifted into the Jackson column. On the other hand, Jackson was more successful in attracting whites. Thus, if the 1988 Jackson candidacy did affect the composition of the Democratic Party, it is more because of his appeal to whites.

Robertson quite definitely attracted new activists to the Republican Party. Whereas 74% of his convention supporters had been active four years or less, the percentages of Bush, Dole, Other Evangelical, and Other Non-Evangelical delegates were 19%, 21%, 31%, and 27% respectively (Table 6.4). Since the Robertson delegates were often charismatic, the Robertson campaign recruited a second wave of evangelicals into the Republican Party. About three-fourths of the Robertson delegates became party activists between 1985 and 1988 whereas those in Other Evangelicals have been moving steadily into the party for at least thirteen years, with only 31% becoming active in the 1985-1988 period.

Region. The delegates' regional residential backgrounds reveal further group differences. Not only were the Gore and black Jackson delegates different from the Dukakis and white Jackson delegates in age, they were also different with regard to their geographic origins. Whereas these first two groups of activists tended to be drawn predominantly from South Carolina (70% and 86% respectively), less than 50% of the Dukakis and white Jackson activists grew up in South Carolina (Table 6.5). Of those delegates whose childhoods were spent outside the South, the pattern is reversed: Gore delegates and black

TABLE 6.5 State of Childhood of Democratic Delegates

	Delegates			
State of Childhood	Dukakis	Gore	White Jackson	Black Jackson
South Carolina	48	70	43	86
Other Southern State	17	17	21	5
Non-Southern State	35	13	36	9
(Total)	100%	100%	100%	100%
(N)	(92)	(135)	(53)	(181)

Source: Surveys by the authors.

Jackson delegates were considerably less likely than the Dukakis and white Jackson delegates to have grown up outside the region. Thus, the new people Jackson drew into the Democratic Party were drawn from the same pool as the Dukakis delegates: relatively young, relatively new to the party, and less southern (and South Carolinian) than their fellow partisans.

Among Republicans, the regional distinction again appeared (Table 6.6). The Robertson and the Other Evangelical delegates were less likely to be home-grown South Carolinians than the other delegates, although, with the exception of Bush supporters, they were about as likely to be native southerners. Thus, Robertson and other Christian Right leaders before him, drew a substantial number of new, non-southern, and non-South Carolinian people into the party.

TABLE 6.6 State of Childhood of Republican Delegates

	Delegates				
				Other	
State of Childhood	Bush	Dole	Robertson	Evan.	Non-Evan.
South Carolina	55	50	42	30	56
Other Southern State	17	12	21	30	13
Non-Southern State	28	38	38	41	31
(Total)	100%	100%	100%	100%	100%
(N)	(267)	(50)	(196)	(61)	(64)

Source: Surveys by the authors.

TABLE 6.7 Party Identification of Democratic Delegates

State		Delegates		
			White	Black
Party Identification	Dukakis	Gore	Jackson	Jackson
Strong Democratic	70	67	72	77
Weak Democratic	10	18	9	19
Indep/Leaning Democratic	15	11	13	3
Independent	3	3	6	1
Republican	1	2	0	0
(Total)	100%	100%	100%	100%
(N)	(91)	(135)	(53)	(274)

Source: Surveys by the authors.

Partisanship, Ideology, and Issue Positions

For political activists, the strength of party attachment is normally an important indicator of intensity of party activity and commitment to future activity. In the case of Jackson and Robertson delegates we consider this variable a reasonably good indirect indicator of their likelihood of remaining active.

Among Democrats, black Jackson activists exhibited the strongest support for the state Democratic Party, and the Gore activists the least (Table 6.7). Thus, although the Dukakis delegates and the white Jackson delegates continued to share a similar attitude, the similarity

TABLE 6.8 Party Identification of Republican Delegates

State		Delegates		Other	
Party Identification	Bush	Dole	Robertson	Evan.	Non-Evan.
Democratic	1	0	2	10	34
Independent	0	0	1	0	0
Indep/Leaning Republican	5	18	9	7	2
Weak Republican	5	6	9	7	2
Strong Republican	89	76	80	77	63
(Total)	100%	100%	100%	100%	100%
(N)	(263)	(49)	(197)	(60)	(64)

Source: Surveys by the authors.

TABLE 6.9   Ideology of Democratic Delegates

	Delegates			
			White	Black
Ideology	Dukakis	Gore	Jackson	Jackson
Extremely Liberal	4	6	29	9
Liberal	38	14	45	50
Slightly Liberal	34	30	14	15
Middle of Road	14	17	8	15
Slightly Conservative	5	17	2	7
Conservative	4	15	2	4
Extremely Conservative	0	2	0	2
(Total)	100%	100%	100%	100%
(N)	(92)	(132)	(51)	(259)

Source: Surveys by the authors.

between the Gore delegates and the black Jackson delegates broke down. The same phenomenon occurred on national party identification; the figures on strong party identifiers were 71% for Dukakis supporters, 62% for Gore supporters, 72% for white Jackson supporters, and 78% for black Jackson supporters.

For Republicans at the state level, the Bush delegates demonstrated the strongest party attachment followed by the Robertson delegates, the Other Evangelical delegates, and the Other Non-Evangelical

TABLE 6.10   Ideology of Republican Delegates

	Delegates				
				Other	
Ideology	Bush	Dole	Robertson	Evan.	Non-Evan.
Extremely Liberal	0	0	0	0	2
Liberal	0	0	1	2	8
Slightly Liberal	0	0	0	2	8
Middle of Road	3	6	0	2	9
Slightly Conservative	9	20	2	0	9
Conservative	69	62	47	53	48
Extremely Conservative	19	12	51	42	16
(Total)	100%	100%	100%	100%	100%
(N)	(265)	(50)	(196)	(60)	(64)

Source: Surveys by the authors.

delegates. The Robertson, Other Evangelical, and Dole delegates were bunched relatively closely together with the Other Non-Evangelicals relatively far down the attachment ladder (Table 6.8). And this pattern repeated itself at the national level: 92% of the Bush delegates, 80% of the Dole delegates, 80% of the Robertson delegates, 82% of the Other Evangelical, and 61% of the Other Non-Evangelical delegates indicated strong support for the national Republican Party. If strength of party identification is an indication of willingness to remain active within the party, the strength of attachment of both sets of Jackson delegates and the Robertson delegates suggests that they will continue to be involved.

Democratic and Republican activists were clearly differentiated by ideology, with the Democrats generally identifying themselves as liberal and Republicans identifying themselves as conservative. However, there were variations within each party. Among the Democrats, white Jackson delegates stand out as the most liberal (64% extremely liberal or liberal), followed by black Jackson delegates (59%), Dukakis delegates (42%), and Gore delegates (only 20%). The Gore delegates were not only the least liberal, they were also the only group of Democrats demonstrating much conservative self-placement, with 17% considering themselves extremely conservative or conservative (Table 6.9).

Just as Jackson supporters, both black and white (but especially white), were the most liberal Democrats, Robertson supporters were the most conservative Republicans, with 98% classifying themselves as extremely conservative or conservative (Table 6.10). Other Evangelical delegates were also quite conservative (95% extremely conservative or conservative), followed by Bush delegates (88%), Dole delegates (74%), and Other Non-Evangelical delegates (64%). These data strongly suggest that the entry of white Jackson activists and Robertson activists into the party arena contributes to greater liberalism within the Democratic Party and to greater conservatism within the Republican Party and could, consequently, have the effect of increasing the distance between the two parties.

An examination of delegates' positions on a number of issues supports this general observation, but it also offers some important refinements, especially for black Jackson delegates. Among Democrats, white Jackson delegates were the most liberal, and Gore and black Jackson supporters were the least liberal across the range of issues (Table 6.11). Proportionately, white Jackson delegates were the most liberal group on fourteen of the nineteen issues, and they were second most liberal on the remaining five. At the other extreme, the Gore

TABLE 6.11 Issue Positions of Democratic Delegates

Percentage Liberal Responses	Delegates			
	Dukakis	Gore	White Jackson	Black Jackson
Social/Moral Issues				
ERA	83%	71%	87%	96%
Abortion Amendment	76	61	85	37
Affirmative Action	61	43	89	97
School Prayer Amend.	67	35	68	22
Sexual Freedom	42	24	54	17
Moral Relativism	46	34	58	45
Family Ties	16	6	23	6
Marijuana Immoral	53	31	65	17
Handgun Control	82	66	89	83
Protect Environment	96	97	98	89
Natl Health Insurance	69	50	81	84
Foreign Policy/Defense Issues				
More Defense Spending	81	62	94	85
Military in Mid-East	71	63	83	55
Military in Latin America	75	55	89	54
INF Treaty	86	70	83	48
SDI	58	42	74	37
Economic Issues				
Balance Budget:				
With Spending Cuts	26	23	39	26
With Tax Increases	42	46	51	33
Public Works Programs	49	41	60	62

Source: Surveys by the authors.

delegates were the least liberal group on nine issues while black Jackson delegates were the least liberal on eleven issues. The black Jackson delegates constitute an interesting case: they were the most liberal group on social issues such as the Equal Rights Amendment and Affirmative Action, but they were the least liberal group on some moral issues, such as an abortion amendment, a school prayer amendment, sexual freedom, and marijuana use, and on all but one of the foreign policy/defense issues. The Dukakis delegates were generally arrayed at the liberal end of the spectrum. In broad terms, then, the two groups of Jackson supporters aligned closely on minority rights issues, but diverged significantly on moral and defense issues. Indeed, on several moral and defense issues, black Jackson and Gore

TABLE 6.12 Issue Positions of Republican Delegates

Percentage Conservative Responses	Delegates				
				Other	
	Bush	Dole	Robertson	Evan.	Non-Evan.
Social/Moral Issues					
ERA	70%	58%	84%	92%	57%
Abortion Amendment	50	52	94	92	58
Affirmative Action	76	79	66	80	67
School Prayer Amendment	75	65	96	91	68
Sexual Freedom	87	81	99	97	88
Moral Relativism	79	75	95	95	77
Family Ties	97	92	99	98	94
Marijuana Immoral	79	76	90	92	71
Handgun Control	52	46	56	88	66
Protect Environment	13	10	9	29	13
Natl Health Insurance	63	68	72	77	63
Foreign Policy/Defense Issues					
More Defense Spending	86	73	88	90	63
Military in Mid-East	45	36	57	45	36
Military in Latin America	75	64	78	72	62
INF Treaty	11	21	57	64	30
SDI	91	85	94	95	79
Economic Issues					
Balance Budget:					
With Spending Cuts	78	75	83	78	61
With Tax Increases	64	53	83	73	66
Public Works Programs	75	63	76	76	56

Source: Surveys by the authors.

delegates took similar conservative positions, while the Dukakis and white Jackson delegates joined at the liberal end. Thus, the white Jackson delegates emerged as change agents. On both minority rights and moral issues they took positions opposed to the traditional white southern subculture.

Among Republicans, the Robertson activists and the Other Evangelical activists were clearly the most conservative groups within a generally conservative party (Table 6.12). Fairly closely aligned, they ranked first or second most conservative on fifteen of the nineteen issues. Their similar conservatism was particularly evident on the social/moral issues and on the foreign policy/defense issues.

The Robertson delegates and the Other Evangelical activists were most sharply differentiated from other Republicans on their support for amendments on abortion and school prayer, the issue of moral relativism, and opposition to the INF Treaty. On a couple of other issues -- especially use of the military in the Middle East and a tax increase to reduce the federal deficit -- the Robertson delegates stood out as more conservative than the other groups, including other evangelicals. Thus, with regard to the moral issues, the Robertson candidacy drew activists into the GOP who reinforced the evangelical/non-evangelical distinction by combining with other evangelicals as a conservatizing force. On certain other issues, the Robertson delegates pulled the Republican Party even further to the right, largely independently of the Other Evangelicals.

Conclusions

As the forgoing analysis demonstrates, the presence of the clerical candidates in the 1988 presidential nominating contests was not just more "politics as usual" wrapped up in a symbolic clerical collar, at least in South Carolina. Both the Jackson and Robertson campaigns were associated with activists who brought some new flavors and twists to their respective parties. However, despite their common ministerial backgrounds, the impact of the Jackson and Robertson candidacies was quite different, which is not surprising in light of their varying theological orientations and campaign directions.

The vast majority of Jackson supporters were black activists with a substantial history of political involvement which, for most, predated Jackson's emergence as a candidate. Jackson's quest for the presidential nomination did less to activate them and the black church networks to which they belonged than to give them a new focus for their energies. For the most part, these activists were fairly liberal on economic and minority rights issues, but more conservative on social and moral issues. In this sense, although Jackson undoubtedly helped to develop and mobilize these tendencies, it is reasonably safe to speculate that these issue positions predated Jackson and would have been promoted by these activists within the Democratic Party independently of Jackson's campaign. Ironically, the new group attracted into the party arena by Jackson's 1988 candidacy consisted of whites with a strongly secular orientation, who can be thought of as change agents within the Democratic Party; they represented a liberalizing force on a great many issues. In recent years, the southern

Democratic Party has become much more liberal than it once was, and Jackson's efforts may well be a contributing factor. In sharp contrast, Pat Robertson's supporters were largely newcomers to party activity, inspired to become active by the close fit between their moral concerns and Robertson's campaign agenda. Earlier research has argued convincingly that as the southern Republican Party has developed into a viable and competitive organization, it has increasingly staked out the region's conservative terrain. As part of this development, people associated with the Christian Right have become fairly heavily involved in Republican politics. In Robertson's candidacy we see further evidence of both of these developments. That is, Robertson's strongly conservative activists served to move the party even further toward that end of the ideological spectrum. In the context of southern politics, this makes the Republican Party more than ever the embodiment of the distinctive elements of the traditional South.[1] And even though our analysis is based on data from one state, these conclusions on Robertson's effect on the Republican Party are generally consistent with the conclusions in other areas of research (see Chapter 1) and with other types of political elites (see Chapter 7).

Appendix:
South Carolina Delegate Surveys

Questionnaires were administered to all delegates attending the two state party conventions and were collected on the day of the conventions in April 1988. The response rates were reasonably high, averaging approximately 60%. The respondents were nearly evenly divided between the two parties -- 680 Democrats and 645 Republicans. In the Democratic convention, Jackson delegates accounted for 54% of the respondents (n = 363), Albert Gore's supporters accounted for 20% (n = 135), and Michael Dukakis's accounted for 13% (n = 91); the remainder (n = 91) supported other candidates or were uncommitted. In the Republican convention, 30% of the delegates supported Robertson (n = 197), 41% supported Bush (n = 266), and the remainder (n = 182) were either uncommitted or supported a variety of other candidates.

Notes

1. A voluminous literature has developed on this point including Black and Black 1987; Steed, Moreland, and Baker 1985; Moreland, Steed, and Baker 1988; Shaffer, 1986; Carmines and Stanley 1990; Bowman, Hulbary, and Kelley 1990; Steed, Moreland, and Baker 1990; Green and Guth 1990; Smidt 1989; Baker, Moreland, and Steed 1989; Baker, Hadley, Steed, and Moreland 1990.

References

Baker, Tod A., Laurence W. Moreland, and Robert P. Steed. 1989. "Party Activists and the New Religious Right," in Charles W. Dunn, ed., *Religion in American Politics*. Pp. 161-176. Washington, DC: CQ Press.

Baker, Tod A., Charles D. Hadley, Robert P. Steed, and Laurence W. Moreland. 1990. *Political Parties in the Southern States*. New York: Praeger.

Black, Earl, and Merle Black. 1987. *Politics and Society in the South*. Cambridge: Harvard University Press.

Bowman, Lewis, William E. Hulbary, and Anne E. Kelley. 1990. "Party Sorting at the Grass Roots: Stable Partisans and Party-Changers Among Florida's Precinct Officials," in Robert P. Steed, Laurence W. Moreland, and Tod A. Baker, eds., *The Disappearing South? Studies in Regional Change and Continuity*. Pp. 54-70. Tuscaloosa, AL: University of Alabama Press.

Carmines, Edward C., and Harold W. Stanley. 1990. "Where Have All the Conservatives Gone?" in Robert P. Steed, Laurence W. Moreland, and Tod A. Baker, eds., *The Disappearing South? Studies in Regional Change and Continuity*. Pp. 21-33. Tuscaloosa, AL: University of Alabama Press.

Charleston News and Courier. 1987. "Charleston Isn't the Problem--for a Change." July 26:12-A.

_____. 1988a. "Who Hijacked the Reagan Revolution?" March 5:5-B.

_____. 1988b. "Unofficial Statewide Returns." March 6:11-A.

Eldersveld, Samuel J. 1964. *Political Parties: A Behavioral Analysis*. Chicago: Rand McNally.

Green, John C., and James L. Guth. 1990. "The Transformation of Southern Political Elites: Regionalism Among Party and PAC Contributors," in Robert P. Steed, Laurence W. Moreland, and Tod A. Baker, eds., *The Disappearing South? Studies in Regional Change and Continuity*. Pp. 34-53. Tuscaloosa, AL: University of Alabama Press.

Kessel, John. 1980. *Presidential Campaign Politics*. Homewood, IL: Dorsey Press.

Moreland, Laurence W., Robert P. Steed, and Tod A. Baker. 1988. "Ideology, Issues, and Realignment Among Southern Party Activists," in Robert H. Swansbrough and David M. Brodsky, eds., *The South's New Politics: Realignment and Dealignment*. Pp. 268-281. Columbia, S.C.: University of South Carolina Press.

Plotkin, Henry A. 1981. "Issues in the Presidential Campaign," in Gerald M. Pomper, ed., *The Election of 1980: Reports and Interpretations*. Pp. 38-64. Chatham, NJ: Chatham House.

Pomper, Gerald M. ed. 1989. *The Election of 1988: Reports and Interpretations*. Chatham, NJ: Chatham House.

Reichley, A. James. 1985. *Religion in American Public Life*. Washington, DC: The Brookings Institution.

Shaffer, Stephen D. 1986. "Partisan Realignment in the South." Presented at the annual meeting of the Southern Political Science Association, Atlanta, Georgia.

Smidt, Corwin. 1989. "Change and Stability Among Southern Evangelicals," in Charles W. Dunn, ed., *Religion in American Politics*. Pp. 147-160. Washington, DC: Congressional Quarterly Press.

Sorauf, Frank J., and Paul Allen Beck. 1988. *Party Politics in America*. Glenview, IL: Scott, Foresman/Little Brown.

Steed, Robert P., Laurence W. Moreland, and Tod A. Baker. 1990. "Searching for the Mind of the South in the Second Reconstruction," in Robert P. Steed, Laurence W. Moreland, and Tod A. Baker, eds., *The Disappearing South? Studies in Regional Change and Continuity*. Pp. 125-140. Tuscaloosa, AL: University of Alabama Press.

Steed, Robert P., Laurence W. Moreland, and Tod A. Baker, eds., 1985. *The 1984 Presidential Election in the South: Patterns in Southern Party Politics*. New York: Praeger.

7

Apostles and Apostates?
Religion and Politics Among Party Activists

John C. Green
James L. Guth
Cleveland R. Fraser

The 1988 presidential campaign was noteworthy, C. Van Woodward observed, because "it was so thoroughly saturated with religious issues, conflicts, personalities, fanatics, candidates, scandals, and demagogues" (1991:11). To many analysts, this dense religious atmosphere was at best incomprehensible, and at worst a crassly generated smoke screen, designed to mask the "real" issues from public view (Wills 1990:15). But behind the most visible events lies an important reality -- religion was a significant source of political division both between and within the major party coalitions.

While hardly novel in historical terms, this religiously based polarization was particularly evident among political activists, the most attentive, sophisticated, and involved strata of the American public. Indeed, we find that among party activists traditional ethnocultural alignments are being replaced by new cleavages between religious conservatives on the one hand, and religious liberals and secular activists on the other (Wuthnow 1988). Although these patterns reveal much about the 1988 campaign, they also provide tantalizing hints about the future, suggesting that the Republican Party may eventually be dominated by "apostles" of religion drawn from many traditions, while "apostates" from many backgrounds may come to characterize the Democrats.

Religion and Party Alignments

Religion has long been a primary basis for party divisions in Western societies. In some nations, political competition has involved the conflict of confessional allegiances, often embodied in hostile ethnic groups. In other countries, the historic battle has been between religious forces, often buttressed by an established church, and secular or anticlerical factions. Whatever the case, religious divisions sometimes cut across cleavages based on social class, but at other times reinforced them (Lipset and Rokkan 1967; Berger 1982).

Despite the evidence from abroad, American scholars long assumed that religion was largely irrelevant to American party alignments (cf. Leege et al. 1991). Progressive historians trained a generation of scholars in an economic interpretation of party conflict, and, whether that perspective really applied to the whole of American history or not, contemporary social scientists have seen religion as a mere concomitant of social status. True, Catholics were Democrats, and northern Presbyterians were Republicans, but that was simply because Catholics were poor and Presbyterians well-off. By the 1970s, however, the new ethnocultural historians had made a convincing argument that religious worldviews and associated cultural preferences of Catholic "liturgicals" and Protestant "pietists" had always been the underlying confessional basis of party alignments and that they retained enormous power even after the New Deal (cf. Kleppner 1979). More recently, the activities of the Catholic Bishops on behalf of "peace and justice" issues and the rise of the Christian Right suggest that these alignments are still important.

In the presidential contests of the 1980s, Republicans wooed religious voters with traditionalist platform appeals on abortion, school prayer, tuition tax credits, and a host of other "cultural" issues. Although scholars disagree on whether this strategy succeeded, many have concluded that religious issues have drawn new voters and activists toward the GOP. For example, in both 1984 and 1988 white "born-again" Christians voted overwhelmingly for the Republican presidential nominees. More importantly, perhaps, scholars have documented the steady shift of theologically conservative Protestants toward Republican self-identification over the past two decades, a change especially evident among younger voters (see Chapter 8).

The preference of many conservative Christians for the GOP has also become evident among religious and political elites such as Protestant clergy (Chapter 5), Republican state convention delegates (Hauss and Maisel 1986), national convention delegates (Kirkpatrick

1976; Skelton 1984), and major campaign contributors (Guth and Green 1986). Activists in interest groups and social movements allied with the GOP are even more religious than the Republicans. Such evidence has led Thomas Edsall (1985) to assert that the Christian Right has achieved a position within the GOP comparable to that of organized labor among the Democrats. The presence of these new religious activists has raised the specter of intense internal factionalism as proponents of the "social agenda" battle either old-style "business" Republicans or new-style "Yuppie" libertarians (Freeman 1986). The GOP's discomfiture over the abortion issue in the 1989 and 1990 elections is often cited as a example of these problems.

Perhaps because of the visibility of the GOP "religious" strategy, less attention has been paid to the flip side of the coin: the growing influence of secular and even "anticlerical" forces among Democrats. The same studies hinting at successful infiltration of the GOP by religious voters and activists have often found non-religious or non-traditional religious people running Democratic party machinery (Guth and Green 1990). Certainly recent Democratic platforms have reflected cosmopolitan values that antagonized even many members of their own coalition. These problems have often been laid to racial, economic, and cultural diversity, and religious cleavages have seldom received much scrutiny. And yet, it has been "the new politics of old values" (White 1988) which has allowed the GOP to exploit Democratic weaknesses, attracting growing numbers of "God and Country" Democrats to candidates Reagan and Bush (*Times Mirror* 1988:10).

The 1988 election presents an excellent opportunity to investigate the role of religion among party cadres. Although many observers were impressed by the presence of two clerical candidates, the focus on Robertson and Jackson obscured some other telling facts. After turning back the presidential bid of an ordained Southern Baptist minister turned charismatic broadcaster, the Republicans nominated for president an observant Episcopal layman who had cultivated conservative religious groups for eight years. And George Bush chose as a running mate a young Indiana Senator, Dan Quayle, a member of an evangelical Presbyterian church, and deeply admired by the Christian Right.

On the Democratic side, the early front-runner was Gary Hart, a lapsed member of the evangelical Church of the Nazarene. After his campaign self-destructed in what many Americans saw as' a moral scandal, the Democrats rejected their own Baptist minister, Jesse Jackson, in favor of Michael Dukakis, who was brought up Greek

Orthodox but had left the faith, a journey paralleling his wife's remove from Judaism. Indeed, Garry Wills called Dukakis the "first truly secular candidate" for President in American history (Wills 1990:60). Thus, not only the party platforms but also the tickets themselves created the appearance of a growing religious divergence between the major parties.

Do these differences in platforms and candidates have a basis in the activist constituencies of the parties? In this chapter, we examine the religious underpinnings of the American party system through an analysis of an increasingly important group of activists: major financial contributors.[1] While contributors do not represent every kind of activist, they are a diverse, affluent, and extremely active set of elites, and one central to recent changes in national politics (Green and Guth 1991a). In the pages to follow we address these questions: (1) How religious are members of the Republican and Democratic activist corps? (2) What social and demographic differences underlie religious divisions? (3) Do religious differences contribute to distinct ideological perspectives between and within the parties? (4) How do religious orientations influence the presidential choices of activists? (5) Which religious groups are most deeply involved in party activity and committed to the parties? (6) Finally, what impact will religious divisions have on future presidential politics in each party?

The Religiosity of Party Activists

At first glance it would seem that the primary influence of religion on party alignments derives from vestiges of the old ethnocultural divide between the high-status Protestant "mainline" churches on the one hand, and, on the other hand, the "coalition of religious minorities" including the Catholic, Jewish and Southern Protestant traditions. Although recent studies of American religion have noted a great deal of change in individual religious choice (Roof and McKinney 1987), Table 7.1 shows that the ancient confessional ties of the parties are mostly intact. Among Republicans, the mainline Protestant denominations are still the church home of almost three-fifths of GOP activists, with Episcopalians, Presbyterians, Methodists and smaller mainline churches comprising the "Republican Party at prayer." More theologically conservative Protestants, such as Baptists, and a miscellany of evangelical, charismatic and fundamentalist churches add a significant minority. Roman Catholics are one of every ten Republican donors, a smaller proportion than among the Democrats,

TABLE 7.1 Religious Denomination of Party Activists

Denomination	Party Republican		Democratic	
Episcopalian	21.2		6.4	
Presbyterian	13.4		5.0	
Methodist	11.9		7.7	
Other Mainline	12.4		7.0	
United Church of Christ		(4.2)		(2.1)
Lutheran		(3.6)		(1.9)
Disciples of Christ		(0.8)		(0.7)
Other		(4.4)		(2.3)
Evangelical churches	11.1		2.4	
Roman Catholic	10.6		17.4	
All Baptists	7.1		6.7	
Mormon	1.5		.2	
Non-Western and New Sects	.7		1.2	
Quaker and Unitarian	.6		5.3	
Orthodox	.5		1.7	
Jewish	2.2		19.5	
"None"	6.8		19.5	
	100.0%		100.0%	
Religious Tradition				
Evangelical	20.0		9.6	
Mainline Protestant	56.2		23.7	
Roman Catholic/Orthodox	11.2		19.1	
Jewish	2.2		19.5	
Liberal/Humanist/New Sects	3.6		8.6	
"None"	6.8		19.5	
	100.0%		100.0%	

Source: Surveys conducted by authors.

although given the enormous numbers of GOP donors, Catholic Republican donors may actually outnumber their Democratic counterparts. Only 7% of the Republicans have no denominational preference.

The Democrats also look familiar. Their historic identity as the refuge of religious minorities is still secure. Catholic donors make up a large contingent, as do Jewish contributors. Evangelical and mainline Protestants are less numerous, although some are present from every major denomination. Like Jewish donors, Greek Orthodox, Quakers, Unitarians, non-Western cults and new religious sects are represented far beyond their numbers in the population. But the vital fact is this: one of five Democrats has no denominational preference at all. Here, then, we find a concentration of a dramatically growing minority of Americans, those without any religious identification, the "Nones" or "Seculars" (see Roof and McKinney 1987; *Times Mirror* 1988).

Of course, broad denominational categories often hide vital theological differences. The Religious Traditions in Table 7.1 represent a summary placement of churches by theological traditionalism. Donors from some parts of the mainline denominational families, such as the firmly orthodox Presbyterian Church in America, are included among evangelicals. The summary measure shows that the GOP boasts a large component of theologically conservative Protestants, while Democrats draw on liberal churches, Catholic and Jewish donors, and "Nones." And as we shall see, many of the liberal and Jewish Democrats are hardly religious at all.

The GOP's attractions for the orthodox and the Democrats' evident appeal to the "Nones" suggests that a new cleavage based on religious traditionalism, or perhaps simple religiosity, may be supplementing, or even supplanting, older confessional attachments. To discover emerging religious cleavages, we looked at other religious traits, finding consistent and clear-cut party differences (Table 7.2). First, Republicans regard religion as very important, with 36% giving it the highest rating on a seven-point scale, compared to only 22% of the Democrats. One-third of the Democrats, on the other hand, give religion a low or very low rating, nearly twice the rate for Republicans. On matters of belief, the differences are even sharper. Over two-thirds of the Republicans hold a high view of Scripture -- "the actual Word of God, to be taken literally, word for word" or "the inspired Word of God, but not all to be taken literally." In contrast, almost one-half the Democrats see the Bible as "an ancient book of fables, legends, history and moral precepts." Nearly one-half the Republicans are sure that there is life after death; Democrats are much less certain and more inclined to think that this world is all there is.

The organizational aspects of religious identity also reveal distinctive partisan patterns. Republicans are regular church attenders, while a majority of Democrats seldom or never darken the door. The results are less clear cut regarding church membership and activism. While more than one-third of Republicans consider themselves "quite active" church members, the Democratic figure is only a few points lower. Democrats, however, are markedly less likely to be members at all; indeed, almost one-half have no such ties.

TABLE 7.2 Religiosity of Party Activists

Religiosity Measures	Party	
	Republican	Democratic
Importance of Religion		.26[a]
Extremely Important	36	22
Very Important	26	27
Somewhat Important	21	18
Not Very Important	8	13
Not at All Important	9	20
	100%	100%
Believe in Life After Death		.26
Yes, and Sure of It	47	33
Yes, but Not Sure	14	14
Undecided	21	18
No, but Not Sure	4	7
No, and Sure of It	15	28
	100%	100%
Nature of Bible		.50
Inspired, literal	18	4
Inspired, but not literal	59	49
Fables, legends	23	47
	100%	100%
Attend Religious Services		.23
More than once a week	10	5
Every week	29	24
Once/Twice a month	18	14
Few Times a year	23	22
Almost never/never	20	36
	100%	100%
Church/Synagogue Member		.17
Active Member	37	31
Member but not Active	30	24
Not a Member	33	45
	100%	100%
Religious Categories[b]		.33
Religious	33	19
Conventional	31	26
Nominal	23	26
Secular	13	29
	100%	100%

[a] Gamma statistic.
[b] See note 2 for construction of traditional religiosity index.

Source: Surveys conducted by authors.

On religious matters, then, Republican activists are much closer than Democrats to the American public, one of the most religiously observant in the Western world. Although direct comparisons are not always possible, the Republicans' responses on the importance of religion look much like those of a cross-section of Americans. On religious attendance and membership, Republicans are very representative of all Americans, 40% of whom attend religious services in a typical week and about 65% of whom belong to a church or synagogue. On life after death and Biblical authority, however, they hold beliefs characteristic of upscale, educated Americans (which they are), rather than the general public (Gallup 1984; Gallup and Castelli 1989). Democrats, on the other hand, tend to represent minority positions on religious practice and belief as well as denomination.

Are these religious differences associated with varying political perspectives? To facilitate further analysis, we used all our religious indicators to calculate a "Traditional Religiosity" index. Although we shall use this interval-level measure in the following analysis, for ease of illustration, we assigned respondents to the four religious categories in Table 7.2, ranging from the most traditionalist to the most secular.[2] The overwhelming majority of Republicans are deeply "Religious" or "Conventional" in religious terms, while over half the Democrats are either "Nominal" or "Secular." These partisan differences, while not astounding, are quite solid. Thus, the major parties are distinguished not only by traditional confessional attachments but also by varying degrees of religiosity as well. Most Republicans regard religion as important, have fairly traditional beliefs, and are quite at home in church, while a majority of Democrats are largely strangers to religious beliefs and institutions.

Demography and Religiosity

Religion is a component of many social milieus, and certain environments are more supportive of religious belief and practice, while others are more hostile. As numerous scholars have demonstrated, the traditionally religious person is most at home in locations "sociologically and geographically distant from the institutional structures and processes of modernity," while Seculars are likely to be closest to modernity (Hunter 1983:60; cf. Roof 1978). Our data generally conform to these expectations (Table 7.3). Religious Republicans are concentrated in the Midwest and South, while their Nominal and Secular co-partisans are proportionately more numerous

TABLE 7.3 Religiosity and Demography Among Party Activists

| | Party and Religiosity | | | | | | | |
| | Republican | | | | Democratic | | | |
Demographic Trait	REL	CON	NOM	SEC	REL	CON	NOM	SEC[a]
Region								
Northeast	20	24	34	32	29	26	38	43
West	17	19	20	20	14	21	20	32
Midwest	24	19	17	13	16	23	16	15
South	39	39	30	36	41	30	26	10
	100%	100%	100%	100%	100%	100%	100%	100%
Size of Place								
Rural, Small Town	29	23	19	20	22	19	18	11
Small/Medium City	39	32	46	37	42	30	32	26
Major Metro Area	32	45	35	43	36	52	50	63
	100%	100%	100%	100%	100%	100%	100%	100%
Mobility								
Always Rural/Town	46%	35%	15%	4%	38%	25%	29%	8%
Rural to Metro	32	41	18	9	11	26	24	39
Always Metro	24	41	22	13	14	24	29	33
One state as adult	52	51	43	36	48	41	29	31
Education								
High School/Less	21	11	6	4	8	4	1	4
Some College	19	19	16	19	11	15	9	8
College Degree	23	23	29	30	18	18	14	20
Postgrad Work	37	48	48	48	62	63	76	67
	100%	100%	100%	100%	100%	100%	100%	100%
Income								
To $50,000	30	12	13	11	25	22	16	24
To $100,000	22	23	21	16	32	31	30	29
To $200,000	24	23	19	14	24	21	28	25
Over $200,000	25	42	47	59	19	26	26	23
	100%	100%	100%	100%	100%	100%	100%	100%
Gender								
Female	25%	19%	19%	8%	33%	31%	30%	36%
Marital Status								
Single, divorced	23%	27%	35%	42%	34%	27%	41%	38%

[a] Key: REL = Religious; CON = Conventional; NOM = Nominal; SEC = Secular.

Source: Surveys conducted by authors.

in the Northeast and West. Religious Democrats are drawn primarily from the South (mostly Protestants) and Northeast (mostly Catholics), although the Northeast, along with the West, is also home to most secular Democrats. Midwestern Democrats tend to be Conventional. Not unexpectedly, Religious Republicans live in rural areas and smaller cities, while many Religious and Conventional Democrats reside in somewhat larger urban places. Secular Republicans and, especially, Secular Democrats are overwhelmingly metropolitan. And geographical mobility, a key attribute of modernity, bolsters secularity. The Religious predominate among activists who have always lived in rural areas or small towns, while those who have moved from rural to metro areas are quite secular, especially among Democrats. Similarly, those who have lived in only one state are more likely to be Religious than are transplants. Women are more numerous among Religious Republicans but more or less evenly distributed among religious categories in the Democratic Party. The Religious are somewhat less educated (in relative terms), especially among Republicans, and their incomes are more modest. Among Republicans especially, there is a clear tendency for the Religious to conform more closely to traditional marriage and family norms, as illustrated by the proportion married "till death do us part" to one spouse. The Nominal and Secular are more likely to be unmarried or to have been divorced. Thus, in many ways, the demography of the Religious and Secular differs, and this provides the social basis for conflicting political perspectives.

Religiosity and Ideology

There is a burgeoning literature on religion's influence on political ideology among elites. Although it is hazardous to summarize, most studies find that religious conservatism influences social attitudes most profoundly, foreign policy questions somewhat less, and economic policy very little (Guth and Green 1986). Efforts to demonstrate such ties have often been hampered by the paucity of religious indicators and issue questions available in surveys. We have a large array of items in all three domains and will use them to assess how religion influences -- or at least is associated -- with political attitudes.

As a first cut, we looked at the self-identified political ideology of the religious groups. On a seven-point scale from "extremely conservative" to "extremely liberal," our religiosity factor score correlates positively with ideology across the sample ($r = .32$). Note, however, in Table 7.4, that this association is much stronger among

Democrats. Although Religious Republicans are more likely to be "extremely" conservative, other differences are minor, while among Democrats, a majority of the Religious are either moderate or conservative and three-fifths of the Secular are "extremely" or "very" liberal. This pattern extends in one form or another to a variety of social, economic, and foreign policy issues.

Social Issues. Not unexpectedly, social issues clearly divide the Religious from the Secular in both parties. Although this comes as no surprise for Republicans, given the reams of newsprint devoted to the cultural chasms in the GOP, such divisions are, if anything, wider among Democrats. A great many Religious and Conventional Democrats oppose abortion on demand, favor school prayer, emphasize strict enforcement of drug laws, and (in data not shown) would prefer mandatory testing for the AIDS virus. Religious Democrats are also less enthusiastic about open immigration and affirmative action programs.

Another fundamental disagreement between parties and between religious groups occurs over the "rights revolution."[3] As Table 7.4 shows, party differences are quite stark: Republicans oppose and Democrats favor what might be called a "Liberal Rights" agenda of expanded rights for minorities such as blacks and Hispanics, gays, criminal defendants, and others. Religion has an important impact as well. Across the entire sample, religiosity is correlated with opposition to Liberal Rights (r=.31). Religious Republicans are only slightly more hostile to extending these kinds of rights than their Secular colleagues; in contrast, Secular Democrats overwhelmingly back minority rights while their Religious counterparts are notably less supportive. When it comes to "Traditional Rights," however, the tables are turned. Religious Republicans and Democrats are much friendlier to the idea of protecting church schools, gun owners, and the nuclear family, among others. Secular Democrats, conversely, lead the opposition.

These patterns are buttressed by other data. We asked donors, for example, how close they felt to some well-known national groups, such as the American Civil Liberties Union (ACLU), the fervent advocate of civil liberties and social-issue liberalism, and inveterate foe of traditionalist forces. As the reader will recall, Michael Dukakis proudly claimed to be an ACLU member during the campaign, a boast which Republican strategists used effectively against him (Wills 1990: ch. 6). The reasons are not hard to find. Among Republicans, as expected, the ACLU is anathema, with a mean rating of 6.06

TABLE 7.4 Religiosity, Ideology, and Social Issues Among Party Activists

Political Attitudes	Republican REL	CON	NOM	SEC		Democratic REL	CON	NOM	SEC[a]	
Ideology										
Extremely Con/Lib	29	17	15	21	.09[b]	6	7	7	24	34
Very Con/Lib	34	35	32	33		19	18	27	33	
Somewhat Con/Lib	18	26	30	36		16	24	32	23	
Moderate	18	21	22	9		41	28	20	12	
Lib/Con	2	1	1	1		19	24	14	8	
	100%	100%	100%	100%		100%	100%	100%	100%	
Social Issues										
No abortion on demand	81	62	50	38	.46	67	36	20	9%	66
Favor School Prayer	97	94	85	62	.45	83	71	49	36	52
Strict Porno Laws	83	75	59	41	.39	--	--	--	--	--
Strict Drug Laws	79	63	58	42	.35	49	48	38	24	27
Enforce Sex Laws	65	44	36	32	.34	28	18	12	9	29
Limit Immigration	47	54	33	52	.08	27	19	21	13	.17
No Affirmative Action	67	69	68	80	-.02	34	29	25	16	.19
Liberal Rights[c]										
Strongly Favor	8	4	4	12	-.06	30	31	45	63	-29
Favor	12	21	31	13		38	33	36	19	
Oppose	33	38	31	31		20	23	11	10	
Strongly Oppose	47	36	35	45		12	13	8	9	
	100%	100%	100%	100%		100%	100%	100%	100%	
Traditional Rights										
Strongly Favor	40	35	28	18	.16	32	22	14	6	33
Favor	28	24	33	31		24	24	17	17	
Oppose	12	15	17	25		30	32	43	35	
Strongly Oppose	20	26	23	27		14	22	26	42	
	100%	100%	100%	100%		100%	100%	100%	100%	

[a] Key: REL = Religious; CON = Conventional; NOM = Nominal; SEC = Secular.
[b] Gamma statistic.
[c] See note 3 for construction of rights indices.

Source: Surveys conducted by authors.

(on a seven-point scale). Religious Republicans are only slightly more critical (6.36) than Secular Republicans (5.62). However, Democrats are more seriously split. Secular donors approve strongly of the ACLU (2.54), while the Religious fall on the negative side (4.70). Similar patterns obtain in activists' evaluations of other interest groups associated with the Democratic left such as the NAACP, NOW, the National Education Association, and the Sierra Club. Thus, in the 1988 campaign at least, advocating civil liberties and social issues hardly bolstered Democratic unity, even among activists.

Economic Issues. More surprising, perhaps, than the religious divisions on social issues is the relation of different religious perspectives to economic and budgetary priorities. As Table 7.5 shows, religious groups within each party differ on these matters, with the Democrats just as divided as the GOP. On what we call the Liberal Budget Agenda[4] (more spending on the environment, education, welfare, transportation, and foreign aid -- all paid for by cuts in military spending), traditional religiosity correlates quite strongly with conservative views across the entire sample (r=.35). Religious Republicans are once again slightly more conservative than less religious activists; Secular Democrats are the vanguard of the Liberal Budget Agenda.

Indeed, Religious and Secular Democrats even prefer different ways of dealing with the federal budget deficit. We asked donors what combinations and kinds of increased taxes, decreased spending, or budgetary devices (such as Gramm-Rudman) would best solve the problem.[5] Republicans were uniformly and strongly against additional taxation, and once again the Democrats were more divided. Secular Democrats and their Nominal allies were much warmer than the Religious Democrats toward new taxes and rejected spending cuts (except for defense, of course). Fully three-fifths of the Secular Democrats strongly backed additional taxation, compared to only one-third of the Religious.

But religion is not always associated with anti-tax, anti-spending views. In both parties, the Religious are friendlier to a Localist Budget Agenda for Social Security, small business aid, farm price supports, and grants to local government. These preferences no doubt reflect in part the occupational and regional locale of the Religious in both parties, but they may also express the localist "plausibility structure" of traditional religion as well, i.e. that religious people are most strongly embedded in local institutions and concerns (Roof 1978). For example, the Religious are more often members of all kinds of local organizations and tend to be much more active in them than their Secular siblings. That they support programs directly benefitting familiar individuals and institutions is not surprising. Perhaps something similar is at work when the Religious in one or both parties take other "local" perspectives: cut off imports to save jobs, aid businesses to keep workers employed, and save jobs over lower prices.

TABLE 7.5 Religiosity, Economic, and Foreign Policy Issues Among Party Activists

	Party and Religiosity							
	Republican				Democratic			
Political Attitudes	REL	CON	NOM	SEC	REL	CON	NOM	SEC[a]
Liberal Budget Agenda[c]								
Much More Spending	1	3	3	9 -.17[b]	29	35	45	67 -30
Somewhat More	12	16	17	14	38	40	41	25
Somewhat Less	34	38	48	35	17	18	10	5
Much Less Spending	53	32	21	14	16	7	5	3
	100%	100%	100%	100%	100%	100%	100%	100%
Localist Budget Agenda								
Much More Spending	20	19	9	5 .28	45	39	34	28 .15
Somewhat More	26	18	20	9	33	29	29	31
Somewhat Less	26	34	27	27	14	19	21	24
Much Less Spending	28	29	44	59	9	14	16	14
	100%	100%	100%	100%	100%	100%	100%	100%
Budget Plans[d]								
Strong Anti-Tax	48	45	31	48 -.08	12	10	6	7 .27
Moderate Anti-Tax	36	33	47	36	23	22	10	5
Moderate Pro-Tax	14	16	22	14	33	30	39	29
Strong Pro-Tax	2	6	1	2	33	39	45	60
	100%	100%	100%	100%	100%	100%	100%	100%
Economic Policy								
Restrict Trade/Jobs	42	33	32	18 -.23	53	51	34	36 -.22
Aid Business/Jobs	45	31	35	21 -.22	63	60	62	52 -.12
Fight Inflation	46	51	63	73 -.18	17	18	21	8 .13
Foreign Policy[e]								
Hardliner	51	41	36	44 .06	10	6	6	6 .33
Moderate Hardliner	30	35	42	33	25	24	17	5
Mod. Accom.	16	19	17	20	34	38	30	22
Accommodationist	4	5	5	4	33	33	48	67
	100%	100%	100%	100%	100%	100%	100%	100%

[a] Key: REL=Religious; CON=Conventional; NOM=Nominal; SEC=Secular.
[b] Gamma statistic.
[c] See note 4 for construction of budget agenda indices.
[d] See note 5 for construction of budget plans index.
[e] See note 6 for construction of foreign policy index.

Source: Surveys conducted by authors.

Foreign Policy. As other scholars have discovered, we find traditional religion associated quite strongly with attitudes on Cold War issues. The Religious in both parties are more favorable to defense spending, deployment of "Star Wars," aid to the Contras in Nicaragua, and more skeptical of arms control and closer ties with the USSR. A composite Foreign Policy score is found in Table 7.5,[5] where we see the expected policy differences between Republicans and Democrats. But also note the greater Democratic divisions. Religiosity correlates fairly strongly with Cold War attitudes across the entire sample ($r = .28$), but it is associated more strongly with attitudes among Democrats than within the more homogenous GOP. Among Republicans, the Religious are slightly more prone than the Secular to adhere to what Holsti and Rosenau (1990) would call the "Hardliner" camp, preferring aggressive military and diplomatic policies; in contrast Secular Democrats clearly prefer an "Accommodationist" perspective, abjuring military force and stressing international cooperation.

Such findings are confirmed by other questions asked in only one survey. For example, among Democrats willingness to use force in the Persian Gulf to protect American interests was much higher among the Religious (47%) than the Secular Democrats (20%). Perhaps most interesting is the strong tendency for Religious Republicans to want closer U.S. relations with Israel (51% compared to only 30% of the Secular Republicans). This posture is an expression of the crucial role Israel plays in some central theological currents on the Christian Right (Turner and Guth 1989). In any case, such views may be an important constraint on the ability of President Bush to maneuver through Middle East policy mine fields.

Candidate Preferences

To this point we have discovered that religious perspectives are linked to systematic political differences. Republicans are more religiously observant than Democrats; religious orientation divides activists in both parties, but especially the Democrats; and the religious prefer more "conservative" options on most social, economic, and foreign policy issues. In fact, the lines of cleavage created by religion tend to be cumulative rather than cross-cutting. So, for instance, Religious Democrats are consistently more conservative across issues, whereas Secular Democrats are consistently more liberal, thus creating clear factions (Shafer 1985).

Given these findings, we are not surprised that religious groups

128

TABLE 7.6 Religiosity and Candidate Choice Among Party Activists

Candidates[a]	Religiosity				Weighted (N)
	REL	CON	NOM	SEC[b]	
GOP First Choice					
Jeane Kirkpatrick	11%	4%	47%	38%	(54)
Pete DuPont	13	31	39	18	(144)
Jack Kemp	26	33	20	21	(325)
George Bush	28	37	22	14	(1205)
Robert Dole	31	37	15	17	(429)
Howard Baker	34	16	46	3	(214)
Paul Laxalt	38	40	22	0	(72)
Al Haig	40	49	2	9	(27)
Ronald Reagan	55	22	23	0	(54)
Pat Robertson	95	5	0	0	(168)
GOP Party Committee					
Candidate Committees	41	27	21	11	(841)
National Committees	28	32	26	14	(1756)
State Committees	36	38	15	11	(403)
Democratic First Choice					
Jesse Jackson (whites)	7%	2%	19%	53%	(174)
Gary Hart	5	25	34	37	(157)
Michael Dukakis	13	22	31	34	(644)
Bill Bradley	8	23	47	23	(101)
Paul Simon	17	21	23	39	(244)
Bruce Babbitt	17	26	30	28	(140)
Mario Cuomo	15	29	35	22	(173)
Joseph Biden	12	43	36	9	(59)
Sam Nunn	27	38	21	14	(115)
Albert Gore	30	28	24	17	(367)
Richard Gephardt	29	34	20	17	(161)
Jesse Jackson (blacks)	31	39	9	21	(154)
Democratic Party Committee					
Candidate Committees	19	27	25	29	(1440)
National Committees	13	25	28	34	(870)
State Committees	27	30	26	17	(440)

[a] Candidate donors are arrayed in order of increasing scores on the original religiosity factor. Jackson donors are divided by race to illustrate radically diverse religious characteristics.

[b] Key: REL=Religious; CON=Conventional; NOM=Nominal; SEC=Secular.

Source: Surveys conducted by authors.

look to different party leaders. We asked respondents to rate twenty-five prominent figures in their party. Religious Republicans give positive ratings to most GOP politicians, but they are the only real support for Pat Robertson, Jesse Helms, and James Watt--who were rated poorly by most other Republicans. Secular Democrats line up behind figures on the left, such as George McGovern, Pat Schroeder, Ted Kennedy, Alan Cranston, and Jesse Jackson; the Religious prefer Sam Nunn, Chuck Robb, Al Gore, and John Glenn. These tendencies are intriguingly like those found among the mass public in the 1984 National Election Study (Woodard 1989).

The same pattern of preferences applies to the potential candidates in 1988. When asked to list their first choice for the GOP and Democratic presidential nominations, Religious and Secular partisans had differing choices. Some long-shot Republican contenders, such as Jeane Kirkpatrick, Pete DuPont, and Jack Kemp, drew backing primarily from Secular Republicans, while Robertson, Haig, Laxalt (and Reagan) attracted mainly Religious and Conventional votes. George Bush and Bob Dole put together religious coalitions very much reflective of the GOP itself (compare to Table 7.1). The Democratic aspirants with the most secular coalitions were Jesse Jackson's white supporters, Gary Hart, Michael Dukakis, and Bill Bradley, while the most religious coalitions were those forged by Sam Nunn, Albert Gore, Dick Gephardt, and Jesse Jackson's black supporters! Given the religious schizophrenia of the Jackson activists, it is no wonder that journalists could never decide whether his was a religious or a secular left campaign (see Chapters 1 and 6).

Some of the strains created by cultural politics within the national parties are reflected not only in the religious makeup of the candidates' core constituencies but also in the distribution of religious groups in the various party committees. Among Republicans in 1988, presidential candidate committees were the most religious, reflecting both the vast number of donors mobilized by Robertson and the massive counter-attack in the evangelical community by Bush and others. Note that GOP state finance committees are also populated primarily by Religious and Conventional Republicans, while the national committees are a microcosm of the party's total financial community. Among Democrats, contributors to the national committees are the most secular, followed by the presidential candidate committees, with donors to state parties being considerably more religious--as in the GOP. On the whole, these data suggest that the Republicans nominated a candidate both personally and politically in the religious mainstream of his party, and, as a result, in the

American religious mainstream; in contrast the Democrats' choice was both personally and politically more secular than Democratic activists, themselves rather atypical in religious terms.

Activism and Partisanship

Of course, selecting presidential nominees is not the only way party activists set the agenda and image for their party. Their involvement in the nuts-and-bolts of party politics is vital in defining the meaning of party. So we need to ask another question: are Religious or Secular partisans disproportionately represented among the most active party cadres? In 1988 there were some obvious features special to that campaign. In the GOP, for example, new Religious activists were slightly more numerous than in previous years (cf. Guth and Green 1989), due to the Robertson mobilization. Here, however, we will look at activists' customary or long-term involvements. After a series of exploratory analyses, we collapsed results for thirty-three items into eight categories.[7] As Table 7.7 shows, neither the Secular nor Religious have an across-the-board advantage in participation, but they do tend to specialize in different kinds of activities.

In both parties, Religious donors are more involved in institutional activities. They work in campaigns at all levels, including the "grunt work" of staffing phone banks and door-to-door canvassing. They are also much more likely to hold party or public office. Secular contributors, on the other hand, prefer "outsider" or less conventional involvements, specializing in contributing, contacting public officials, demonstrating, and, in a few cases, deserting to third parties. Such specialization might suggest that the religious in both parties are more committed to the party as an institution.

Whether that surmise is correct can be assessed by the degree of psychological commitment to the party and approval of its policies. The standard seven-point partisanship scale shows that Religious Republicans are slightly more likely than the Secular to think of themselves as "strong" partisans (73% to 68%). They are also much more approving of party positions on social issues, somewhat more positive on foreign policy, and just as pleased with GOP economic policy. This positive attitude is no doubt colored by the extraordinarily high job ratings Religious Republicans gave Ronald Reagan: 71% thought the retiring President did an "excellent" job, compared to only 51% among the Secular.

TABLE 7.7 Religiosity and Activism Among Party Activists

Type of Activism[a]	Party and Religiosity									
Percent Active	Republican					Democratic				
	REL	CON	NOM	SEC		REL	CON	NOM	SEC[b]	
Religious *Specialize*										
Campaigning	33%	31%	27%	17%	.17[c]	50%	45%	41%	34%	.18
Grunt Work	27	23	20	21	.11	42	47	38	36	.11
Party Service	23	21	19	12	.14	25	26	20	18	.13
Public Office	12	15	10	6	.14	26	26	15	13	.27
Secular *Specialize*										
Contributing	39%	52%	53%	51%	-.16	45%	49%	50%	51%	-.06
Contacting	30	39	31	41	-.07	45	61	54	47	.04
Protest	28	23	27	37	-.06	18	28	31	38	-.24
Third Party	1	0	0	4	-.40	0	1	2	5	-.56

[a] See note 7 for contruction of activism indices.
[b] Key: REL = Religious; CON = Conventional; NOM = Nominal; SEC = Secular.
[c] Gamma statistic.

Source: Surveys conducted by authors.

Among Democrats the situation is a little more complex. Secular Democrats are more often "strong" partisans at the national level than are the Religious (64% to 52%), but 54% of both groups claim to be "strong" Democrats in local politics--far above the 42% for both Conventional and Nominal Democrats. On both the Liberal Rights and the Liberal Budget Agenda, the Secular are most pleased with party policy and performance, with Religious Democrats much less so. The gaps are greatest on party handling of social issues, including abortion, prayer in school, gay and civil rights. Only on parts of the Localist Budget Agenda do the Religious Democrats match the Secular in party approval. These patterns suggest the political drift of each coalition: Religious Republicans are the most satisfied with the GOP's performance, while Secular Democrats most favor the Democrats' direction.

Conclusions

Clearly the religious atmosphere of the 1988 election resulted from more than the crass calculations of political strategists. If our findings are any indication, the campaign both reflected and advanced a new religious polarization in party politics. Scholars and journalists, long unaccustomed to thinking of religious and partisan preference in the same context, have been slow to perceive that a new divide is opening beneath the crust of the ancient ethnocultural alliances, with religious traditionalists on the one side, and religious liberals and secularists on the other. The evidence we have found is persuasive. First, the Republican Party is the preferred home of the most orthodox and observant political activists among Protestants, with other religious traditions not far behind.[8] Indeed, it is hardly surprising that the social conservatism of recent Republican administrations, which attracted traditionalist voters, should have even stronger appeal among more sophisticated and committed politicos. Just as important, the Democratic Party -- especially in its national activist corps -- draws heavily and disproportionately from secular activists, and is radically unlike the American public in religious composition (Green and Guth 1988; Guth and Green 1990). The dilemma thus created for Democratic presidential aspirants is well-captured by Michael Dukakis' proud claim to ACLU membership: identification with a noted "enemy of religion" may advance one's prospects with many Democratic activists, but it hardly helps in the general election.

A second critical observation follows. New lines of cleavage between parties create dissension within the parties. Much has been made of the "country club" versus "polyester" division within the GOP. As we have seen here (and shown more extensively elsewhere) this division is real enough (Guth and Green 1989). But many observers have missed a key point: religion and cultural values divide the Democrats even more severely, whether in the mass public or among activists. And religious differences are a vital component of virtually every other split afflicting Democrats: regional factionalism, racial polarization, social issue dissensus, foreign policy disagreements, and budget quarrels. Indeed, the fundamental differences in worldview between the "brie and chablis" set and the "God and country" folk may be much more difficult to accommodate than some of the policy perspectives associated with them.

Of course, there are religious people among Democrats as well, and they are often crucial to campaign efforts: black church networks, the liberal Protestant and Catholic peace and justice activists, and the small-town Sunday school teachers of the South and Midwest. The institutional activism of these groups, embedded in local communities, may help account for the continued success of the Democratic Party at the subnational level (cf. Green and Guth 1991a). While it is possible that religious voices could have more influence in the Democratic party (and for that matter, secular voices receive a better hearing in the GOP) party politics is moving in the opposite direction, aided and abetted by social trends (see Chapter 12). And if these trends continue unabated, apostles of religion may become the norm in the GOP, the party of "order and tradition," while religious apostasy may dominate the Democrats, the party of "rights and reform."

Notes

1. The data come from two 1986-88 mail surveys of stratified random samples of 6,800 contributors to state and national party committees and to multi-candidate PACs sponsored by several presidential hopefuls. The return rates were 46.0% for the Republican and 45.7% for the Democratic sample, excluding undeliverable mail. Inspection of the original mailing lists revealed one modest response bias: undelivered mail was concentrated in the central cites of major metropolitan areas. The Republican and Democratic party questionnaires varied somewhat, but were both ten pages long with over four hundred items. Due to oversampling of smaller finance committees, we have used Federal Election Commission data for the 1987-88 election cycle to weight the sample so as to approximate the final distribution of donors in the entire Republican and Democratic financial communities. Weightings available from authors on request.

2. The religiosity score was developed using a principal components analysis of the five religious measures in Table 5 plus a seven-point denominational traditionalism scale (see Green and Guth 1991b). The analysis produced a single factor with an eigenvalue of 3.74, accounting for 62.3% of the variance. All six measures loaded strongly: importance of religion (.86), church attendance (.85), Biblical literalism (.77), life after death (.77), church membership and activism (.73), and denominational traditionalism (.73). We recognized that inclusion of the denominational traditionalism scale required somewhat arbitrary assignments of some religious groups, especially non-Protestants, and we therefore ran all the analyses with that variable omitted with virtually identical results. Although we use respondents' actual scores in the later analysis, we divided the factor scores into quartiles to produce the categories in Table 7.2, a division which illustrates well the differences among activists. For example, the Religious donors exhibit the following traits: they interpret the Bible as either literal or authoritative (99%), believe in life after death (98%), regard religion as very important (95%), attend services weekly or oftener (89%), and are "quite active" in their church (81%). On the other hand, the Secular respondents represent the other extreme: they regard the Bible as fable (93%), don't believe in life after death (80%), see religion as of little or no importance (93%), seldom or never go to church (99%), and are not members of a church (93%).

3. The two rights factors result from a factor analysis of thirteen questions on whether further federal legislation was needed to protect the rights of specific groups.

These items were cast in seven-point Likert scales, ranging from "very desirable" to "very undesirable." The factors had eigenvalues of 6.23 and 1.71, explaining 47.9 and 13.2% of the variance, respectively. A varimax rotation revealed a "Liberal Rights" factor, on which these variables loaded: rights for blacks and Hispanics (.85), gays (.84), single mothers (.78), employed women (.78), criminal defendants (.73), homemakers (.67), "non-Christian sects" (.67), and the handicapped (.66). The second factor is a "Traditional Rights" dimension, with heaviest loadings from protection for church schools (.80), gun owners (.74), divorced fathers (.57), crime victims (.55), and the traditional nuclear family (.55). Respondents were assigned two factor scores, which were then divided into quartiles for the analysis in Table 7.4.

4. The two budget measures were derived from a factor analysis of eleven types of federal programs cast in seven-point Likert scales, ranging from "spend more" to "cut a lot." The factors had eigenvalues of 4.86 and 1.22, explaining 44.2 and 11.1% of the variance, respectively. A varimax rotation produced the "Liberal Budget Agenda" factor, with heavy loadings on environmental spending (.76), cuts in defense (.70), regulatory programs (.69), education (.67), social welfare (.64), foreign aid (.59), and transportation (.50), and a "Localist Budget Agenda," with heaviest loadings from farm programs (.78), small business aid (.72), social security (.68), and assistance to local government (.57). The factor scores were then divided into quartiles for Table 7.5.

5. The Budget Plans factor was derived from a factor analysis of eleven items on how the federal budget might be balanced, cast in seven-point Likert scales, ranging from "very best" to "very worst." The factor had an eigenvalue of 3.66, explaining 45.7% of the variance. These items loaded heavily: increased income tax (.82), higher corporation tax (.77), line-item veto (-.74), constitutional amendment (-.72), Gramm-Rudman (-.61), excise tax increases (.58), spending cuts (-.56), and combinations of tax increases and spending cuts (.54). Respondents' factor scores were divided into quartiles for presentation in Table 7.5

6. The Foreign Policy score is a recoded factor score derived from a factor analysis of questions dealing with foreign policy issues. Experimentation produced one major factor, incorporating support for Star Wars funding (.84), increased defense spending (.78), dislike for warmer relations with the Soviet Union (.75), willingness to take strong action against the Sandinistas in Nicaragua (.72), and skepticism concerning strategic arms talks (.68). The principal component had an eigenvalue of 2.86, explaining 57% of the variance. The factor scores were divided by quartiles to create the categories in Table 7.5.

7. The first seven categories listed in Table 7.7 were isolated by factor analysis of the activism questions in both surveys. Campaigning includes involvement in seven types of electoral contests, from the Presidential election to local races. Grunt work includes routine electoral activities such as staffing telephone banks and door-to-door canvassing. Party services incorporates several items on holding party office. Public office includes three items on running for and holding elected and appointive office. Contributing includes four items on donating to party committees. Contacting includes three items on communicating with political influentials. Protest includes extra-party activities such as demonstrations, contributing to single-issue PACs, and participating in special caucuses. The Table reports the percentage of those who report "often" being active in these ways.

8. Interestingly, in this sample Catholic Republicans are considerably more traditionalist and observant than Catholic Democrats, a tendency which has not yet appeared in the mass public (see Chapter 10).

References

Berger, Suzanne, ed. 1982. *Religion in West European Politics*. London: Frank Cass.

Edsall, Thomas. 1985. "Pulpit Power: Converting the GOP." *Washington Post National Weekly Edition*, July 8:8

Freeman, Jo. 1986. "The Political Culture of Democrats and Republicans." *Political Science Quarterly*, 101:327-344.

Gallup, George, Jr. 1984. *Religion in America*. Princeton, NJ: Princeton Religion Research Center.

_____, and Jim Castelli. 1989. *The People's Religion: American Faith in the 90's*. New York: Macmillan.

Green, John C., and James L. Guth. 1988. "The Christian Right in the Republican Party: The Case of Pat Robertson's Supporters." *Journal of Politics*, 50:150-165.

_____. 1991a. "Who is Right and Who is Left: Activist Coalitions in the Reagan Era," in Benjamin Ginsberg and Alan Stone, eds., *Do Elections Matter?* Pp. 32-56. Armonk, NY: M.E. Sharpe.

_____. 1991b. "Religion, Representatives, and Roll Calls." *Legislative Studies Quarterly*. (Forthcoming).

Guth James L., and John C. Green. 1986. "Faith and Politics: Religion and Ideology Among Political Contributors." *American Politics Quarterly*, 14:186-199.

_____. 1989. "God and the GOP: Varieties of Religiosity among Political Contributors," in Ted G. Jelen, ed., *Religion and American Political Behavior*. Pp. 233-241. New York: Praeger.

_____. 1990. "Politics in a New Key: Religiosity and Participation Among Political Activists." *Western Political Quarterly*, 43:153-179.

Hauss, Charles S., and Sandy Maisel. 1986. "Extremist Delegates: Myth and Reality," in Ronald B. Rapoport, Alan I. Abramowitz, and John McGlennon, eds., *The Life of the Parties*. Lexington: University Press of Kentucky.

Holsti, Ole, and James Rosenau. 1990. "The Structure of Foreign Policy Attitudes Among American Leaders." *Journal of Politics*, 52:94-125.

Hunter, James D. 1983. *American Evangelicalism*. New Brunswick, NJ: Rutgers University Press.

Kirkpatrick, Jeane J. 1976. *The New Presidential Elite*. New York: Russell Sage Foundation.

Kleppner, Paul. 1979. *The Third Electoral System, 1853-1892*. Chapel Hill: University of North Carolina Press.

Leege, David C., Joel A. Lieske, and Kenneth D. Wald. 1991. "Toward Cultural Theories of American Political Behavior: Religion, Ethnicity and Race, and Class Outlook," in William Crotty, ed., *Political Science: An Assessment*. Chicago: Northwestern University Press. (Forthcoming).

Lipset, Seymour, and Stein Rokkan, eds. 1967. *Party Systems and Voter Alignments*. New York: The Free Press.

Roof, Wade Clark. 1978. *Community and Commitment: Religious Plausibility in a Liberal Protestant Church*. New York: Elsevier.

_____, and William McKinney. 1987. *American Mainline Religion: Its Changing Shape and Future*. New Brunswick: Rutgers University Press.

Shafer, Byron E. 1985. "The New Cultural Politics." *PS*, 28:221-31.

Skelton, George. 1984. "GOP Faces Ideological Divisions in '88." *Los Angeles Times* July 21.

136

Times Mirror. 1988. "The People, Press and Politics: Post-Election Typology Survey." November. Unpublished Report.

Turner, Helen Lee, and James L. Guth. 1989. "The Politics of Armageddon," in Ted G. Jelen, ed., *Religion and Political Behavior in the United States*. Pp. 187-208. New York: Praeger.

White, John Kenneth. 1988. *The New Politics of Old Values*. Hanover, NH: University Press of New England.

Wills, Garry. 1990. *Under God: Religion and American Politics*. New York: Simon and Schuster.

Woodard, David. 1989. "Evangelical Politics: The Role of the Media," in Corwin E. Smidt, ed., *Contemporary Evangelical Political Involvement*. Lanham, MD: University Press of America.

Woodward, C. Vann. 1991. "In God We Trust." *New York Review of Books*, February 14:11-13.

Wuthnow, Robert. 1988. *The Restructuring of American Religion*. Princeton: Princeton University Press.

PART FOUR

Religion and the Electorate in 1988

8

Religious Tradition, Denomination, and Commitment: White Protestants and the 1988 Election

Lyman A. Kellstedt
Corwin E. Smidt
Paul M. Kellstedt

As the 1988 presidential campaign began it appeared that religion might play a powerful role in shaping the outcome. For the first time in American history, two prominent presidential candidates were clergymen. Jesse Jackson, a liberal Democrat, and Pat Robertson, a conservative Republican, were both Baptist ministers. Despite their different political leanings, both candidates made use of biblical passages in their campaign speeches, and both viewed "the religious commitment of their followers as a strategic resource for political mobilization" (Hertzke 1988:4). Jackson consistently drew an impressive proportion of the Democratic vote and, in the end, posed the only serious challenge to the Dukakis nomination. Similarly, Robertson's forces were able to capture the Michigan Republican Party organization in 1987 as a prelude to the 1988 campaign, and, in February 1988, Robertson out-polled Vice-President Bush in the Iowa caucuses. Nevertheless, neither Robertson nor Jackson captured his party's nomination.

In contrast, a variety of other factors suggested that religion would play a minimal role in the 1988 election. Neither of the two nominees, Bush and Dukakis, emphasized their religious credentials. Likewise, the Christian Right, which had been the focus of so much media attention in the 1980 and 1984 elections, received little scrutiny in 1988. The Moral Majority, the flagship of the Christian Right, was hardly evident in the campaign and disbanded shortly after the election. Finally, the Bakker and Swaggart scandals discredited televangelists generally and stymied their efforts to mobilize their viewers politically. It is not surprising, then, that many observers believed that religion would be inconsequential in the election of 1988. What impact did religion have on political behavior in the 1988 presidential election? This essay will focus on the role of two groups of white Protestants, evangelical and mainline. It begins by placing these religious traditions in historical, socio-demographic, and political context. It will examine the role of the two religious subgroups in the Super Tuesday primaries, with a particular focus on support for Pat Robertson and Jesse Jackson. The essay will examine next the role of white Protestants in the fall campaign, and, finally, the future of evangelical and mainline Protestantism in the political process.

American Protestantism

To the casual observer, there may be no apparent reason to differentiate between evangelical and mainline Protestantism. But there are several reasons why such a distinction is necessary to understand American Protestantism. First, political differences between these two Protestant traditions have existed since the nineteenth century (Swierenga 1990:157). Members of evangelical denominations have been predominately Democratic in partisan identification, while members of mainline denominations have been largely Republican (Kellstedt and Green 1990).

Second, theological differences separate evangelical and mainline Protestants. The former tend to be more particularist or exclusivistic theologically, holding that "Christ is the only way unto salvation." Mainline Protestants, on the other hand, are often more universalistic, there being "many roads unto salvation." In addition, evangelicals emphasize religious conversion as a necessary step for salvation, a "born-again" experience that can often be pinpointed in time. For mainline Protestants, conversion is less specific in time and place. Faith is more likely to be described in terms of religious commitment, family upbringing, or church membership. Biblical beliefs and practices also differentiate the two traditions. Evangelical Protestants emphasize that the Bible is the Word of God, while mainline Protestants have been more willing to hold that the Bible either contains the Word of God or becomes the Word of God to the believer. Finally, evangelicals are more oriented toward the sharing of their faith than mainline Protestants, while the latter are more likely to espouse the "social gospel" of reform.

Third, evangelicals have been located largely outside the mainstream of American society since the Fundamentalist-Modernist debate of the early twentieth century (culminating in the Scopes Trial of 1925), while mainline Protestants have been at the center of American culture, holding positions of influence and power. Mainline Protestants are better educated, wealthier, somewhat older, and more likely to live outside the South than evangelical Protestants (Kellstedt and Noll 1990). These social differences are also reflected in denominational affiliation with different religious organizations. Evangelical denominations often belong to the National Association of Evangelicals, while most mainline denominations belong to the National Council of Churches.

Many differences exist within each branch of Protestantism as well. Under the umbrella of evangelicalism is found the Southern Baptist Convention, the largest Protestant denomination (which rejects the label "evangelical") as well as smaller groups such as the fundamentalists and Pentecostals. Denominational families also divide the mainline group, with Presbyterians, Lutherans, Methodists, and Episcopalians exhibiting important theological differences. Because of these differences, we focus on the religious traditions as a whole as well as upon prominent subgroups within each.

The past thirty years reflect a period of change and continuity for both evangelicals and mainline Protestants. On the one hand, evangelicals have grown dramatically in numerical strength relative to mainline Protestants, who have experienced membership decline. While evangelicals constituted slightly more than one-third of all white Protestants in the 1950s, they accounted for nearly one-half in the 1980s. On the other hand, there has been great continuity in the demographic characteristics of the two groups. In the 1950s, more than one-half of evangelicals resided in the South, compared to only one-fifth of mainline Protestants, and these patterns remained relatively unchanged in the 1980s. Mainline Protestants were, and continue to be, better educated than their evangelical brethren.[1] Evangelicals had a higher proportion of younger respondents than mainline Protestants in the 1950s, and this pattern has changed little over time. What is evident in American Protestantism, then, is a southern, less educated, younger evangelical community, and a more northern, better educated, older mainline community. These differences will be taken into account when analyzing the political attitudes and behavior of evangelical and mainline Protestants in the 1988 presidential election.

Politically, mainline Protestants began and ended the period as

Republican Party identifiers. They have been a bastion of the Republican coalition since the advent of survey research in the 1930s. On the other hand, evangelical Protestants have historically identified as Democrats and continued to do so through the 1980 election, but made a dramatic switch toward the Republicans by 1984 (Kellstedt and Green 1990). Mainline Protestants have also had higher turnout rates than evangelicals throughout the past several decades. Finally, both mainline and evangelical Protestants have voted for Republican presidential candidates in every election but one from 1956 to 1984,[2] despite the fact that evangelicals identified as Democrats through most of the period. The evangelical vote for Reagan was particularly high in 1984, approaching 80% for regular church attenders (Kellstedt and Green 1990).

The Measurement of Religion

Religion is a complex phenomenon, and at least five facets are relevant for understanding political behavior. The first is denominational affiliation. For most individuals, religion means affiliation with a group larger than oneself, and for most Americans such a group is a denomination. The mechanism by which these affiliations have political relevance may be either social in nature (e.g., through the formation of primary group friendships) or psychological in nature (e.g., through identification with a larger religious group).

A second facet of religion involves the grouping of Protestant denominations into two broad religious traditions, evangelical and mainline. These traditions are comprised of social networks or subcultures which have been created around and across various denominational structures. Each tradition has different publishing houses, periodicals, colleges, organizational umbrellas, communication networks, and, as we will show, a distinct political perspective.

Doctrinal beliefs, a third facet of religion, are often assumed to influence behavior. Two of these beliefs are particularly important within American Protestantism: beliefs about the Bible and beliefs about conversion. As noted earlier, evangelical and mainline Protestants usually hold different beliefs in these areas.

A fourth facet is religiosity. Here, frequency of church attendance plays a central role. Believers learn about the faith by attending church regularly, for it is difficult, if not impossible, to pick up religious cues without sitting in the pews (Wald, Owen, and Hill 1988, 1990). Thus, church attendance conditions the relationship between religion and political behavior; evangelical and mainline Protestants who attend church regularly are more likely to exhibit the attitudes and behaviors of their respective religious traditions than those who rarely attend (Kellstedt 1989:105).

A fifth facet is religious salience, the perceived importance of religion to the individual. Generally, the more important one's religion, the stronger the religious belief and the greater frequency of religious practice. Recent research has shown that religious salience correlates highly with various social and political attitudes and behaviors, including attitudes toward abortion, racial relations, partisanship, voting turnout, and vote choice (Leege, Kellstedt, and Wald 1990; Jelen, Kellstedt, and Wilcox 1990).

We will analyze how these five facets of religion affected the political behavior of evangelical and mainline Protestants in the 1988 presidential election using data from the 1988 American National Election Study (see the Appendix for further details and denominational codings).

American Protestants and the 1988 Primary Elections

The 1984 presidential election was disastrous for the Democratic Party in the South; Reagan carried the 14 southern and border states with 62.5% of the vote, his best regional showing. In response, various Democratic-controlled southern state legislatures decided to hold 1988 presidential primaries on the same Tuesday in early March. As a consequence, more than one-third of the national convention delegates were chosen on or near "Super Tuesday." Southern Democrats, in particular, hoped that the Super Tuesday primary would: (1) "ensure the nomination of a moderate-to-conservative candidate" who could carry the South in the general election (Castle 1987:6), and (2) spark increased voter turnout in the Democratic primaries, "especially among moderate and conservative Democrats who voted for Reagan in 1984" (Galston 1988:3). Among the key targets were the large numbers of evangelicals who voted heavily for Reagan in 1984 and had begun to identify with the Republican Party.

To what extent were the Super Tuesday primaries successful in wooing evangelical Protestants back to the Democratic Party? Did evangelicals, given their history of low turnout, choosing to participate in the primaries in large numbers? How did evangelicals compare to mainline Protestants? To what extent did Jesse Jackson and Pat Robertson receive support among white evangelical and mainline

Protestants on Super Tuesday? Table 8.1 provides some answers to these questions.

Democrats could take some comfort from these findings. Less than one-half of evangelicals voting on Super Tuesday chose to participate on the Republican side, a pattern similar to the mainliners. Apparently, southern Protestants had not permanently cast their lot with the GOP. However, Table 8.1 also provide some sobering signs for the Democrats, particularly concerning the probability of any Democratic candidate winning the white Protestant vote in the fall election. First, the mean partisan identification score for evangelicals, while significantly less Republican than that for mainline Protestants, was still in the direction of the GOP, consolidating the changes of the 1980s. And the turnout among evangelicals was likewise approaching that of the mainline. Moreover, Dukakis, the eventual Democratic nominee, did not receive widespread support among either evangelical or mainline Protestants who voted in the Democratic primaries. In fact, Gore fared as well as Dukakis among those who cast Democratic ballots. Finally, a clear majority of non-voting Protestants stated that they would have voted in the Republican primaries had they gone to the polls.

Although Bush did not receive overwhelming support among white Protestant voters on Super Tuesday--only about one in four cast their ballots for him--he far out-distanced his nearest Republican competitor. And when all respondents were asked who they would like to see elected President, a clear plurality of both evangelical and mainline Protestants indicated Bush. In fact, Bush was nearly a three-to-one favorite over his nearest challenger among evangelical and mainline Protestants alike. Given such patterns, the outlook for the eventual Democratic candidate among white Protestants was rather bleak as early as March 1988.

Finally, despite the fact that most Super Tuesday primaries were held in the "Bible Belt," neither Jackson nor Robertson did particularly well. Jackson received a relatively small percentage of support among evangelical and mainline Protestants voting in the Democratic primaries (6% and 10%, respectively). Nevertheless, Jackson managed to carry five southern states on Super Tuesday, due largely to his overwhelming support among black voters. Robertson, on the other hand, received much greater support among evangelical than mainline Protestants voting in the Republican primaries (23% versus 4%). Yet even this level of evangelical support must have been disappointing to Robertson. Among evangelicals, the supposed base of Robertson's support, Bush out-polled Robertson over two-to-one.

TABLE 8.1 White Protestants and the Super Tuesday Primaries

	Evangelical Protestants (N = 548)	Mainline Protestants (N = 454)
Partisan Identification[a] (Mean Score)	3.08*	3.32*
Voted in Primary	42%	47%
Primary Voters Who Voted in Republican Primary	44	46
Non-Voters Who Would Have Voted in Republican Primary	58	62
Primary Voters: Democratic Primary Vote Choice		
Dukakis	22	40
Gore	38	32
Jackson	6	10
Other Democrat	33	19
Republican Primary Vote Choice		
Bush	48	57
Dole	16	29
Robertson	23	4
Other Republican	12	10
All Respondents: Would Like Elected President		
Bush	43	41
Dukakis	9	14
Dole	8	12
Gore	13	8
Robertson	4	2
Jackson	3	4
Other Republican	4	8
Other Democrat	16	12

[a] Scores for individuals ranged from 0 (strong Democrat) to 6 (strong Republican) with a mid-point of 3.0.

* Differences between evangelical and mainline Protestants are statistically significant at the .01 level or better.

Source: The 1988 American National Election Study Super Tuesday Survey.

Before examining the behavior of white Protestants in the fall, we might ask what happened to the Robertson and Jackson supporters. Did they refuse to participate in the fall campaign because their preferred candidate lost in the primary season? Or did they turn out for their party's candidate? The Robertson and Jackson primary supporters show some evidence of low turnout, one sign of disaffection from parties and presidential candidates. Of those Robertson supporters who voted, a majority supported Bush. White backers of Jesse Jackson, however, gave Bush approximately 46% of their votes, a healthy figure and possibly the result of disaffection with the Democratic Party and its presidential candidate (data not shown).

American Protestants and the 1988 General Election

During the fall campaign, religion did not seem a particularly important force. Americans paid little attention to the fact that Dukakis' affiliation with the Greek Orthodox Church, like Kennedy's Roman Catholicism, was outside conventional American Protestantism. Perhaps more importantly, neither the Christian Right nor any other religious groups received much media attention during the course of the 1988 general election. Nevertheless, appearances can be deceiving. Religion may have an impact on political behavior at the individual level even when there are no overt efforts to mobilize voters on this basis. Did evangelicals continue their movement toward the Republican Party in 1988? Did mainline Protestants sustain their strong affinity for the Republican Party? Did mainliners continue to vote at greater rates than evangelicals? Was the political behavior of Protestants affected by facets of religion such as doctrinal beliefs, church attendance, and religious salience? Did the socio-demographic characteristics, which tend to differentiate evangelical and mainline Protestants, account for the differences in political behavior between the two groups? These questions serve as the focus of the remaining analysis.

The partisan identification, voter turnout, and vote choice of both groups of Protestants are examined in Table 8.2, along with some of the larger denominations within each of these traditions. First, mainline Protestants remain significantly more Republican in identification than evangelicals. While the mean partisan identification score was 3.40 among mainliners, it was 3.16 among evangelicals. Despite such differences, the GOP gains made among evangelicals between 1980 and 1984 were still evident in 1988. It appears that

TABLE 8.2 Partisanship, Turnout, and Vote Choice for White Protestants

Religious Group	Partisan Id.[a]	Voted	Voted Bush	N
All Evangelicals	3.16*	63%*	70%	484
Reformed	4.62	92%	80%	13
Non-Denominational	3.59	73%	76%	68
Churches of Christ	3.13	67%	61%	45
Other Baptists	3.12	62%	75%	102
Southern Baptists	2.99	62%	68%	143
Pentecostal/Holiness	2.76	52%	65%	90
All Mainline	3.40*	79%*	64%	520
Congregationalists	4.35	85%	76%	26
Episcopalians	3.61	72%	71%	49
Presbyterians	3.54	87%	64%	79
Lutherans	3.32	85%	63%	117
Methodists	3.18	75%	59%	196

[a] Scores for individuals ranged from 0 (strong Democrat) to 6 (strong Republican) with a mid-point of 3.0.
* Differences between evangelical and mainline Protestants are statistically significant at the .01 level or better.
Source: The 1988 American National Election Study.

evangelicals have joined the coalition of groups associated with the Republican Party.

In addition to the differences between evangelical and mainline Protestants, there is also much diversity *within* each camp. For example, among evangelicals, the relatively small and northern Reformed family (mainly the Reformed Church in America and the Christian Reformed Church) is more strongly Republican than any other subgroup. Non-denominational Protestants are also strongly Republican, a group that has grown substantially over the past three decades in many parts of the country. They include fundamentalists as well as other kinds of evangelicals who share a strong belief in the inerrancy of the Bible, acknowledge a born-again experience, and have very high rates of church attendance.

While the Reformed and non-denominational Protestants are more Republican than evangelicals as a whole, the Pentecostal/Holiness families and the Southern Baptists are more Democratic. The Pentecostal/Holiness category combines the Church of God-Holiness, Free Methodists, Nazarenes, and Salvation Army with the Pentecostal-Assemblies of God churches. The Holiness and the

Pentecostal families are somewhat distinct theologically in that the latter emphasize the Baptism of the Holy Spirit, speaking in tongues, and faith healing. However, both groups tend to be "perfectionist" in lifestyle, low in social status, and similar politically. Pentecostal churches served as Pat Robertson's natural base, a distinct disadvantage given their Democratic leanings.

Note that the Southern Baptist Convention, the largest Protestant denomination, is also more Democratic than the other evangelicals. Yet this predominantly southern denomination is about equally divided between Republican and Democratic partisans. There is evidence of substantial movement of Southern Baptists toward the Republican Party in the past decade among both the laity (Kellstedt and Noll 1990) and the clergy (Guth 1985). Thus, Southern Baptists are shifting towards the partisan home of the traditional mainline, namely, the GOP. Finally, the Churches of Christ and Baptists outside the Southern Baptist Convention have scores on the partisan measure near the mean for all evangelicals.

Among the mainline groups, there is less deviation than among evangelicals. The three strongest subgroups in Republican partisanship are the original "big three" of American Protestantism: Congregationalists, Episcopalians, and Presbyterians. Dominant from the time of the Founding, these groups have been Republican almost since the party's origin. Less Republican in orientation, but still solidly so, are the Lutherans and Methodists. Lutherans, conservative and orthodox in orientation, but not evangelical, have maintained a commitment to the GOP over the past generation (Kellstedt and Noll 1990). The Methodists, evangelical at their founding but mainline in outlook today, have less of the upper-status character commonly associated with Episcopalians and Presbyterians. Not surprisingly, they are less Republican.

Evangelicals have for several decades voted at lower rates than their mainline counterparts. This pattern continued in 1988 with the differences between the two Protestant traditions attaining statistical significance (Table 8.2). These differences remain despite the apparent politicization of evangelicals over the past decade.[4] Among evangelicals, only the small Reformed family had turnout rates higher than those for the mainline groups, while non-denominational Protestants approached the percentages for the mainliners. Interestingly, the Pentecostal/Holiness family exhibited a particularly low turnout. This pattern is important in that the largest segment of this family, the Pentecostals, constituted the natural base of support for Pat Robertson. But as noted above, the partisan identification data suggest that this group is oriented toward the Democratic Party. Taken together, these findings suggest two reasons for Robertson's poor showing: his natural base was Democratic and relatively apolitical.

Mainline Protestants vote at very high rates. Given that they have traditionally been dominant players in American politics, it is not surprising that Presbyterians, Congregationalists, and Lutherans have the highest turnout rates among the mainline. But Episcopalian turnout, especially when compared to their behavior over the past generation, was low in 1988 (Kellstedt and Noll 1990). Methodists rank near the low end of the mainline spectrum, as expected.

Both evangelicals and mainliners gave George Bush a lower percentage of their votes (70% and 64%, respectively) than they had given Ronald Reagan in 1984 (75% and 71%, respectively). Nevertheless, white Protestants supplied the crucial votes for the Bush victory. Jews, blacks, and those with no religious preference gave strong majority support to Michael Dukakis, while white Catholics were equally divided (see Chapters 9,10 and 11). It is important to note that evangelicals in the last two presidential elections have given a greater share of their votes to Republican candidates than have mainline Protestants. In addition, the evangelicals are growing in numbers, making their votes particularly valuable. Only their somewhat lower turnout rates might slow the emergence of evangelicals as central players in the Republican coalition.

Within the evangelical camp, the small Reformed family voted most heavily for Bush in 1988, followed by the Other Baptists and Non-denominational Protestants. In contrast, the Southern Baptists, Pentecostal/Holiness families, and Churches of Christ gave Bush less support than evangelicals as a whole, but at rates comparable to the mainline. Among mainline Protestants, the Congregationalists and Episcopalians voted most heavily for the Republican candidate, followed by Presbyterians and Lutherans, while the Methodists ranked lowest of all white Protestants. Still, the white Methodist vote for Bush was five percentage points above the national average.

The Impact of Religious Commitment

Religious traditions and denominational families clearly influenced the partisanship, voting turnout, and vote choices of white Protestants in the 1988 election. Individuals differ, however, in the intensity of their religious commitments, and these differences could well qualify the relationships noted above. If religion truly does matter politically, then those voters who are religiously committed should exhibit different political characteristics than those voters who are relatively uncommitted.

The measures of religious commitment used here include religiosity, religious salience, and doctrinal orthodoxy. Religiosity is exemplified by frequency of church attendance and is a relatively straightforward measure of religious commitment. Religious salience represents the importance of religion to the individual. Finally, the religious doctrine score combines attitudes toward the Bible with born-again identification.[5] Our hypothesis is that these three religious variables influence partisanship, turnout, and vote choice, both within and across religious traditions and denominations. Those who attend church more than once a week (high religiosity), claim that religion provides a "great deal" of guidance for day-to-day living (high salience), and those who hold high views of the Bible and claim a born-again experience (high doctrinal orthodoxy) will identify more often as Republicans, vote at higher rates, and vote more Republican than those who do not.

To test these hypotheses, the nine largest groups in Table 8.2 were studied in detail.[6] The three measures of religious commitment were first tested separately on each of the three measures of political behavior for a total of eighty-one separate tests of the hypotheses. These hypotheses held with rare exception.[7] However, for ease of presentation, we used a composite index of religious commitment which combined all three indicators and was dichotomized into high and low religious commitment.[8] Tables 8.3, 8.4, and 8.5 report the results of this analysis using multiple classification analysis.[9]

We examine the impact of religious tradition, denomination and religious commitment on partisan identification in Table 8.3. The results are impressive: high levels of religious commitment are linked to Republican partisanship for both evangelical and mainline Protestants.[10] Nevertheless, religious traditions and denominational groups still differ in partisanship even after controls are introduced for religious commitment and socio-demographic factors. And even after socio-demographic controls, religious commitment is still closely related to partisanship within each religious tradition and for each denominational family.

Voter turnout is also influenced by religious commitment. Table 8.4 examines this relationship within different levels of church attendance[11] while controlling for socio-demographic variables. For all categories except the Presbyterians, low church attendance is associated with the lower turnout rates. Moreover, in almost every instance, turnout increases as church attendance increases. Despite this, the differences

TABLE 8.3 Partisanship by Religious Commitment for White Protestants

| | Partisan Identification[a] Adjusted for Age, Sex, Education, and Region | | |
| | Religious Commitment[b] | | |
	Low	High	Beta
All Evangelicals	2.97	3.51	.13*
(N)	(287)	(160)	
Non-Denominational	3.54	3.73	.04
(N)	(37)	(22)	
Other Baptists	2.84	3.58	.17*
(N)	(61)	(31)	
Southern Baptists	2.73	3.51	.18*
(N)	(92)	(41)	
Pentecostal/Holiness	2.49	3.19	.16*
(N)	(40)	(45)	
All Mainline	3.37	3.86	.08
(N)	(427)	(67)	
Presbyterians	3.49	4.74	.18*
(N)	(66)	(9)	
Lutherans	3.25	3.88	.12*
(N)	(91)	(20)	
Methodists	3.12	3.57	.08
(N)	(159)	(28)	

[a] Table entries are group partisan identification scores produced by multiple classification analysis. See note 9 for further explanation.
[b] Religious Commitment index includes church attendance, religious salience, and doctrinal orthodoxy. See note 8 for further explanation.
* Significant at .05 level

Source: The 1988 American National Election Study.

between evangelical and mainline Protestant groups persist. Mainline Protestants vote at greater rates than evangelicals even when controlling for church attendance and socio-demographic characteristics. Thus, religious tradition and denominational affiliation in conjunction with church attendance had a cumulative effect in increasing turnout in 1988.

How did religious commitment influence vote choice? Table 8.5 presents the percentages of votes cast for Bush for each religious

TABLE 8.4 Voting Turnout by Church Attendance for White Protestants

| | *Voting Turnout Percentages*[a] *Adjusted for Age, Sex, Education, and Region* | | | |
| | *Church Attendance*[b] | | | |
	Low	Medium	High	Beta
All Evangelicals	57%	70%	74%	.16*
(N)	(213)	(90)	(45)	
Non-Denominational	57%	70%	74%	.21*
(N)	(22)	(18)	(11)	
Other Baptists	57%	71%	79%	.19*
(N)	(53)	(15)	(18)	
Southern Baptists	64%	66%	67%	.03
(N)	(70)	(25)	(24)	
Pentecostal/Holiness	39%	56%	63%	.21*
(N)	(27)	(20)	(24)	
All Mainline	74%	89%	89%	.18*
(N)	(303)	(109)	(40)	
Presbyterians	87%	99%	82%	.17*
(N)	(49)	(15)	(8)	
Lutherans	77%	93%	96%	.23*
(N)	(57)	(36)	(9)	
Methodists	69%	85%	85%	.17*
(N)	(108)	(44)	(17)	

[a] Table entries are mean percentage turnout produced by multiple classification analysis. See note 9 for further explanation.
[b] Low church attendance = attended "once or twice a month" or less; Medium = attended "most weeks" or weekly; High = attended church greater than weekly.
* Significant at the .05 level.
Source: The 1988 American National Election Study.

tradition and for each of the seven denominational families within the two levels of religious commitment, while controlling for the various socio-demographic variables. In all cases except the Southern Baptists, the higher the religious commitment, the greater the Bush vote.[12] The impact of religious commitments upon voting for Bush was particularly strong in the Presbyterian and Pentecostal/Holiness denominations. Even after controlling for religious commitment and socio-demographic characteristics, differences between religious traditions and among denominations remain. Thus, religious traditions and denominational

TABLE 8.5. Vote Choice by Religious Commitment for White Protestants

	Percentage Voting for Bush[a] *Adjusted for Age, Sex, Education, and Region*		
	Religious Commitment[b]		
	Low	High	Beta
All Evangelicals	65%	78%	.15*
(N)	(133)	(118)	
Non-Denominational	71%	82%	.12*
(N)	(20)	(17)	
Other Baptists	69%	85%	.20*
(N)	(30)	(24)	
Southern Baptists	69%	67%	.02
(N)	(46)	(29)	
Pentecostal/Holiness	40%	78%	.36*
(N)	(10)	(27)	
All Mainline	63%	75%	.09*
(N)	(285)	(55)	
Presbyterians	61%	92%	.22*
(N)	(54)	(8)	
Lutherans	58%	79%	.18*
(N)	(65)	(19)	
Methodists	57%	62%	.04
(N)	(97)	(21)	

[a] Table entries are mean percentage vote for Bush produced by multiple classification analysis. See note 9 for further explanation.

[b] Religious Commitment index includes church attendance, religious salience, and doctrinal orthodoxy. See note 9 for further explanation.

* Significant at the .05 level.

Source: The 1988 American National Election Study.

affiliations in conjunction with religious commitment, operate cumulatively to increase the Republican vote.

Clearly, evangelical and mainline voters still differ in partisanship, vote turnout, and vote choice. Denominational differences exist as well within the two religious traditions. Controlling for religious commitment (or church attendance in the case of turnout) served only to the enhance relationships. Protestants who have high religious

TABLE 8.6 Issue Positions by Religious Commitment for White Protestant Republican Identifiers

	Evangelical Protestants Religious Commitment		Mainline Protestants Religious Commitment	
	Low (N=130)	High (N=91)	Low (N=236)	High (N=45)
Ideology				
% Conservative	43*	74*	54	58
Government Guarantee of Jobs				
% Favoring	11	8	12	4
Abortion				
% Pro-Life[a]	55*	87*	29*	66*
% Pro-Choice	26*	7*	41*	14*
Social Issues[b]				
% High	28*	72*	19*	49*
Defense Spending				
% Favoring Increase	47	36	35	44

[a] Pro-life includes opposition to abortion in all circumstances or except in cases of rape or where the mother's health is in danger. Pro-choice positions favor abortion with no restrictions.

[b] High scores on the social issues index include: negative attitudes toward homosexuals and feminists; positive attitudes toward anti-abortionists, school prayer, and traditional views on women's issues; and opposition toward a law protecting homosexuals.

* Differences are statistically significant at the .01 level

Source: The 1988 American National Election Study.

commitment tend to be more Republican, to vote more regularly, and to vote more for the Republican candidate than do Protestants who exhibit low religious commitment. Finally, controls for social/demographic variables do not alter these conclusions significantly. The analysis presented so far has shown that important political differences exist between white evangelical and mainline Protestants, although they are becoming more alike in partisanship, and both were important to the Bush victory in 1988.

But are the two Protestant traditions on the same wavelength in reasons for their support for the Republican Party? Do evangelical and mainline Protestants who classify themselves as Republicans express similar stands on major public issues of the day? Table 8.6

shows important areas of agreement in political perspective. On ideological self-identification and opposition to government involvement in providing jobs, the two groups are similar. Both traditions identify as "conservative," although, among evangelicals great differences exist between the high and low religiously committed, with the former holding pronounced conservative leanings. Neither religious tradition favors government involvement in the economy.

Nevertheless, there are also important issue cleavages evident among Protestant Republicans, especially on abortion and a broader social issues agenda. Although the religiously committed in both traditions are most in favor of a pro-life position on abortion and a conservative social issue agenda, evangelicals clearly are the most conservative. Finally, Republican evangelicals were somewhat more willing in 1988 to increase defense spending than mainline Protestant Republicans, though these differences are not statistically significant.

Conclusion

This essay has highlighted the importance of white Protestants to the Republican Party victory in 1988. Both evangelical and mainline Protestants were critical components of Bush's winning coalition. The support for Bush evident among mainline Protestants continued a long tradition of support for GOP presidential candidates. For evangelicals, identification with the Democratic Party coupled with support for Republican presidential candidates also has had a long history. By 1984, however, evangelicals had moved towards identification with the Republican Party. This increased Republicanism continued in 1988 as well.

This analysis has also shown that religion played an important role in the 1988 election, despite the fact that it receded from public attention in the fall campaign. The evangelical and mainline traditions and their denominational affiliates differed in 1988 in partisan identifications, vote turnout, and vote choice. Mainline Protestants were more likely to vote and to identify with the Republican Party than evangelicals. Nonetheless, just as in 1984, evangelicals gave a higher percentage of their votes to the GOP presidential candidate than did the mainline Protestants. In addition, this analysis has shown that religious commitment works cumulatively with religious tradition and denominational affiliation to influence partisanship, turnout, and vote choice, and that controls for socio-demographic variables do not significantly alter these relationships.

Finally, these findings suggest that the basis of cohesion among Protestant Republicans rests upon economic, and not social issues. In the future, white Protestant Republicans should not differ much in regard to traditional New Deal economic issues, but conflict is likely if abortion and other social issues come to the fore. These latter issues are shaped by the perspective of religious traditions, denominational affiliations, and religious commitment. As a result, the Protestant coalition of the Republican Party could well dissipate if social issues are placed at the forefront of a presidential campaign.

Appendix:
Denominational Coding

This essay is based on data taken from the 1988 National Election Study fall election and Super Tuesday surveys conducted by the Center for Political Studies at the University of Michigan. Denominations were classified as follows (whites only):

Evangelicals: Southern Baptists, all other Baptists, Reformed, Christian Reformed, Christian, Mennonite, Amish, United Missionary, Protestant Missionary, Church of God, Nazarene, Free Methodist, Church of God in Christ, Plymouth Brethren, Pentecostal-Assemblies of God, Church of Christ, Salvation Army, Seventh Day Adventists, Other Fundamentalists, Non-denominational Protestants, Community Church, Other Protestants.

Mainline: Protestants (no denomination given), all Presbyterians, Lutherans, Congregationalists (United Church of Christ), Episcopalians, Evangelical and Reformed, Methodists, Evangelical and United Brethren, Disciples of Christ, Church of the Brethren.

Notes

1. Proportionately such educational differences have narrowed considerably over time. While slightly less than one-half of white mainline Protestants reported some college education in the 1980s, slightly more than one-third of the evangelicals did so.

2. The exception was the 1964 Goldwater debacle, when both groups voted Democratic.

3. We employ the standard partisan identification scale: Strong Democrat (0); Not Very Strong Democrat (1); Independent, Leans Democrat (2); Independent (3); Independent, Leans Republican (4); Not Very Strong Republican (5); Strong Republican (6). In the analysis that follows, mean scores on the partisanship measure are employed. If a group has a score below 3.0, it tends in the Democratic direction; conversely, if the score is above 3.0, it tends in the Republican direction.

4. Ralph Reed of the Christian Coalition, a new Christian Right group concerned with the development of a grassroots base, estimated in communication with the authors that the Moral Majority registered 1.5 million voters in its years of existence. We have no reason to doubt these statistics, but we know of no way to document them.

5. Technically, a born-again identification does not directly tap the religious doctrine that Christians must experience conversion to be saved. However, the willingness to state that one is a born-again Christian is likely to be highly correlated with the belief

that one must experience conversion. Consequently, for ease of discussion, we have simply labeled the responses to the Bible and born-again items as tapping religious doctrine.

6. Because of the small N's associated with some denominations, we limited the analysis to the four largest groups within the evangelical camp (i.e., the Non-Denominational, Baptist, Pentecostal/Holiness, and Southern Baptist families) and the three largest mainline denominations (i.e., the Presbyterian, Lutheran, and Methodist families), in addition to the broader evangelical and mainline categories.

7. In partisanship, the expected hypothesis failed only twice. Non-denominational Protestants who attended church more than once per week and Southern Baptists in the high doctrinal category were both less likely to identify as Republicans. For vote turnout, the hypothesis again failed only twice. Non-denominational Protestants who attended church more than weekly and Methodists in the high doctrinal category were less likely to vote. For vote choice, the hypothesis failed four times, for high doctrinal mainline Protestants as a whole: for high doctrinal Presbyterians and Methodists, and for high church attending Southern Baptists. Thus, out of 81 tests, the hypotheses failed only 8 times.

8. The three indicators of commitment are positively correlated and meet acceptable standards of reliability, an alpha coefficient of above .6. Respondents who attended church more than weekly, said that religion provides a great deal of guidance in their lives, and scored high on the "orthodoxy" measure were given a value of 3 on this index; at the opposite end of the index, individuals who failed to reach the highest category in religiosity, salience, or orthodoxy were given a 0. Scores of 1 were for respondents who scored high on one of the three variables, while scores of 2 were respondents who scored high on two of the three variables. For ease of presentation, the index was dichotomized into low (scores of 0 and 1) and high (scores of 2 and 3) values. As expected, a higher percentage of evangelical than mainline Protestants fall into the "high" religious commitment category. While 36% of the evangelicals fell into the high commitment category, only 14% of the mainline Protestants did so. Moreover, all evangelical denominational families scored higher than any mainline subgroups. Evangelical groups ranged from 53% in the high category for the Pentecostal/Holiness family to a low of 31% for Southern Baptists. Among mainline Protestants, Lutherans led Methodists and Presbyterians with the highest percentage of respondents falling within the high commitment category--18%.

9. The results of the Multiple Classification Analysis are straightforward. Mean scores for the religious groups on the partisan measure are presented for each level of religious commitment, controlling for age, sex, education, and region. This analysis accomplishes two things: (1) it measures the differential impact of religious tradition or denominational affiliation as opposed to religious commitment, and (2) it controls for the effects of demography which were shown earlier to differentiate evangelical and mainline Protestants.

10. The statistical package which performed these analyses, SPSSx, does not provide a measure of statistical significance for the beta coefficients. Performing a difference of means test suggests that the .05 level of significance would be reached when the beta coefficient is .09 or higher.

11. We substituted church attendance for religious commitment in this table. A behavioral measure seemed better for an analysis with a behavioral dependent variable, namely, voter turnout, than did the broader religious commitment measure.

12. If the Southern Baptists are removed from the evangelical group, the low

158

commitment category gave Bush 62% of their vote, while the high commitment segment gave him 80% of their vote. The latter is a remarkably high percentage for any significant subgroup in the population. However, this percentage of votes still falls below the 92% reported to have been cast for Dukakis by those blacks interviewed in the National Election Study.

References

Castle, David. 1987. "A Southern Regional Presidential Primary in 1988: Will It Work as Planned?" *Election Politics*, 4:6-10.

Galston, William. 1988. "Did Super Tuesday Work?" *Election Politics*, 5:2-5.

Guth, James. 1985. "The Christian Right Revisited: Partisan Realignment among Southern Baptist Ministers." Paper presented at the annual meeting of the Midwest Political Science Association, Chicago.

Hertzke, Alan. 1988. "Jackson, Robertson, and the Politics of Community: Religious Mobilization and the 1988 Presidential Campaign." Presented at the meeting of the International Political Science Association, Washington, DC.

Jelen, Ted, Lyman Kellstedt, and Clyde Wilcox. 1990. "Racism and Religion: Some New Evidence for an Old Question." Presented at the annual meeting for the Association for the Sociology of Religion, Washington, DC.

Kellstedt, Lyman. 1989. "Evangelicals and Political Realignment," in Corwin Smidt, ed., *Contemporary Evangelical Political Involvement*. Pp. 99-117. Lanham, MD: University of Press of America.

Kellstedt, Lyman, and John C. Green. 1990. "Waiting for Realignment: Partisan Change among Evangelical Protestants 1956-1988." Presented at the Citadel Symposium on Southern Politics, Charleston.

Kellstedt, Lyman, and Mark Noll. 1990. "Religion, Voting for President, and Party Identification, 1948-1984," in Mark A. Noll, ed., *Religion and American Politics*. Pp. 355-379. New York: Oxford University Press.

Leege, David, Lyman Kellstedt, and Kenneth Wald. 1990. "Religion and Politics: A Report on Measures of the Religiosity in the 1989 NES Pilot Study." Presented at the annual meeting of the Midwest Political Science Association, Chicago.

Swierenga, Robert P. 1990. "Ethnoreligious Political behavior in the Mid-Nineteenth Century: Voting, Values, Culture," in Mark A. Noll, ed., *Religion and American Politics*. Pp. 355-379. New York: Oxford University Press.

Wald, Kenneth D., Dennis E. Owen, and Samuel S. Hill, Jr. 1988. "Churches as Political Communities." *American Political Science Review*, 82:531-548.

_____. 1990. "Political Cohesion in Churches." *Journal of Politics*, 52:197-215.

9

Religion and Electoral Politics Among Black Americans in 1988

Clyde Wilcox

During the 1988 presidential primaries, exit polls showed that more than 90% of black voters cast ballots for the Reverend Jesse Jackson. After the 1988 general election, exit polls revealed that nearly 90% of black voters supported Democratic candidate Michael Dukakis. No other demographic group rivaled blacks in the consensus of their voting. Clearly race was a very strong factor in 1988, apparently leaving little room for religion to influence vote choice in the black community. Yet religion played a role in increasing participation among blacks and in molding affect toward candidates as well.

There has been considerable debate among sociologists and political scientists about the role of religion in black politics. Some have argued that the otherworldly focus of religion in the black community serves to blunt pressures for political and social change (Marx 1969; Frazier 1974; Nelsen and Nelsen 1975). Others have reported that black churches enhance feelings of black identification and racial consciousness, and thus stimulate political participation (Olson 1970; Wilcox and Gomez 1990; Wilcox 1990a).[1] This study will show that religion stimulates political participation among black Americans.

The Black Church and Politics

To understand the role of religion in black politics, it is first necessary to review the recent history of the black church as a political institution. Especially in the South, the leadership cadre of the early civil rights movement came from politicized pastors who headed organizations like the Southern Christian Leadership Conference. Morris (1984) reports that black pastors trained and recruited movement volunteers, allowed churches to be used for meetings, and played a vital role in communications networks.

In the 1970s competing leadership groups emerged in the black community (especially in the North), but Wald (1987) reports that black pastors remained important. Many prominent black leaders, including Jesse Jackson, Andrew Young, and Congressman William Gray were ordained ministers, and the leadership of the NAACP, PUSH, and other civil rights groups included many pastors. Even those pastors who did not seek public office or an active leadership role in civil rights organizations played important political roles by urging political involvement and sometimes endorsing candidates.

Why have clergy played such an important role in black politics? Many black churches are institutions with important political resources. For example, the Shiloh Baptist Church in Washington, D.C. has a large community outreach program with 90 social services and over 5,000 parishioners. In Brooklyn, the East Brooklyn Churches can turn out thousands for a rally and register 10,000 new voters in a year (Wald 1987). Black churches frequently urge political involvement to redress racial discrimination. This "prophetic" motif in black Protestantism has a long tradition of promoting justice, equality, and compassion (Wald 1991), and pastors frequently encourage their flock to achieve these qualities through political action. Voter registration booths are often set up outside churches and their outreach organizations, and pastors may devote sermons to the importance of voting. Collection plates may be passed on behalf of black candidates, who are often allowed to address the congregation (see Chapter 2).

This clerical activity clearly affects black electoral behavior. Walton (1985) reported that blacks in the 1970s cited their church or minister as a major influence on their thinking more often than any other source. In the 1990 Washington mayoral race, radio interviews with congregants in many black churches indicated that some (though certainly not all) church members were influenced by their pastor's endorsement. But political activity by religious elites is not the only important characteristic of religion among blacks. Blacks exhibit higher rates of public, and especially, private religiosity than do whites, and are more orthodox in belief. This religious involvement and orthodoxy has important political implications in its own right.

There have been, however, fewer academic studies of religion and politics among blacks than among whites because most national surveys include fewer than 200 black respondents, reflecting the fact that blacks constitute only 13% of the American public, rather than bias on the part of survey researchers. Unfortunately, this situation makes analysis of the connection between religion and politics in the black community tenuous. In this chapter, I will use data from the CBS-*New York Times* and the ABC News exit polls for presidential primaries and caucuses in 1988, a special American National Election Study survey of Super Tuesday states in March 1988, the regular American National Election Study general election survey in October and November 1988, and my own survey of blacks in Washington, D.C. in March 1988. In addition, I will discuss some results from the National Black Election Study, conducted as a supplement to the regular American National Election Study in 1984.

Religion in the Black Community

Blacks are more likely than whites to attend evangelical Protestant churches, to attend church regularly, and to be active in their church (Table 9.1). Approximately one-half of blacks attend a racially integrated church, although most of these integrated churches have a majority of black members. Blacks are much more likely to say that religion is highly salient to their lives and to hold more orthodox beliefs. They are much more likely than whites to believe that the Bible is the inerrant word of God, to report having a born-again experience, to be very certain of the existence of God, and to have no doubts about their faith.

The private religious behavior of blacks is also different from that of whites. Blacks are much more likely to watch religious television shows, to pray, to say grace before meals, and to try to "save souls." Blacks are also more likely to say that religion influences their lives and that the Bible or their church is important to their decisions, although they are less likely to actually read their Bibles when compared to whites.

As noted above, sermons with political messages are more common in black churches. These political sermons usually urge blacks to participate in politics and may also involve the endorsement of candidates. In a survey of blacks in Washington, D.C. in March 1988, 60% reported that their pastor encouraged them to vote and become involved in politics. Fully one in five said that their pastor endorsed candidates in church, and 40% indicated that their pastor had at least some influence on their politics. In the National Black Election Study

162

TABLE 9.1 Racial Differences in Religious Beliefs and Behavior

	Whites	Blacks
Religious Affiliation		
Evangelical Denomination	28%	69%**
Catholic	23	10**
Member of Church	62	62
Active in Church	45	54*
Attend church at least twice monthly	44	54*
Integrated Church	39	48*
Religious Beliefs		
Religion Highly Salient[a]	33	57**
Born Again	34	57**
Bible Inerrant	36	59**
Sure God Exists	62	75*
No Doubt about Faith	26	37*
Religious Behaviors		
Watch Religious TV[a]	27	65**
Pray More than Daily	24	36*
Say Grace	48	74**
Read Bible	38	25*
Try to Save Souls	44	66*
Helps Decide Issues:		
the Bible	31	59**
the Church	28	36*

[a] Items from American National Election Study; all other items from General Social Survey.
* Differences between blacks and whites significant at .05; ** differences between blacks and whites significant at .01.

Sources: The 1988 American National Election Study and the General Social Survey, 1972-1988.

of 1984, respondents reported similarly high rates of pastoral involvement. More than one-third reported that their pastor had discussed the presidential campaign in church, and two-thirds said that their pastor had encouraged them to vote. Nearly one-quarter had attended a candidate rally or meeting on church property, one in ten had performed work in support of a candidate on church grounds, and one in five had attended a church service in which funds were collected on behalf of a candidate.

What are the implications of these religious characteristics for black political attitudes? Among whites, high levels of religiosity and doctrinal orthodoxy are associated with conservative positions on social, economic, and foreign policy issues. Among blacks, these religious traits do not influence economic or foreign policy issue positions, and religion exerts an uneven influence on social issue attitudes (Cook and Wilcox 1990). Blacks are less supportive of legal abortion, and this difference is entirely due to their higher levels of religious orthodoxy and involvement (Wilcox 1992). Unlike whites, however, blacks with high levels of religious involvement are not less supportive of gender equality, or even of equal protection for homosexuals.[2]

Race and Political Attitudes

Although partisanship has lost some of its power to predict vote choice in the past two decades, it is still an important factor. Blacks have supported the Democratic Party since the New Deal, but when the Democrats backed civil rights legislation in 1964 and 1965, and the Republican presidential nominee Barry Goldwater favored a states' rights position, black loyalty to the Democratic Party reached an astonishing level. In the 1964 election, many surveys could not locate a single black voter who supported Goldwater! This Democratic partisanship remained in force in 1988. Fully 40% of blacks called themselves strong Democrats in 1988 (compared to 14% of whites). Overall, 83% of blacks either identified as Democrats or leaned to the Democratic Party, with only 12% supporting or leaning toward the Republicans. The comparable figures for whites were 42% and 47%.

Partisanship is not the only political attitude on which blacks differ from whites; blacks are also much more likely to call themselves liberals. This liberal identity is mirrored in specific attitudes. Blacks are more supportive of spending on social welfare programs, education, and child care, and less supportive of defense spending. Not surprisingly, there are huge racial differences in attitudes toward programs designed to aid blacks. Not all blacks support such programs, and not all whites oppose them, but these programs are a central political issue in the black community.

Finally, on social issues, blacks are more conservative than whites on abortion and school prayer, but more liberal on gender equality and homosexual rights. Although most whites see these four issues as closely linked, blacks perceive them as two distinct sets of issues. Abortion and school prayer for blacks are linked to religious beliefs, while the issues of gender equality and homosexual rights involve political equality. Black experiences with racial discrimination have led them to oppose gender discrimination as well, and their support of legal guarantees of racial equality generalizes to support for similar legal protection of homosexuals. It should be noted that support for legal rights for homosexuals does not translate into an endorsement of homosexual behavior. Blacks actually display less affect towards homosexuals in this survey than whites, but they still endorsed legal protection of homosexuals.

These political attitudes generally reinforce Democratic partisanship. The national Democratic Party is closer to the modal black position on defense spending, spending for social programs, discrimination on gender and sexual preference and, most importantly, civil rights and affirmative action. The Republicans have the advantage on abortion and school prayer, but these issues are far less important to most black voters. Moreover, although blacks are less supportive of legal abortion than whites, they do not generally take a consistent pro-life position like that advocated by Republican presidential candidates in the 1980s.

Religion and the 1988 Primary Elections

In 1984 and 1988 Reverend Jesse Jackson mounted large, relatively well-financed campaigns for the Democratic presidential nomination. These campaigns attracted a good deal of support from black religious elites. Jackson appeared in large, urban black churches on Sundays and was given the pulpit to preach and exhort the crowd. Pastors endorsed him openly and urged their followers to vote. They also passed the collection plate to raise funds for his campaign (Wilcox 1991). Not surprisingly, the vast majority of blacks voted for Jesse Jackson during the 1988 primaries. Jackson's campaign engendered a racial pride among many black voters, and his campaign sounded many themes important to the black community -- an end to discrimination, programs to help blacks enter the American mainstream, and cuts in defense spending coupled with increased spending on education and social programs.

Religion seems to have played no role in black vote choice, nor, in fact, did many other variables. Jackson won nearly identical percentages of the vote from those who attended church regularly and those who never attended, those with orthodox and less orthodox religious views, the wealthy and the poor, the well-educated and the less so. There was also no correlation between vote for Jackson and attitudes on racial issues, spending on social programs, or any other issue. Those blacks with the strongest sense of black identification were somewhat more likely to vote for Jackson, but little else predicted a Jackson vote.[3]

Yet religion did have a role. Although most blacks who voted cast ballots for Jackson, not all were equally enthusiastic. To measure enthusiasm for Jackson in 1988, I have used responses to an item that asked all respondents to rate him on an imaginary feeling thermometer that ranges from 0° (very cool) to 100° (very warm). I have adjusted this scale, so that possible scores range from -100 to 100.[4] Table 9.2 shows the relationship between this scale and several religious variables.

Those who held orthodox views of the Bible were cooler toward Jackson than those who held less orthodox views. Conversely, those who were born-again were slightly, but not significantly, warmer towards him. Jackson got his greatest support among secular blacks who never attend church or among regular church-goers, but he did much less well among those who attended more than weekly. One reason may be that abortion attitudes are strongly related to feelings

TABLE 9.2 Religion, Affect for Jackson, and Turnout among Blacks

	Affect for Jackson[a]	Turnout Primaries	Turnout General
Bible			
Inerrant	13.8	45%	65%
Inspired	19.1	34	56
Other	30.8	22	22
Born-Again			
Yes	19.0	48	65
No	13.2	28	54
Attendance			
More than Weekly	12.7	68	80
Regularly	21.8	45	65
Seldom/Occasionally	15.0	31	55
Never	19.2	19	31

[a] Mean affect for Jackson; scale ranges from -100 to 100 with higher scores indicating greater support for Jackson.

Source: The 1988 American National Election Study.

toward Jackson, with pro-life blacks markedly cooler than those who are pro-choice. These results are confirmed when we control for other variables: holding constant age, region, sex, education, income, partisanship, and attitudes toward other political issues in a multivariate regression analysis, religion and abortion attitudes were significant predictors of warmth toward Jackson.

On first glance, however, the patterns here are confusing. Why are born-again blacks warmer, while those who believe that the Bible is inerrant are cooler? Why does Jackson do best among those who never attend or regularly attend, but worst among those that attend church more than weekly? It is impossible to answer these questions definitively, for there have been no large, national surveys of blacks that include a range of religious variables. Nonetheless, the findings of other studies help sort out the results.

My research on the religious and political attitudes of blacks in Washington, D.C. suggests that although an inerrant view of the Bible often goes hand-in-hand with a born-again experience among whites, this is less true among blacks. Blacks in charismatic churches are more likely than other blacks to report a born-again experience but less likely to believe that the Bible is inerrant. Such charismatic churches frequently preach a message of equality and liberation, and in Washington, D.C., charismatic churches served as an important base for the Jackson campaign (Wilcox 1990a). Other conservative black churches, however, preach Biblical inerrancy and interpret the Scriptures in ways that advocate conservative positions on social issues. In these churches, Jackson's endorsement of legal abortion and his welcoming gays and lesbians into the Rainbow Coalition may have decreased black warmth toward his candidacy.

The curious relationship between church attendance and support for Jackson may also be explained in part by different types of black churches. Not all churches offer their members the opportunity to attend services more than once a week; churches that preach an inerrant Bible and conservative positions on social issues are the most likely to offer church services throughout the week. Thus, the decline in support for Jackson among those who attend very frequently is closely linked to religious doctrine and disappears when doctrine is controlled.

Those secular blacks who support Jackson presumably do so based on racial identity and policy preferences, not religion. Among those who do attend church, however, more frequent exposure to church sermons that may endorse Jackson seems to lead to greater support. Elsewhere I have reported that those blacks in Washington D.C. who frequently attended churches in which the pastor took political positions and endorsed candidates were significantly warmer toward Jackson than other blacks (Wilcox 1990a).

It should be noted that blacks who believed the Bible to be inerrant and who were pro-life voted for Jackson in roughly the same proportion as those who were less orthodox and were pro-choice. The decreased enthusiasm for Jackson that their religion engendered did not result in their voting for other candidates. This does not mean, however, that religion was irrelevant to actual political behavior in the primaries.

Voter turnout was highest among those who attended church regularly, and thus, frequent church attenders helped increase Jackson's vote total. In the Super Tuesday primaries, frequent attendance was a significant predictor of turning out for Jackson (Wilcox 1990b). Across all primary elections, both frequency of attendance and doctrinal orthodoxy are significant predictors of higher turnout. Of course, some of the correlation between church attendance and turnout is spurious -- active personalities may lead to involvement in religion and in politics. Yet elsewhere I have found that even when rates of other types of activity are held constant, frequent church attendance is associated with higher rates of voting (Wilcox and Gomez 1990). Moreover, that study demonstrated that church attendance indirectly stimulated other types of political involvement by contributing to a sense of pride and racial identity.

In my survey of blacks in Washington, turnout (and other political activities) were associated with frequency of church attendance, participation in a charismatic church, and orthodox views of the Bible. Moreover, those blacks who attended churches in which the pastor encouraged political involvement had especially high rates of participation. Although very frequent attendance and orthodox views of the Bible led to cooler feelings toward Jackson, they still led to slightly higher rates of turnout and therefore contributed to his vote totals.

It appears, then, that religion influenced black attitudes toward Jackson as well has his actual vote total. Secular blacks and those who attended church regularly, particularly charismatic churches, were warm toward Jackson. Those who attended churches where pastors preached politics and endorsed candidates were more likely to support Jackson and more likely to actually vote. But those with orthodox religious views and conservative positions on social issues, especially those who attended conservative churches more than once a week, voted for Jackson with significantly less enthusiasm. Their high turnout, however, meant that orthodox religion increased Jackson's vote totals.

Religion and Black Support for Robertson

One other presidential candidate claimed some religious support among blacks, although he garnered few black votes in the primaries. Reverend Pat Robertson's charismatic religion and conservative position on abortion had some appeal to blacks. Robertson's *700 Club* co-host Ben Kinchlow was black, and he explicitly targeted black voters in Louisiana and other southern states. Robertson's supporters generally supported black candidates in Republican intra-party battles, and they were responsible for the nomination of a black candidate for the U.S. Senate in the Virginia Republican Party in 1988. Although Robertson's campaign was ultimately unsuccessful in wooing strongly Democratic black voters from their chance to vote for Jesse Jackson, Robertson was actually fairly popular among blacks. In a nonpartisan primary without Jackson, Robertson might have attracted some limited black support.

During the Super Tuesday primaries, fully one in four blacks rated Robertson as their favorite Republican candidate (the figure for whites was 10%). Nearly one-third rated him relatively warmly on a feeling thermometer relative to other white candidates. Support for Robertson was closely related to religion. Those blacks who believed the Bible to be inerrant and/or who were born-again were warmer toward Robertson, as were those who took conservative positions on social issues such as abortion (Wilcox 1990b).

In a survey of blacks in Washington, D.C. just prior to the Super Tuesday primaries, I found that fully one-third had watched Robertson's *700 Club*, and 13% claimed to watch it regularly (Wilcox 1990c). More than a third of blacks preferred Robertson to George Bush in March, and nearly one in six preferred him to Michael Dukakis.[5] Robertson's support was tied exclusively to religion, with those who frequently watched religious television and those who had high levels of private religiosity most supportive.

This level of support for Robertson is surprising. Robertson was a Republican candidate who opposed affirmative action, favored cuts in many social programs, and increased spending on defense. Still, the Washington survey revealed that few blacks knew much about Robertson's positions on these issues -- and just over one-half knew that he was a Republican. Such low levels of information about candidates during the primary season is common -- few southern whites knew much about Robertson at the time of the Super Tuesday primaries either. But more than one-half of Robertson's support among Washington, D.C. blacks came from liberals who supported him on religious grounds but who took very different political positions. Much of this support, however, would have evaporated as potential voters became aware of Robertson's actual political positions during the campaign. This suggests that Robertson's support doubtlessly overstated the number of votes he might have received had Jackson not run for president. Nonetheless, religious involvement and orthodoxy translated into greater warmth for Robertson among blacks than among whites.

Religion and the General Election

On election day some 90% of blacks cast their ballots for Michael Dukakis. Vote choice was not directly related to any religious variables. A probit analysis revealed that only partisanship and family income predicted vote choice among blacks in 1988. As in the primaries, however, some blacks cast less enthusiastic votes for Dukakis than others. Most black voters preferred Dukakis by a solid margin and rated him on average more than 25° warmer on the 100° feeling thermometer than they rated Bush.

The reasons for this preference were not primarily religious. In a multivariate regression analysis that held constant demographic variables, political attitudes, and religious characteristics, the strongest predictors of the degree of preference for Dukakis were partisanship, feelings toward Reagan, affect for blacks, attitudes toward racial policies, and spending for the poor. Only one religious variable was related to attitudes toward the candidates. Those blacks who reported a born-again experience favored Dukakis by a slightly bigger margin than those who did not report such an experience. However, turnout was again related to frequency of church attendance. In addition, those with orthodox doctrinal views and high personal religiosity were more likely to vote in the general election. Religion was as important as strength of partisanship and education in predicting turnout among blacks. Thus, as with Jackson, religion swelled Dukakis's vote totals by increasing turnout.

Conclusions

Black Americans voted in overwhelming numbers for Jesse Jackson in Democratic primaries. Clearly, race was a powerful predictor of primary vote choice, and against this remarkable homogeneity of preference, religion had little room to influence candidate choice. Most blacks supported Jackson regardless of their policy positions or religious beliefs. This widespread support may have been due to racial identity and pride, although Jackson's campaign articulated issues of great importance to the black community.

Nonetheless, religion influenced black attitudes and behaviors in the primaries in two ways. First, religion influenced the degree of enthusiasm for Jackson. Those who frequently attended charismatic churches where the pastor endorsed candidates were warmer to Jackson. Orthodox views of the Bible and very frequent church attendance (along with conservative positions on abortion), however, decreased enthusiasm for Jackson. Second, frequent attendance and religious orthodoxy increased levels of turnout in the primaries. Although those blacks who believed in the inerrancy of Scriptures and who attended church more than weekly were cooler toward Jackson, they turned out in higher numbers and therefore contributed to his support. Had Jackson run against another black candidate with more conservative positions on religious and social issues, this greater reserve might have translated into a loss of votes. Against a field of white candidates, none known for their civil rights activism, religious orthodoxy increased his vote totals.

Religion helped Jackson in one other important respect. By most accounts money collected in black churches was vital to his campaign. Campaign appearances in black churches across the country were valuable opportunities to mobilize volunteers, and they helped reach potential supporters. When black churches made available their basements for his campaign workers, the campaign saved needed resources (see Chapter 1).

In the general election, the Democratic partisanship of blacks led them to vote in overwhelming numbers for Dukakis. Blacks favored Dukakis because they associated Bush with the dismal civil rights record of the Reagan administration and because they believed that Dukakis would support spending on social programs. Although religion played only a minor role in generating warmth for Dukakis, it contributed to his vote totals by encouraging turnout in the general election.

Thus, the principal impact of religion on black political behavior in 1988 was to stimulate voting. Since preferences for Jackson and Dukakis were widespread, higher turnout benefitted both candidates. Black churches in 1988 frequently preached the duty of voting and set up voter registration booths on church property. Such efforts had an impact on turnout and, therefore, on the vote totals of Jackson and Dukakis.

Notes

1. For a review of this debate see Taylor, Thornton, and Chatters (1988).
2. Elsewhere I have argued that because black churches preach racial equality and the importance of government action to guarantee that equality, religion is associated with support for a more general societal equality and for government action to protect minorities in general (Wilcox 1990d).
3. Jackson also won an overwhelming majority of black votes in the 1984 Democratic primaries, but his percentage was higher in 1988. In part this may be due to the nature of his competition. In 1984 Jackson opposed Walter Mondale, an established leader with a strong record on civil rights. In 1988, Jackson faced a field of relative unknowns, none of whom had reputations as civil rights leaders (Reed 1986).
4. The adjustment was made by subtracting the individual's average score for a range of social groups from the feeling thermometer for Jackson. This was done to adjust for individual differences in responses to feeling thermometer items. Previous research (Wilcox, Sigelman and Cook 1989) has revealed that some individuals assign all groups and individuals high scores, while others use a lower range.
5. It should be noted that in March Dukakis was seen as Jackson's principal rival for the nomination. By the time of the November election, most blacks rated Dukakis more warmly than Robertson.

References

Cook, Elizabeth Adell, and Clyde Wilcox. 1990. "Religious Orientations and Political Attitudes among Blacks in the District of Columbia." *Polity*, 22:527-544.
Frazier, E. 1974. *The Negro Church in America*. New York: Schoken.
Marx, Gary. 1969. "Religion: Opiate or Inspiration of Civil Rights Militancy among Negroes?" *American Sociological Review*, 32:64-72.
Morris, Aldon. D. 1984. *The Origins of the Civil Rights Movement*. New York: The Free Press.
Nelsen, H., and A. Nelsen. 1975. *The Black Church in the Sixties*. Lexington, KY: University of Kentucky Press.
Olson, M. 1970. "Social and Political Participation of Blacks." *American Sociological Review*, 35:682-697.
Reed, Adolph, Jr. 1986. *The Jesse Jackson Phenomenon*. New Haven: Yale University Press.
Taylor, R., M. Thornton, and L. Chatters. 1988. "Black American's Perceptions of the Sociohistorical Role of the Church." *Journal of Black Studies*, 18:123-138.

172

Wald, Kenneth. 1987. *Religion and Politics in the United States*. New York: St. Martins.

_____. 1991. "Ministering to the Nation: The Campaigns of Jesse Jackson and Pat Robertson," in Emmett Buell and Lee Sigelman, eds., *Nominating a President in 1988*. Pp. 119-149. Knoxville, TN: University of Tennessee Press.

Walton, H. 1985. *Invisible Politics: Black Political Behavior*. New York: St. Martins.

Wilcox, Clyde. 1990a. "Religious Sources of Politicization among Blacks in Washington, D.C." *Journal for the Scientific Study of Religion*, 29:387-395.

_____. 1990b. "Religion and the Preacher Vote in the South: Sources of Support for Jackson and Robertson in Southern Primaries." Presented at The Citadel Symposium on Southern Politics, Charleston, SC.

_____. 1990c. "Blacks and the New Christian Right: Support for the Moral Majority and Pat Robertson among Washington, DC Blacks." *Review of Religious Research*, 32:43-56.

_____. 1990d. "Race, Gender Role Attitudes and Support for Feminism." *The Western Political Quarterly*, 43:113-123.

_____. 1991. "Financing the 1988 Prenomination Campaigns," in Emmett Buell and Lee Sigelman, eds., *Nominating a President in 1988*. Pp. 91-118. Knoxville, TN: University of Tennessee Press.

_____. 1992. "Race, Region, Religion, and Abortion Attitudes." *Sociological Analysis*. (Forthcoming).

Wilcox, Clyde, and Leopoldo Gomez. 1990. "Religion, Group Identification and Politics among American Blacks." *Sociological Analysis*, 51:271-287.

Wilcox, Clyde, Lee Sigelman, and Elizabeth Adell Cook. 1989. "Some Like it Hot: Individual Differences in Responses to Group Feeling Thermometers." *Public Opinion Quarterly*, 53:246-257.

10

Catholic Voting Behavior in 1988: A Critical Swing Vote

Henry C. Kenski
William Lockwood

The Roman Catholic Church is the largest religious denomination in the United States, with an estimated membership equal to one-fourth of the total population (Wald 1987). Historically, Catholics have been at the very heart of the Democratic electoral coalition both in size and dependability. Indeed, since the New Deal "loyalty to the Democratic Party has been something on the order of a theological commitment for a large share of America's Catholic community" (Dionne 1981:308). Until 1970, for example, Catholics provided more than one-third of the Democratic presidential vote despite constituting only one-quarter of the population (Axelrod 1986). But Catholic voting behavior, once so reliably Democratic, has undergone significant change, so that by 1988 Catholics were an important swing vote with Democratic leanings. In order to assess this change, we will first discuss the socio-demographic and political context of American Catholics, then consider partisanship and vote choice in 1988, followed by information on candidate image, issues, and religiosity.

American Roman Catholics: A Profile

Understanding the shift of Catholics from staunch Democratic loyalists to Democratic swing voters necessarily begins with an awareness of their upward economic and educational surge since 1960 (Greeley 1990; Gallup and Castelli 1987). Historically, Catholics have been an immigrant people, with many falling into the lowest educational and income categories. Although Catholics today still rank behind certain Protestant denominations like Episcopalians and Presbyterians in socioeconomic status, they are on a par with Lutherans and Methodists, and ahead of Baptists. However, these aggregate figures mask important differences among Catholics.

Previous research has shown that it is useful to separate Catholics by race (Kenski and Lockwood 1988). Nationally, 88% of the population identify as white, 8% black, and 4% as other races, including Hispanics and Asians. Catholics, by contrast, are 89% white, only 3% black, but with 8% in the other category, twice the proportion of the population at large.[1] For our purposes, we will divide Catholics into two categories, whites and non-whites. This division reveals important demographic and political differences that are lost when Catholics are aggregated.

Both the upward mobility of white Catholics and socioeconomic lag of non-whites are revealed in the patterns of education and income. White Catholics are a mirror image of the national educational profile: 37% are college graduates or have post-graduate training, 29% have some college, and 34% have completed high school or less. On the other hand, non-white Catholics are markedly less well-educated, with only 30% college graduates or better, 29% with some college, and 40% with high school or less. Much the same pattern appears for annual family income. White Catholics are actually slightly more affluent than the population as a whole, with 37% having incomes of $40,000 or more, 39% $20,000 to $39,999, and only 24% less than $20,000, compared to figures for all Americans of 35%, 37%, and 29%, respectively. Not surprisingly, non-white Catholics are much less affluent, with only 24% over $40,000, 37% in the middle range, and 40% under $20,000. These figures reflect in part the age distribution of the population. White Catholics very closely resemble the age profile of the country, with 31% fifty years or older, 47% thirty to forty-nine years old, and 22% under thirty. Non-white Catholics are much younger, with 18% over fifty years old, 48% middle-aged, and 34% under thirty.

In sum, white Catholics are remarkably similar to all other Americans; in contrast non-white Catholics are less well educated, less affluent and younger, holding much the same relationship to the general population as other non-whites, and as white Catholics held a generation ago. The socioeconomic gains of white Catholics help explain the decline of their support for the Democratic Party, and the lower status of non-white Catholics helps account for their stronger support for the Democrats.

Poll data since 1932 underscore the changes in Catholic political behavior since the New Deal (Gallup and Castelli 1987). An estimated 80% of Catholics voted for Roosevelt in 1932 and 1936 and about 73% in 1940 and 1944, dropping off slightly to about 66% for Truman in the four-person 1948 race. Even in Eisenhower's landslide victories of 1952 and 1956, the Democrats won a majority of the Catholic vote, 56% and 51% respectively. The high points in Democratic voting were in 1960 and 1964, when John F. Kennedy, the first Roman Catholic elected to the White House, and his successor, Lyndon Johnson, won stunning proportions of the Catholic vote, 78% and 73% respectively. In a difficult three-way race in 1968, Hubert Humphrey claimed 59% of the Catholic vote.

The Catholic vote began to swing away from the Democrats in 1972, the first presidential election since 1932 in which a majority of Catholics did not vote Democratic; only 48% cast ballots for McGovern. Although Carter won back 57% of the Catholics in 1976, Reagan took a plurality of Catholics in the three-way 1980 race with 47% and then picked up 61% in the 1984 landslide. In 1988, Gallup's final poll suggests parity, with the Catholic vote splitting: 51% Democratic and 49% Republican (Gallup Opinion Index 1988). Network polls tended to agree, with one exception, the CBS/*New York Times* poll giving Bush 53% of the Catholic vote. We will explore these results below, with an additional concern for the behavior of non-white Catholics.

Vote Choice and Partisanship in 1988

Much like opinion polls, the literature on Catholic voting behavior is characterized by conflicting interpretations. On the one hand, Greeley argues strenuously that Catholics are still solidly Democratic, and he minimizes events such as the 1984 presidential elections with the assertion that "one election does not a trend make" (1985:36). He concedes that Catholic presidential voting for the Democratic ticket is not as impressive as it is for congressional races, but he stresses that Catholics are nevertheless more Democratic than both the nation overall and white Protestants. Hoffman (1986) also stresses the more Democratic orientation of Catholics at the presidential level, but he focuses more on Republican successes in capturing Catholic Independents.

On the other hand, Petrocik argues that Catholics were unusually supportive of Reagan but that "their Republican vote was not unprecedented" (1987:367). In this view, Republicans have achieved parity with the Democrats among Catholics. Between these extremes is the continuing research by Axelrod (1986) and by Erickson, Lancaster, and Romero (1989), who find Catholics becoming less Democratic over time but still more Democratic than the nation overall. Other writers who are less quantitatively oriented (Reichley 1985; Dionne 1981) have advanced similar views.

Very little has been written on the Catholic vote in Senate and House races or on split-ticket voting. Greeley claims (1990) that about three-fifths of the Catholics routinely vote for Democratic House and Senatorial candidates. Kenski (1988) and Kenski and Lockwood (1989) find the Catholic congressional vote to be slightly less Democratic, and at the other extreme is Petrocik (1987:370), who argues that the Catholic House vote is evenly divided, with the Republicans receiving 53% in 1986. Although our primary focus is on the presidential vote, we also examine 1988 sub-presidential voting.

Table 10.1 uses the ABC News General Election Exit Poll to summarize the 1988 voting patterns among Catholics. With respect to the overall pattern, it is clear that Catholics are more Democratic than all American voters, with some 51% of Catholics voting Democratic for president, 58% for the Senate, and 57% for the House. Disaggregating the data reveals that only 48% of white Catholics voted Democratic in the presidential race, and also voted less for Democratic Senate and House candidates (mid-fifties range). Still, white Catholics were far more supportive of the Democrats than white Protestants (see Chapter 8). On the other hand, non-white Catholic voters were much more Democratic, with some three-quarters voting Democratic for the president, Senate and House. The importance of racial identification is underscored by these numbers, although non-white Catholics did not vote as Democratic as non-white Protestants (see Chapter 9).

A split ticket-measure was created by tabulating respondents' vote for the presidency and the Senate, with two consistent party votes yielding either a Straight Democrat or a Straight Republican label, and a vote for each party resulting in a split ticket designation. About one-fifth of all Catholics split their tickets, closely resembling the voters overall. On the other hand, more Catholics voted a straight Democratic ticket (44%) than a straight Republican ticket (35%), modestly at variance from the general population. Once again, white Catholics are less Democratic (41% straight ticket) than non-white Catholics who are pronounced straight ticket Democrats (66%).

TABLE 10.1. Catholics and the Democratic Vote

Group	Pres.	Senate	House	Straight Democrat	Split	Straight Republican	(N)[a]
All Voters	46%	53%	52%	40%	20%	40%	(20,701)
All Catholics	51	58	57	44	21	35	(5,711)
White Catholics	48	56	55	41	22	37	(5,250)
Non-white Catholics	74	76	77	66	16	18	(661)
Democrats							
All Voters	82	83	89	75	17	8	(8,870)
White Catholics	79	80	86	70	20	10	(2,446)
Non-white Catholics	90	91	95	84	14	3	(468)
Republicans							
All Voters	8	20	13	4	19	77	(7,411)
White Catholics	9	22	12	5	21	74	(1,652)
Non-white Catholics	11	23	17	6	22	72	(108)
Independents							
All Voters	43	53	50	36	27	37	(3,809)
White Catholics	44	56	54	37	27	36	(1,037)
Non-white Catholics	74	69	56	62	16	22	(66)

[a] Percentages are based on sample data weighted to national population size. N's in parenthesis are the original unweighted data.

Source: ABC News 1988 General Election Exit Poll.

Party identification is still an important factor in voting decisions among Catholics, although perhaps less so than in the past. For example, more than 80% of self-identified Democrats favored the Democratic candidate for president, Senate, and House, and three-quarters of these supported a straight Democratic ticket. Republican identifiers were the mirror image and offered little support for Democratic candidates, registering a 77% straight Republican vote. Hoffman (1986) was correct in his emphasis on the critical role of self-identified Catholic Independents, as only 44% supported Dukakis. White Catholics deviated only a little from this pattern, while non-whites showed more variation. Non-white Democrats voted more Democratic and non-white Republicans only modestly so, but non-white Independents voted dramatically more Democratic than other Independents. Taken together, these patterns suggest that race is far more important than religion for non-white Catholics.

Do these voting patterns reflect changes in party identification among Catholics? The answer is yes (Kenski and Lockwood, 1989). Using data from 1952 to 1986 from the American National Election Studies, we find that Catholic voters have paralleled the national trend of decreased Democratic identification, increased Independent identification, and some increase in Republican identification as well. Still, a plurality of Catholic voters remain Democratic and are still more likely to be Democratic than their Protestant counterparts. The ABC News General Election exit poll data confirm this pattern in 1988. As a group, Catholics continue to have a Democratic plurality, with a solid advantage over Republicans of 48% to 32%, compared to a 42% to 38% margin among all voters. Catholic Independents are about equal to the population as a whole (19% to 18%, respectively). White Catholics show a smaller Democratic margin (45% to 33%), while non-white Catholics are still solidly Democratic (70% to 18%).

Candidate Image

Party identification is not the only factor that influences voting behavior. Many scholars have pointed to candidate image and issues as factors that can reinforce or undermine partisanship. Lopatto (1985) was among the earliest scholars to suggest that, beginning in the early seventies, Catholic voters were becoming less enthusiatic about the traditional Democratic liberal candidates like Humphrey and McGovern. To evaluate candidate perceptions in 1988, we used the American National Election Study thermometer measures to tap feelings towards candidates (ranging from 0° for "cool" feeling towards a candidate to 100° for the "warm" feeling, and 50° neutral). In Table 10.2, we look at the feelings of Catholics voters towards the two national presidential nominees, Bush and Dukakis; two very visible and ideological candidates, Reagan and Kennedy; and two candidates with strong religious orientations, Pat Robertson and Jesse Jackson. Unfortunately, the sub-samples were too small to present findings for non-white Catholics, although we can infer something about them by comparing white Catholics to all Catholics.

Bush and Reagan are clearly the most popular candidates with a mean rating of 60° or higher rating among all voters; all Catholics and white Catholics actually have slightly higher ratings. Republican Pat Robertson emerges as the least popular political candidate with a mean overall rating of 32.6°, and he had very little appeal to Catholics

TABLE 10.2 Mean Candidate Ratings for Catholics

Group	Bush Degrees	N	Reagan Degrees	N	Robertson Degrees	N
All Voters	61.6[a]	1218	62.3	1221	32.6	1083
All Catholics	61.8	307	63.3	308	27.3	260
White Catholics	62.1	289	64.3	289	27.2	246

	Dukakis Degrees	N	Kennedy Degrees	N	Jackson Degrees	N
All Voters	56.4	1212	50.3	1186	49.9	1201
All Catholics	58.7	306	54.8	300	50.3	302
White Catholics	57.8	288	53.9	284	49.2	283

[a] Entries are mean degrees of "warmth" towards a candidates, ranging from 0° ("cool") to 100° ("warm").

Source: The 1988 American National Election Study.

and white Catholics, who gave him extremely low mean ratings, 27.3° and 27.2° respectively.

Dukakis received respectable but not overpowering evaluations, the highest of all Democratic candidates, but definitely lower than Bush and Reagan. He received a mean score of 56.4° from voters overall,and slightly higher ratings from Catholics (58.7°) and white Catholics (57.8°). Kennedy's evaluations approximated the neutral point (50.3°) overall, with higher evaluations from his coreligionists, Catholics (54.8°) and white Catholics (53.9°). Jesse Jackson rated a little lower overall than Kennedy at 49.9° degrees, doing better among Catholics overall (50.3°) but a little worse among white Catholics (49.2°). Taken together these figures suggest that non-white Catholics had predictably higher ratings of Democratic candidates, particularly Jesse Jackson, and lower ratings of Republicans.

These candidate evaluations are for groups overall, of course, and within each group a candidate could tap stronger feelings. For example, exit poll data from the primaries shows Jackson receiving a stronger support from Catholics (18%) than from white Protestants (10%) and Jewish voters (8%). Similarly, Pat Robertson did better than expected in the Iowa caucus where some of his first-time primary voters were Catholics (Pomper 1989). Overall, Catholics have had generally positive views of recent Republican presidential candidates; still, they also held more favorable views of Democrats than the population at large.

TABLE 10.3 Issues and Factors in the Presidential Vote

	All Voters	% Mentions White Catholics	Non-White Catholics
Issues			
Helping the Middle Class	33	35	42[a]
Economic Prosperity and Jobs	32	32	33
Punishing Criminals	25	24	26
Not Raising Taxes	19	18	16
The Federal Budget Deficit	16	16	9[a]
Environment and Pollution	14	12	13
Defense Spending	10	9	10
Abortion	9	10	7
U.S.-Soviet Relations	8	9	3[a]
TOTAL RESPONSES[b]	165%	166%	158%
Factors			
Dukakis' Liberal Views	31	29	33
Experience	27	29	14[a]
The Vice Presidential Candidates	18	18	16
He is My Party's Candidate	17	17	20
He Cares About Poor People	16	15	26[a]
Patriotic Values	11	10	6[a]
I Like Him as a Person	11	11	11
The Debates	9	10	10
Jesse Jackson's Role	6	3	10
TOTAL RESPONSES[b]	144%	142%	146%
(N)	(11,539)	(2,666)	(411)

[a] Percentages at least 5% greater than or less than the national sample distribution.

[b] A total of 200% is theoretically possible, but it is considerably less here because many respondents failed to give two responses.

Source: CBS News/*New York Times* 1988 General Election Exit Poll.

Issue Positions

Issues are another factor that influences voting behavior, and some issues, particularly abortion, have been closely linked to Catholics. Generally speaking, however, Catholic issue positions are remarkably like other Americans, so white Catholics tend to hold centrist views, and non-whites tend to be more liberal. These tendencies are shown in Tables 10.3 and 10.4. Table 10.3 presents the findings of a multiple-response measure in the CBS News/*New York Times* Election Exit Poll

TABLE 10.4 Items Perceived as Important in the Presidential Vote

| | % Mentions | | |
Item	All Voters	White Catholics	Non-white Catholics
Abortion	29%	29%	21%[a]
Death Penalty	24	24	15[a]
Illegal Drug Problem	23	25	24
Dukakis/Bush Debates	23	26	35[a]
My Candidate's Political Party	21	21	18
Education	20	20	24
Health Care	19	21	20
Social Security	17	19	18
Environmental Problems	17	18	16
College Costs	11	12	16[a]
Pledge of Allegiance	11	9	6[a]
Prison Furloughs	11	11	5[a]
Foreign Competition	11	13	10
Quayle for Vice President	11	12	8
Bentsen/Quayle Debate	10	11	12
My Candidate's Personality	10	10	9
Iran-Contra Affair	10	10	11
None of These	10	10	9
Bentsen for Vice President	9	10	11
ACLU Stand	8	7	3[a]
Capital Gains Tax	7	7	5
(N)	(22,785)	(5,250)	(660)

[a] Percentages at least 5% greater than or less than the national sample.

[b] Percentages are based on sample data weighted to national population size; N's listed in parenthesis are for weighted data.

Source: ABC News 1988 General Election Exit Poll.

in 1988. Each voter was allowed 0, 1, or 2 boxes on separate lists of the "issues" and "factors" which mattered most in deciding their presidential vote. The data are arranged from the most- cited to the least-cited issues and factors. "Helping the middle class" tops the issue list for Catholics while "US-Soviet Relations" ranks last; in the factors list, "Dukakis liberal views" ranks first, and "Jesse Jackson's role" comes in last. White Catholics closely approximate the distributions for all voters on such "issues" and "factors," while non-white Catholics are more likely to deviate 5% above or below the national percentages. For example, non-white Catholics were more likely to stress the issue of helping the middle class but less likely to mention the federal budget deficit or U.S.-Soviet relations. On factors, non-white Catholics are more concerned about the candidate who is seen as caring for poor people and less interested in experience and patriotic values.

Table 10.4 summarizes the ABC News 1988 General Election Exit Poll data, which asked respondents dichotomous questions about the importance of 20 issues or factors in their vote. The data are again arranged from the most- to least-cited items. Among white Catholics abortion heads the list with 29% and the capital gains tax rated last with 7%. Here again, white Catholics hardly differ from the public at large, with non-whites once again more distinctive. The latter are more likely to have stressed the Dukakis-Bush debates and college costs and less likely to have singled out the death penalty, pledge of allegiance, prison furlough, and the Dukakis ACLU stand.

The abortion issue has been a controversial subject throughout the 1980s. While the ABC News data reveal that it was the issue most often mentioned by Catholics, the CBS News/*New York Times* data suggest that other issues and factors were more influential. Neither exit poll, however, provides information about voters' specific attitudes towards abortion. For this we turn again to the 1988 American National Election Study which includes an abortion approval question ranging from pro-choice (abortion always permissible), pro-life (abortion never permissible), and several "it depends on the circumstances" alternatives.

Among white Catholics, 33% believe abortion is always permissible, 50% say it depends on the circumstances, and only 17% believe abortion is never permissible. These figures are quite similar to the public at large (36%, 53%, and 11% respectively). White Catholics register a higher pro-life position than white Protestants or voters overall, but clearly the majority place themselves in the "depends" category. To assess the effect of respondents' abortion attitudes on their party vote choices, we performed a hierarchical log-linear analysis of abortion approval by party vote (data not shown). This analysis revealed that the effect of religious affiliation on party voting depends upon an individual's attitude toward abortion. For the majority of voters, who approve of abortion under some circumstances, the likelihood of voting for a particular party is about the same as for the overall religion category to which they belong. Thus, such Catholics were still more likely to vote Democratic. However, for voters holding a pro-life position, religion-based differences in party voting are greatly intensified. Pro-life Catholics are much more likely to vote Democratic, and pro-life Protestants are much more likely vote Republican than would be expected from their religious affiliation alone. Among the small proportion of Catholic voters who never approve of abortion, there was more Democratic loyalty than among Catholics overall. Finally, among those who feel that a woman should always be able to obtain an abortion, religious affiliation loses its

TABLE 10.5 Religiosity and Democratic Vote Among Catholics

Church Attendance	Group	President	(N)	Senate	(N)
Weekly or Almost	All Voters	45%	(497)	57%	(351)
	Catholics	55	(138)	66	(116)
Occasionally	All Voters	48	(495)	59	(347)
	Catholics	52	(146)	61	(113)
Never	All Voters	43	(117)	52	(83)
	Catholics	46	(22)	53	(19)

Religious Salience	Group	President	(N)	Senate	(N)
Religion provides:					
A Great Deal of Guidance	All Voters	44%	(177)	59%	(138)
	Catholics	55	(53)	67	(46)
Quite a Bit of Guidance	All Voters	52	(227)	57	(155)
	Catholics	59	(79)	63	(62)
Some Guidance	All Voters	41	(252)	57	(185)
	Catholics	48	(87)	63	(70)
No Guidance	All Voters	46	(446)	56	(297)
	Catholics	47	(86)	54	(70)

Source: The 1988 American National Election Study.

impact on party vote; these individuals are equally likely to vote for either party. Within this group, representing about one-third of voters, the traditional party loyalties of Catholics appear to be reduced. This group, however, is not likely to have been drawn to the Republican Party because of abortion, since George Bush did not share their position. Taken together, these findings provide evidence that abortion did not have a major impact on religion-based party vote choices during the 1988 elections.

Inspection of various other issue questions in the ABC News and CBS News/*New York Times* General Election Exit Polls, coupled with the 1988 American National Election Study, reveals that Catholic voters exhibit centrist or moderate liberal positions across a wide range of issues. Non-white Catholics, of course, are decisively more liberal. We agree with Leege and Welch (1989: 138-139) that "Catholics are more Democratic and slightly more liberal in ideology and on most issue positions than white gentile non-Catholics." In short, Catholics have become more Republican without becoming substantially more conservative on a broad spectrum of policy issues.

Religiosity and the Catholic Vote

The change in Catholic voting behavior suggests that religious affiliation no longer translates directly into support for Democrats. This fact has led some researchers to conclude that religiosity is now more important than religious affiliation in voting behavior. For example, Petrocik and Steeper (1987) suggest that church attendance has become an important determinant of party preference since 1980, with regular attenders more likely to be Republican. However, Table 10.5 reports data from the 1988 American National Election Study that fail to confirm this finding for Catholics. Larger proportions of Catholic votes for Republicans appear to be found among less frequent attenders, and the most frequent attenders are the most Democratic.

Similar results are seen for the effect of religious salience on Catholic voting behavior. Two questions in the 1988 American National Election Study were used to create a four-category scale indicating the amount of guidance over everyday life that religion provided (Table 10.5). Once again, increased religious salience is associated with higher Democratic support among Catholics. The largest Democratic support is found in the "quite a bit" and "a great deal of guidance" categories. Although the situation is unclear for non-white Catholics, these data suggest that greater religiosity buttresses traditional Catholic attachments to the Democratic Party.

Summary

Gallup and Castelli (1987:190) have written that "Catholics are now a two-party church. They are poised to keep the Democratic Party from going too far to the left and to keep the Republican Party from going too far to the right." We agree, but with the caveat that this two-party church still leans more Democratic than Republican. Democrats still dominate the congressional arena, while Republicans have achieved parity in presidential contests. In this regard, Catholics, and particularly white Catholics, resemble the population as a whole.

Our socio-economic profile underscores the importance of dividing Catholics by race, and reveals that white Catholics are remarkably similar to all voters with respect to education and age; but they are, however, slightly more affluent. Non-white Catholics, by contrast, are less well-educated, less well-off financially, and younger than white Catholics and the population at large, much as is the case for other non-whites. The upward economic and educational surge of white Catholics has undermined a critical anchor point for traditional Democratic partisanship, while the socioeconomic lag for non-white Catholics provides class underpinnings for the kind of Democratic Party support that has substantially declined in the electorate since the New Deal.

In 1988 Catholics divided their votes between the parties, with a very slight edge for Dukakis. The latter's margin was due to the heavy support from non-white Catholics, as only 48% of white Catholics cast their ballots for the Democratic presidential ticket. But in the congressional arena Catholics once again supported Democrats at a rate above the national average. Thus, white Catholics are still more Democratic in their voting than their Protestant counterparts, and they still retain a Democratic tendency in partisan identification. Non-white Catholics are, of course, decidedly more Democratic. Given the relative youth of this group, non-white Catholics are the best hope for maintaining the Democratic edge in the "two-party" Catholic Church.

As for candidate images, Catholics, particularly white Catholics, gave high ratings to Bush and the highest to Reagan, but they also registered higher scores for Dukakis than voters overall. Catholics were fairly neutral about Jesse Jackson and were somewhat negative about Pat Robertson. On issues, white Catholics were found in the middle of the political spectrum, approximating voters overall, while non-white Catholics are considerably more liberal. When the two groups of Catholics are combined, Catholics emerge as slightly left of center. Abortion did not, however, have a major impact on religion-based party vote choices in the 1988 election. Finally, religiosity had modest impact on the behavior of Catholics in 1988. Frequent church attenders and those to whom religion is salient are more Democratic, while most Republican Catholics are found in the ranks of the least religious. Thus, while sociodemographic factors, the candidates, and the issues influenced Catholic behavior in much the same way as for other Americans, religiosity intensified traditional Catholic commitments to the Democratic Party.

Overall, Catholics remain a critical swing vote in presidential elections. The Democrats must do better than parity among Catholics to win the White House and they must reach the 6 to 8% of Catholics who currently vote Democratic in congressional races but Republican in presidential elections. Conversely, Republicans must do better in the congressional arena since they cannot hope to control Congress without parity in Catholic support. "One thing is clear," according to Gallup and Castelli (1987:191) "no Democrat will ever be elected president without heavy Catholic support, and no candidate-- Democratic or Republican--can take the Catholic vote for granted."

Notes

1. For most of our analysis we will use the 1988 ABC News General Election Exit Poll (N=22,785). Overall, 28.4% of the sample is Catholic, 25.3% white, and 3.1% non-white. We will also use the 1988 American National Election Study and CBS/*New York Times* General Election Exit Poll where appropriate.

References

Axelrod, R. 1986. "Presidential Election Coalitions In 1984." *American Political Science Review*, 80:281-284.

Dionne, E.J., Jr. 1981. "Catholics and the Democrats: Estrangement but not Desertion," in S.M. Lipset, ed., *Party Coalition in the 1980s*. Pp. 307-325. San Francisco: Institute for Contemporary Studies.

Erikson, R.S., T.D. Lancaster, and D. Romero. 1989. "Group Components of the Presidential Vote, 1952-1984." *Journal of Politics*, 51:337-346.

Gallup, G., Jr., and J. Castelli. 1987. *The American Catholic People*. New York: Doubleday.

Gallup Opinion Index. 1988. Report No. 278:6-7.

Greeley, A.M. 1990. *The Catholic Myth: The Behavior and Beliefs of American Catholics*. New York: Charles Scribner.

_____. 1985. *American Catholics Since the Council*. Chicago: The Thomas More Press.

Hoffman, T.J. 1986. "Contemporary Political Attitudes of American Catholics." Presented at the annual meeting of the American Political Science Association, Washington.

Kenski, H. 1988. "The Catholic Voter in American Elections." *Election Politics*, 5:16-23.

Kenski, H., and W. Lockwood. 1988. "Re-Imagining American Catholicism: The American Bishops and the Seamless Garment," in I.H. Shafer, ed., *The Incarnate Imagination: Essays in Theology, the Arts, and Social Sciences*. Pp. 87-104. Bowling Green, OH: Popular Press.

_____. 1989. "The Catholic Vote from 1980-1986: Continuity or Change?" in T. Jelen, ed., *Religion and Political Behavior*. Pp. 109-138. New York: Praeger.

Leege, D.C., and M.R. Welch. 1989. "Religious Roots of Political Orientations: Variations Among American Catholic Parishioners." *Journal of Politics*, 51:137-162.

Lopatto, P. 1985. *Religion and the Presidential Election*. New York: Praeger.

Petrocik, J.R. 1987. "Realignment: New Party Coalitions and the Nationalization of the South." *Journal of Politics*, 49:347-373.

Petrocik, J.R., and F.T. Steeper. 1987. "The Political Landscape in 1988." *Public Opinion*, 10:41-44.

Pomper, G.M. 1989. "The Presidential Nominations," in G.M. Pomper, ed., *The Election of 1988: Reports and Interpretations*. Pp. 33-71. Chatham, NJ: Chatham House Publishers.

Reichley, A.J. 1985. *Religion in American Public Life*. Washington, DC: Brookings Institution.

Wald, K.D. 1987. *Religion and Politics in the United States*. New York: St. Martin's Press.

11

Jews and the 1988 Election: More of the Same?[1]

Lee Sigelman

As November 8, 1988 approached, the evaporation of Michael Dukakis's once seemingly insurmountable lead over George Bush alerted all but the most blindly loyal Democrats that the Republicans were about to capture the White House for the fifth time in their last six tries and the seventh in their last ten. Widely expected to be among the many sources of this Republican victory was much stronger than usual backing from the Jewish community -- no trivial matter because, even though Jewish Americans are few in number, theirs is the strength of many. Although Jews comprise only two to three percent of the American population, they account for much larger proportions of political activists, financial contributors, and voters. And they are strategically placed in large states that are keys to victory in a presidential election. Indeed, if Jews in New York had divided their votes evenly between Jimmy Carter and Gerald Ford in 1976 instead of casting 80% of their ballots for Carter, Ford would have won New York State and, with it, the presidential election (Solomon 1988:276).

When the dust finally settled in 1988, Bush had routed Dukakis, as expected, but had been treated much more poorly than expected by Jewish voters. Estimates of the two-party division among Jews in 1988 varied, with one post-election poll pegging it as low as 64%-36% for Dukakis, another as high as 77%-23%, and the rest splitting the difference between these extremes (see Table 11.1). Notwithstanding these differences, every poll told essentially the same story. While the nation as a whole was experiencing another Republican landslide, approximately seven out of every ten Jewish voters were supporting the

TABLE 11.1 Estimates of the Jewish Presidential Vote in 1988

Survey	% for	
	Bush- Quayle	Dukakis- Bentsen
American Jewish Congress	23	77
CNN/*Los Angeles Times*	25	75
ABC News/*Washington Post*	29	71
NBC News/*Wall Street Journal*	29	71
Market Opinion Research	31	69
News Combo	31	69
CBS News/*New York Times*	36	64

Sources: Lerman (1984); Penn and Schoen (1988:26); Rothenberg and Licht, with Newport (1982:20-24)

losing Democrats. The long anticipated and, in some quarters, eagerly awaited Republican conquest of the Jews would be delayed by at least four more years.

So, one might well ask, what else is new? Six decades and sixteen presidential elections have now passed since the Republicans last mustered a majority of Jewish voters. Even when most others have forsaken them, as has often occurred in recent elections, the Democrats have been able to count on the Jews.

Was 1988 simply more of the same? The ultimate result -- another trouncing for the Democrats, another handsome Democratic showing among Jews -- certainly had a familiar look to it. But while the 1988 presidential race did continue along a well-trodden path, the path branched off in some new directions along the way. To understand what happened, and what might have happened but did not, we must grasp both the long-term dynamics of the Jewish vote and the specific forces that emerged in 1988.

Liberalism: The "Lay Religion" of American Jews

It is impossible to state with any precision how, prior to the advent of modern opinion polling earlier in this century, the public, including Jews, felt about various political issues. Even today it is difficult to say exactly where Jewish Americans stand politically; because Jews account for only a tiny fraction of the public, the sample for a typical national

TABLE 11.2 The Jewish Democratic Presidential Vote, 1928-1988

Year	Democratic Nominee	%
1928	Smith	72
1932	Roosevelt	80
1936	Roosevelt	85
1940	Roosevelt	95
1944	Roosevelt	90
1948	Truman	67[a]
1952	Stevenson	70
1956	Stevenson	67
1960	Kennedy	82
1964	Johnson	90
1968	Humphrey	82
1972	McGovern	65
1976	Carter	70
1980	Carter	45[a]
1984	Mondale	70
1988	Dukakis	70

[a] In 1948 and 1980 the Jewish Democratic vote was shared respectively by Henry Wallace and John Anderson, each of whom carried approximately 15-20% of the Jewish vote. Figures at five-point intervals represent a consensus of several sources, while those at odd intervals are compromise figures based on differing estimates. All figures in this table should be understood as rough approximations.

Sources: Lerman (1984); Penn and Schoen (1988:26); Rothenberg and Licht, with Newport (1982:20-24).

survey contains too few Jews to permit reliable estimates of their opinions and attitudes. However, by fitting together scattered pieces of evidence and, where possible, by analyzing data from special surveys, it is possible to compose a reasonably detailed political portrait.

The primary features in this portrait are the steadfast Democratic sympathies and unusually liberal leanings of many Jewish Americans. In elections from the Civil War through 1924, Jews usually aligned with the Republicans, the party of Lincoln. But in 1928 they were drawn to the Democratic banner by the liberal Catholic New Yorker, Al Smith. Then in 1932 their love affair with Franklin Delano Roosevelt and the Democratic party began. Jews in the 1930s and 1940s were said to have three *velten* (worlds): *die Welt* (this world), *yenna Velt* (the world to come), and Roosevelt (Cohn 1958:622), and it is estimated that Roosevelt received an *average* of more than 85% of the Jewish vote in his four presidential races (Solomon 1988).

No other Democrat except Lyndon Johnson in 1964 has matched Roosevelt's showing, though Kennedy and Humphrey were also special Jewish favorites (see Table 11.2). Of all the Democratic nominees since Smith, only the unpopular Jimmy Carter in 1980 failed to win majority approval from Jewish Americans, and even Carter won a clear-cut plurality of Jewish votes. What seems remarkable was not that Carter -- a born-again Christian with a "soft" Middle East policy, presiding over a nation mired in double-digit inflation and the Iranian hostage crisis -- failed to carry a majority of the Jewish vote in 1980, but that he was even able to win a plurality.

Not only do most Jews vote for the Democratic presidential candidate once every four years, they are also much more likely than most other Americans to view themselves as members of the Democratic Party. According to a national survey of Jews and gentiles conducted in 1988 (Cohen 1989), one-quarter of all white Americans, Jew or gentile, think of themselves as political Independents. Among white gentiles, the remaining three-quarters are evenly split between Republicans and Democrats; but among Jews, those who identify with the Democrats outnumber Republicans by better than four to one. And along with these pro-Democratic sentiments comes a strong dose of old-fashioned liberalism. Although Jews are not the diehard left-wingers they are sometimes made out to be, they are, on average, a good deal more liberal than other white Americans. According to the same 1988 poll, approximately one-half of white gentiles consider themselves middle-of-the-roaders ideologically, more than one-third describe themselves as conservatives, and fewer than two in ten label themselves as liberals. Among Jewish Americans, too, almost one-half are middle-of-the-roaders, but the proportions of conservatives and liberals are almost exactly reversed; one Jew in three describes himself or herself as a liberal, twice the proportion as among white gentiles. By comparison, black Americans are even more pro-Democratic and liberal than Jewish Americans are. Responding to the same 1988 survey, 84% of blacks identified as Democrats, 11% as Independents, and only 5% as Republicans; 44% of blacks called themselves liberals, 33% middle-of-the-roaders, and only 23% conservatives.

An even better sense of the distinctiveness of Jewish Americans can be gained by comparing the way they describe themselves politically to the self-descriptions given by members of other racial, ethnic, and religious groups (see Table 11.3). Jews stand out from every other group, first and foremost, in their widespread support for Israel, a theme to which we shall return below. But they also rank at or near

TABLE 11.3 Political Self-Descriptions by Religious Group

Self-Description	Groups						
	1	2	3	4	5	6	7
Pro-Israel	86%	27%	17%	20%	23%	20%	36%
Anticommunist	73	54	55	62	74	71	80
Supporter of the Civil Rights movement	61	51	84	55	44	37	33
Supporter of the peace movement	57	55	62	52	47	39	40
Environmentalist	50	48	31	33	41	31	39
Feminist/supporter of the women's movement	47	30	41	28	28	41	20
Supporter of business interests	29	26	28	20	33	28	29
Supporter of the Gay Rights Movement	28	17	11	8	8	11	3
Union supporter	21	24	42	27	31	42	21
Supporter of the anti-abortion movement	18	15	31	33	39	31	45
NRA supporter	4	24	16	15	27	16	39

Group memberships are as follows: (1) Jewish, (2) no affiliation, (3) black Protestant, (4) Hispanic Catholic, (5) white Catholic, (6) white non-evangelical Protestant, (7) white evangelical Protestant. To facilitate comparison, the self-identification items are listed in order of frequency for Jewish respondents.

Source: National Gallup survey, 1987, for the *Times Mirror* Study of the American Electorate. See Gallup and Castelli (1989:214-218); Ornstein, Kohut, and McCarthy (1989:126). Respondents were handed a card and asked the following question: "Now I'd like to ask you a question about how you regard yourself. On a scale from 1 to 10, where '10' represents a description that is perfect for you and '1' a description that is totally wrong for you, how well do each of the following describe you? First, to what extent do you regard yourself as..." Each number given in the table is the percentage of respondents in a particular group that circled 8, 9, or 10 for a particular self-description.

the top of the seven groups in their identification with the civil rights movement, the peace movement, the environmental movement, and especially the feminist movement and the gay rights movement. And they fall at or near the bottom of the seven groups in their support for the anti-abortion movement and the National Rifle Association. On the most heated issues facing the nation, then, Jews are -- to a far greater extent than white Protestants and, indeed, to an extent unmatched by virtually any other racial, ethnic, or religious group -- carriers of the liberal creed.

In their decidedly liberal political leanings, Jews constitute a dramatic exception to the rule that in American politics the more prosperous a group is, the greater its support for conservative causes and Republican candidates (see Fisher 1979:99). Jewish Americans, as a group, have "made it" economically, but one would never know it from their political behavior. Pondering this anomaly, Milton Himmelfarb (1985:40) once quipped that Jews resemble Episcopalians economically but act like Puerto Ricans politically. However, after Jews turned out in large numbers for Walter Mondale in 1984, Himmelfarb was forced to reconsider: "Jews vote like Hispanics," he decided, "only more so."

Debate has raged for years about why Jews are so liberal and pro-Democratic, and scores of historical, cultural, economic, and social explanations -- some complementary, some contradictory -- have been offered for the "American Jew's lay religion" (Yaffe 1968:245) of seemingly unswerving allegiance to liberal causes. The only certainty at this point is that as the two parties headed into the 1988 presidential race, the record of the last sixty years was one of virtually unalloyed Democratic dominance of the Jewish vote.

The Sources of Republican Optimism

Why, then, did the Republicans approach the 1988 election with such high hopes of making major inroads among Jewish voters? As we look back on what turned out to be yet another rejection by Jews in 1988, the Republicans' initial optimism may appear to have been no more than wishful thinking, but they actually had good reasons for expecting Jewish voters to rally to their cause in 1988. Two of these reasons, partially separate but also intermingled, were Israel and Jesse Jackson.

During the post-World War II era, Jewish Americans have been almost unanimously in favor of strong U.S. support for Israel (Lewis 1988), but the electoral impact of this issue has been blunted by repeated assurances from both parties that the security of Israel would continue to be a cornerstone U.S. policy in the Middle East. Because both parties have been so solicitous of Israel's interests, Jewish voters have been free to choose between the parties on the basis of other issues (Mann 1989:4). In the 1980s, however, there were signs of an emerging gap between the parties in Middle East policy. In contrast to the Carter administration, whose relatively even-handed approach to the Middle East discomfited many Jews, the Reagan administration took a tough pro-Israel stance. Continuing in this tradition, the Republicans in 1988 adopted what the Executive Director of the American Israel Public Affairs Committee hailed as the "best platform ever on US-Israel relations by either party" (quoted by Eizenstat 1989: 101).

It hardly seemed unreasonable, then, for Republicans to expect an expression of Jewish gratitude in the voting booth. Reinforcing this expectation was the suspicion that Jesse Jackson, an outspoken advocate of Palestinian self-determination, would exercise great influence in a new Democratic administration (Balinska 1988). A 1979 photo of Jackson embracing PLO leader Yasir 'Arafat, widely circulated in 1984 by Jews Against Jackson (an affiliate of the Jewish Defense League), still stuck in the craw of many Jews, as did his infamous reference to New York City as "Hymietown," his failure to disassociate himself from Black Muslim minister Louis Farrakhan, and reports that Operation PUSH had received funds from the Arab League (Kovler 1985). According to a survey conducted approximately six months before the election, six Jews in ten considered Jackson an anti-Semite, and only one in ten disagreed (Cohen 1989). Jews were dismayed at the prospect that Jackson might be catapulted into a position of power. Some 58% of Jews anticipated voting Democratic in November, 25% were undecided, and only 16% said they would probably vote Republican. But these predictions were made under the assumption that Jackson would not be on the Democratic ticket. When the same question was repeated, but with the proviso that Jackson *would* be on the Democratic ticket, only 24% of Jews expressed a willingness to vote Democratic and 44% said they would vote Republican (Cohen 1989:9).

The Jackson situation put the eventual nominee, Michael Dukakis, in a strategic bind: to retain the support he needed from Jews and other whites, he would have to distance himself from Jackson, but in doing so he would run the risk of alienating black voters. The Republican campaign in the Jewish community sought to capitalize on Dukakis's dilemma by focusing on the GOP's support for Israel and playing on fears of Jackson (Helmreich 1989).

However, Israel and Jackson were not the sole bases for Republican optimism about the Jewish vote. During the Reagan years, Jews, like other white middle class groups, had prospered, so any tendency to engage in pocketbook voting would work to the Republicans' advantage (Balinska 1988). Over the long run, Jews, having spent the better part of the twentieth century climbing the socioeconomic ladder, had attained a position of relative affluence, and an economic program oriented largely to the poor and the working class no longer addressed Jewish needs as directly as it once had (Cohen 1989). Reflecting their altered social and economic circumstances, Jews had, some thought, turned into stand-patters, far more eager to preserve than to transform the existing social and economic order: "They have 'made it' and do not welcome upheavals in societal relationships," Herbert Solomon (1988:281) wrote. "The conservative philosophy of maintaining the status quo, therefore, now meshes neatly with Jewish needs." Solomon expected "a new political era for Jews in the United States" to be inaugurated on November 8, 1988, and in this expectation he was by no means alone.

What Went Wrong?

The Republicans' hopes of finally achieving their long-awaited breakthrough in the Jewish community were dashed for several reasons. In the first place, the issue of Israel did not play out as they had expected. In part, this was because, even though most Jews are concerned about the welfare of Israel, Israel is by no means their *only* standard for appraising presidential candidates. Indeed, when asked whether a commitment to social equality, religious observance, or support for Israel is most central to their identity as Jews, 50% of Jews nationwide cited social equality; only 17% named support for Israel, and another 17% religious observance (Lewis 1988; *Los Angeles Times* 1988). Reflecting these priorities, when the same Jewish respondents were asked which of several issues would be the most important to them in selecting a presidential candidate, only about one in five chose support for Israel (*Los Angeles Times* 1988).[2]

So while Israel was obviously a salient topic for many Jews, by no means was it their sole preoccupation. Accordingly, even if the Republicans were seen as holding an edge over the Democrats in terms of their stance toward Israel, that edge could still be overridden by a Democratic advantage on other issues -- most notably, on the social issues that have traditionally been of such concern to Jewish voters. But the Democrats did not really have to override a Republican edge on Israel, since the Republicans never enjoyed an edge in the first place. It is common for voters to decide who they are going to vote for without knowing very much about the candidates' positions on the issues, even on issues of great importance to them, as Israel is to Jews. Having selected a candidate, such voters often simply assume that their favorite candidate shares their own views on the issues (Berelson, Lazarsfeld, and McPhee 1954). Something along these lines seems to have taken place as Jews made up their minds about the 1988 presidential candidates. Notwithstanding their concern about the security of Israel, two out of every three Jews settled on a candidate without knowing where their favorite stood on support for Israel. Early in the campaign, when asked which candidate was most supportive of Israel, about one Jew in five named Bush, but almost exactly the same number named Dukakis (Lewis 1988; *Los Angeles Times* 1988). So neither candidate entered the general election campaign holding an edge on Israel. As the campaign wore on, had either Bush or Dukakis begun to be viewed as hostile to Israel, there undoubtedly would have been a negative reaction from Jewish voters (Lipset and Raab 1985:145). But this never happened.

Nor did the Democrats have to face the full force of the Jewish disdain for Jesse Jackson, since Jackson did not end up on the Democratic ticket and was assigned a fairly low-key role in the general election campaign. To be sure, many Jews were concerned about Jackson's role in the Democratic Party (American Jewish Congress 1988), and four Jews in ten felt that his influence on the campaign was negative. But surprisingly, almost three in ten considered his impact positive, and the rest considered it inconsequential (Helmreich 1989). Perhaps more importantly, the Republicans' efforts to capture Jewish votes were undermined by a Jackson-style problem of their own: the candidacy of televangelist Pat Robertson and, more generally, the party's continuing association with the Christian Right. Like Jackson, Robertson and his conservative Christian allies deeply unsettled many Jews, even though conservative Christians voiced strong support for Israel. For one thing, as Steven Cohen put it:

> Many Jews have a visceral aversion to political leaders like Jackson and Robertson who make their Christian identity a vital and public part of their political personas. To be acceptable to Jews . . . a deeply religious politician should not appear to allow personal religious beliefs to dictate public policy positions. Mario Cuomo is very popular among Jews; Jimmy Carter was always suspect (Cohen 1989:8).

Understood in historical context, it hardly seems surprising that most Jews prefer a secular political style, whether of the left or the right. But their widespread concern about Robertson was at least as much a matter of substance as of style. Robertson's vision of a nation governed by conservative Christian moral standards genuinely alarmed many Jews, only a tenth of whom said they would vote Republican if Robertson were on the ticket (Cohen 1989:9). Robertson, like

Jackson, failed to capture his party's presidential or vice-presidential nomination in 1988, but his efforts and those of other Christian Right leaders over the years solidified the conservative Christian hold over the national Republican Party. Herbert Solomon's analysis of the resulting credibility gap which the Republicans faced when they tried to court Jewish voters merits careful consideration:

> To put it plainly, Jews still do not trust conservatives. . . . It is not the old anti-Semitism of 50 years ago nor the anti-Zionist form of recent years that [is] so worrisome. It is, rather, the new political thrusts by Christian Fundamentalists and Evangelical Protestants to 'Christianize' America. It is here that Republicans, who have become partners with the Religious Right, are irritating Jewish sensibilities. . . . [I]n their alliance with the Religious Right, they are forced into placating their Evangelical partners by constant affirmations of Jesus-centered policies. To a majority of Jews this direction of the Republican Party appears more menacing than the 'soft' anti-Semitism of Jesse Jackson or of the left in general (Solomon 1988:285-286).

By simultaneously attempting to win Jewish votes and to hold on to their conservative Protestant base, then, the Republicans placed themselves in a strategic bind very similar to the one the Democrats faced in trying to maintain Jewish support without alienating blacks. In the end, the Democrats were much more successful than the Republicans in winning Jewish votes, but since it came as part of a Republican landslide this was hardly the type of "success" the Democrats had hoped for. For their part, the Republicans were, as former Democratic operative Stuart Eizenstat put it, left to ponder the possibility that their quadrennial campaign for Jewish support might prove no more productive than "chasing for the proverbial pot of gold at the end of the rainbow. Just when they think they are close, the prize remains out of reach" (Eizenstat 1989:107).

Is There a "Jewish Vote"?

For the last six decades Jews, along with blacks, have been the most reliable members of the Democratic coalition (Erikson, Lancaster, and Romero, 1989). Accordingly, Jews, like blacks, are typically treated by professional politicians and political analysts alike as a voting bloc. But are Jews really as homogeneous politically as they are often made out to be? Beneath the surface of the Jewish vote lie some social and political cleavage lines that are at least as divisive as anything to be found among Protestants or Catholics.

For example, in 1988 71% of the votes of Jews residing in the eastern United States went to the Democrats, as did 68% and 76%, respectively, of the midwestern and western Jewish vote. However, southern Jews, like their gentile neighbors, were somewhat more restrained in their enthusiasm for the Dukakis-Bentsen ticket: 63% of Jews south of the Mason-Dixon line voted Democratic.[3] Similarly, there was a twelve percentage point gap between Jewish women (76%) and men (64%) in Democratic voting -- a gender gap somewhat larger than that usually observed among gentiles.

Because, as noted earlier, Jews as a group are both unusually prosperous and unusually pro-Democratic, it is widely believed that Jews are impervious to the lure of pocketbook voting (the tendency to vote for or against the party in power based on calculations of financial self-interest). Among all voters in 1988, pocketbook voting was very much in evidence, as the likelihood of supporting the Democrats declined steadily from the lower to the higher income brackets. Income-based differences among Jewish voters, while less dramatic, were nonetheless perceptible: of Jews with incomes of $20,000 or less, 79% voted Democratic; the counterpart figure for Jews with incomes topping $40,000 was 69% -- again, not a night-and-day difference, but one well worth taking into account.

A further source of political differentiation among Jews, and an intriguing one at that, was age. The Bush-Quayle ticket's greatest appeal to Jews was to those below 30: the Republicans drew a respectable 39% among Jewish voters in the 18-24 age range, and did even better -- 44% -- among those between 25 and 29. By contrast, among Jews who had passed their thirtieth birthday, the Republicans managed only 28%. Nor did this difference simply reflect a broader trend that crossed religious lines, for the age-based gap in vote choice was more pronounced among Jews than other voters. This age gap is intriguing, since younger voters are by definition the wave of the future. If the Republicans are able to maintain or even increase their popularity among younger Jewish voters, the long-standing Democratic dominance of the Jewish community will progressively erode. It is for this reason that some see in the Republicans' otherwise bleak 1988 showing among Jews a future silver lining (Helmreich 1989).

This brings us to a final source of political differentiation among Jews: the distinctions among the Orthodox, Conservative, Reform, and unaffiliated. Orthodox Jews are to other Jews more or less as fundamentalist Protestants are to other Protestants, though Orthodox Jews stand out starkly from the mainstream of American life because of their strict observance of religious practice. Reform Jews, on the other hand, approach Judaism more or less as members of liberal

Protestant denominations approach Christianity. Conservatives occupy something of a middle ground between the Orthodox and the Reformed. Nationwide, the Orthodox account for approximately 10% of Jews, with Conservative, Reformed, and unaffiliated Jews apportioned more or less equally among the remaining 90% (Cohen 1989:38).

What it means to be Jewish has been a vexing issue for many centuries, but it is clear at the very least that Jews have progressively been assimilated into the broader American culture and that many of those who do identify as Jews do not actively practice Judaism as a religion. The ranks of the unaffiliated are growing. Thus, for example:

- The percentage of Americans identifying as Jews has declined substantially during the post-World War II era, falling from approximately 5% in 1947 to approximately 2% today.
- Of all major American religious denominations, only Episcopalians are involved in a greater proportion of mixed marriages than Jews are.
- One self-identified Jew in four never attends religious services, and 52% attend only a few times per year -- a much lower attendance profile than that of the average non-Jew.
- Only 44% of American Jews are members of a synagogue, whereas 69% of the general population cite membership in a congregation.[4]

On the other hand, being Jewish, understood in a religious sense, is for many Jews a -- perhaps *the* -- central fact of life. Earlier it was noted that most Jews consider commitment to social equality to be a more vital aspect of being Jewish than either religious observance or support for Israel. However, among Orthodox Jews exactly the opposite is the case. The Orthodox, as Table 11.4 makes clear, are preoccupied with religious observance and are less immersed in worldly issues such as social equality and the welfare of Israel. Reform and non-affiliated Jews, by contrast, tend to view religious observance as relatively incidental to the maintenance of their Jewish identity; they see Jewishness as very much a matter of this world.

Liberalism on social and political issues is not at all characteristic of Orthodox Jews. Heilman and Cohen (1989), in a survey conducted in 1979-80, distinguished among traditionalist, centrist, and nominal Orthodox Jews, based on observance of various ritual practices --

TABLE 11.4 Qualities Considered Central to Jewish Identity

	Orthodox	Conservative	Reform	Non-affiliated
As a Jew, which of the following qualities do you consider most important to your Jewish identity: a commitment to social equality, or religious observance, or support for Israel, or what?				
Equality	18%[a]	44%	65%	63%
Religion	51	19	10	5
Israel	9	21	16	12
Something else	5	6	4	6
Not sure, refused	17	10	5	14

[a] Entries are percentage of respondents listing qualities as important.

Source: Los Angeles Times. 1988. "Poll Number 149: Israel and the Palestinians."

traditionalists being the most observant of the Orthodox, nominals being the least so. For purposes of comparison, they also surveyed non-Orthodox Jews (that is, Conservative, Reform, and unaffiliated Jews), but they were unable to reach the ultra-Orthodox (who, it is safe to assume, hold the most conservative social and political views of any Jewish group). Some items culled from this survey (see Table 11.5) underline the diversity of social and political views that can be found within the Jewish community. To cite only one example, nine out of ten traditional Orthodox Jews condemned homosexuality, as did two-thirds of centrist and nominal Orthodox Jews; but only 40% of the non-Orthodox agreed. More generally, between the traditionally and the nominally Orthodox and, to an even greater degree, between the Orthodox and the non-Orthodox, fundamental differences of social and political outlook can be seen. Indeed, on many issues Orthodox Jews (and especially the ultra-Orthodox) have more in common with the Christian Right than with other Jews (Balinska 1988:7).

Such deep-seated denominational differences in basic social and political orientations are bound to have an effect on election day. In New York City, the Democratic percentage of the votes in election districts dominated by affluent, highly assimilated Jews often topped 80% -- ranging all the way up to 97% on the Upper West Side -- but plummeted below 20% in parts of Brooklyn and Queens dominated by Orthodox and ultra-Orthodox Jews (Balinska 1988:7).[5] Nationwide, one poll estimated that the Dukakis-Bentsen ticket carried better than three-quarters of the votes of unaffiliated, Reform, and Conservative Jews, but barely managed to scrape together a majority among

TABLE 11.5 Social and Political Positions of Jews by Affiliation

Percent Agree	Non-Orthodox	Nominal Orthodox	Centrist Orthodox	Traditional Orthodox
Homosexuality is wrong.	40%	64%	66%	92%
The government should give aid to nonpublic schools.	34	46	65	75
The government should not pay for abortions.	33	44	45	64
A wife should make her own decisions even if she disagrees with her husband.	78	71	65	46
The Equal Rights amendment (ERA) should be passed.	61	48	47	29

Source: Heilman, Samuel C., and Steven M. Cohen. 1989. *Cosmopolitans & Parochials: Modern Orthodox Jews in America.* (Chicago: University of Chicago Press):167. © 1989 The University of Chicago Press. Reprinted with permission.

Orthodox Jews; another poll pegged the Democrats' share of the Orthodox vote nationwide at only one in four (Balinska 1988:7).

In sum, political and social differences abound in the Jewish community. These differences stem, to some extent, from the same factors that operate in every racial, ethnic, and religious group -- region, gender, income, and so on. But they also stem from factors peculiar to the Jewish community, like the age patterning of the 1988 vote and the denominational differences we have just examined. For all these reasons, there is, in the words of Nathan Perlmutter (1985:17), "a vulnerability to positing the Jewish vote as if Jews were a monolithic entity. They aren't, any more than other American groups, and in their parts Jews often reflect the American electorate." Even though Jews, in the aggregate, are ardent Democrats, there are far greater political differences among them than have ordinarily been recognized. As their assimilation into the broader American culture continues apace, it seems reasonable to expect that they will become even more politically diverse in decades to come. As for the Republicans' hopes of winning Jewish Americans over to their side, the realization of this goal seems unlikely in the near future unless there is a truly major reversal of form by either or both of the parties -- say, the abandonment of Israel by the Democrats or a falling out between the Republicans and the Christian Right. Short of that, the best prediction is simply that what has been happening for some six decades will keep on happening, as Jews continue trooping to the polls to cast their ballots for the Democratic presidential nominee.

Notes

1. Thanks are due to John Green, James Guth, Martin Hochbaum, and Carol Sigelman for their helpful comments on an earlier draft of this chapter.
2. Similar priorities emerged in the News Combo Poll, a post-election telephone survey of Jews sponsored by three Jewish newspapers. The candidates' stands on social issues were cited by News Combo Poll respondents as the factor that had done most to determine their vote, with the economy running second and Israel third as primary concerns (Helmreich 1988).
3. These figures and others in this section that are not otherwise identified are drawn from the 1988 ABC News presidential election exit poll. The ABC figures were used in preference to those from other exit polls because of the large size of the ABC sample. The figures given here vary slightly from those presented by Himmelfarb (1989).
4. These examples are all drawn from Gallup and Castelli (1989).
5. These election district figures, however, must be approached with caution. Although the districts are numerically dominated by Jews, they also include more than a few gentiles.

References

American Jewish Congress. 1988. "Jewish Community Vote Heavy for Dukakis." News release, November 9. Mimeo.

Balinska, Maria. 1988. "The Jewish Vote in the 1988 United States Presidential Election." *Institute of Jewish Affairs Research Report*, no. 9 (December).

Berelson, Bernard R., Paul F. Lazarsfeld, and William N. McPhee. 1954. *Voting: A Study of Opinion Formation in a Presidential Campaign*. Chicago: University of Chicago Press.

Cohen, Steven M. 1989. *The Dimensions of American Jewish Liberalism*. New York: American Jewish Committee.

Cohn, Werner. 1958. "The Politics of American Jews," in Marshall Sklare, ed., *The Jews: Social Patterns of an American Group*. Pp. 614-626. New York: The Free Press.

Eizenstat, Stuart E. 1989. "The Presidential Election of 1988," in William Frankel, ed., *Survey of Jewish Affairs 1989*. Pp. 101-107. Oxford: Basil Blackwell.

Erikson, Robert S., Thomas D. Lancaster, and David W. Romero. 1989. "Group Components of the Presidential Vote, 1952-1984." *Journal of Politics*, 51:337-346.

Fisher, Alan M. 1979. "Realignment of the Jewish Vote?" *Political Science Quarterly*, 94:97-116.

Gallup, George, Jr., and Jim Castelli. 1989. *The People's Religion: American Faith in the 90's*. New York: Macmillan.

Heilman, Samuel C., and Steven M. Cohen. 1989. *Cosmopolitans & Parochials: Modern Orthodox Jews in America*. Chicago: University of Chicago Press.

Helmreich, William B. 1989. "American Jews and the 1988 Presidential Elections." *Congress Monthly*, January:3-6.

Himmelfarb, Milton. 1985. "Another Look at the Jewish Vote." *Commentary*, December:39-44.

_____. 1989. "American Jews: Diehard Conservatives." *Commentary*, April:44-49.

Kovler, Peter. 1985. "The Jackson Phenomenon," in William Frankel, ed., *Survey of Jewish Affairs 1985*. Pp. 158-168. Cranbury, NJ: Associated University Presses.

Lerman, Tony. 1984. "American Jewish Voters and the Democratic Tradition: An Analysis of the Jewish Vote in the 1984 Presidential Election." *Institute of Jewish Affairs Research Report* no. 14 (December).

Lewis, I.A. 1988. "American Jews and Israel." *Public Opinion*, July/August:3-55.

Lipset, Seymour Martin, and Earl Raab. 1985. "The American Jews, the 1984 Elections, and Beyond," in William Frankel, ed., *Survey of Jewish Affairs 1985*. Pp. 141-157. Cranbury, NJ: Associated University Presses.

Los Angeles Times. 1988. "Poll Number 149: Israel and the Palestinians March 25-31, April 4-7." Mimeo.

Mann, Theodore R. 1989. "In the Mainstream and Out." *Congress Monthly*, January:4-5.

Ornstein, Norman, Andrew Kohut, and Larry McCarthy. 1988. *The People, the Press, & Politics: The Times Mirror Study of the American Electorate, Conducted by The Gallup Organization*. Reading, MA: Addison-Wesley.

Penn, Mark J., and Douglas E. Schoen. 1988. "Prospects for the Jewish Vote in 1988." *Election Politics*, Spring:24-26.

Perlmutter, Nathan. 1985. "A 'This World' Symposium: Jews and American Politics, 1984 and After." *This World*, Winter:15-17.

Rothenberg, Stuart, and Eric Licht, with Frank Newport. 1982. *Ethnic Voters and National Issues: Coalitions in the 1980's*. Washington, DC: Free Congress Research & Education Foundation.

Solomon, Herbert. 1988. "The Republican Party and the Jews." *Judaism*, 37:276-287.

Yaffe, James. 1968. *The American Jews*. New York: Random House.

PART FIVE

Religion and the Future of American Politics

12

The Bible and the Ballot Box:
The Shape of Things to Come

John C. Green
James L. Guth

New political relationships are most easily recognized in dramatic events, such as wars, depressions and landslide elections, but evidence of new developments also appears in routine politics. Such is the case with religion and American electoral politics: the 1988 election reveals that a fundamental change is transpiring between the Bible and ballot box. The United States is moving away from the ethnocultural foundations of political alignments, based on conflict between religious traditions, toward a more European pattern, in which conservative parties draw heavily from religious groups and leaders, while parties of the left are supported by more secular forces (Berger 1982). And as in Europe, these "confessional" alignments are being produced by modernization, albeit modified and delayed by unique American circumstances. Such a religious-secular cleavage is still embryonic and may constitute only one element of emerging party coalitions, but its harbingers are everywhere.

Religion, Modernization, and Political Alignments

Historically, of course, American parties did not sort voters into religious and secular camps. The reason was simple: Americans were one of the most religious peoples in the developed world. The United States has always been a paradox to social scientists -- deeply religious

207

yet thoroughly modern, believing in God and the machine with equal fervor. Unlike most of Europe, where modernization was accompanied by -- and perhaps resulted in -- extensive and progressive secularization, American religion has adapted to modernity, thereby maintaining the loyalty of most Americans.

Such adaptability had many sources. The absence of a strong state church gave the political "left" few reasons to promote anticlerical or secularist ideologies, and equally important, no single religious group could count on much symbolic or material support from the state (Murrin 1990). Instead, religious voluntarism left entrepreneurs to shape institutions and beliefs to "market" demands: there was a religious product for all tastes -- and if not, one would soon appear (Hatch 1989). And, as Louis Hartz (1964) pointed out long ago, America was a "fragment" society, and our "fragments" were often religious, abandoning older locales to seek religious autonomy, and once in America, they often found religious commitments a crucial source of identity. These conditions produced a dynamic mixture of religious commitment, rivalry, and experimentation which still continues (Wuthnow 1986).

In this environment, religion played a prominent role in politics, operating along three important pathways (Wald 1987:24-27). Religious beliefs often influenced politics directly, particularly when articulated and applied to contemporary problems by religious leaders. Religious organizations often supplied vital resources to political movements and to more durable party organizations, mobilized and directed by religious activists. And religious identifications were often a crucial source of political allegiance in the mass public. Religion had its greatest impact on politics when the pronouncements of leaders, the resources of activists, and the identifications of believers operated in a mutually-reinforcing fashion (Wald, Hill and Owen 1988).

The classic "ethnocultural" or "ethnoreligious" electoral alignments in the United States embodied just such a convergence of religious factors. From the origins of American parties down to the mid-twentieth century, party coalitions were alliances of ethnocultural communities: distinctive social groups whose special beliefs and autonomous organizations buttressed exclusive identifications (Kelley 1979). Religion was one of many conjoined factors, including ethnicity, culture, and, often, social class, that molded cohesive electoral blocs. Unique worldviews, defense of cultural practices, and hostility toward rival groups connected ethnocultural communities to party coalitions (McCormick 1986:38-40).

While these alliances evolved over time, and differed from place to place, two constellations predominated. On the one side were "pietist" Protestants with a reformist bent, who supported first the Whigs and then the Republicans, and on the other, a collection of religious minorities, including Catholics, Jews, and many Southern Protestants, often "liturgical" in outlook, who, together with a few Jeffersonian rationalists and freethinkers, saw the Democratic Party as a refuge from the meddling of moral reformers, the protector of ethnic customs, and the guardian of "personal liberty" (Swierenga 1990). And although the influences of region and class sometimes cut across these alignments, they just as often reinforced them. Even the "class politics" of the New Deal can be seen as a minor reshuffling of these ethnocultural alignments (cf. Petrocik 1981).

The key political characteristic of ethnocultural politics is solidarity. Indeed, religion is often hard to distinguish from other solidary forces since religious beliefs and organizations are at the center of community life. Religious leaders serve dual political roles, embodying the community's distinctive ethos and acting as brokers with outside interests. And religious organizations control resources not dependent upon the good will of the larger society, providing the basis for religious activists, who articulate community values and interests in politics. Thus, religious leaders and activists can evoke group identification to mobilize voters. Not surprisingly, this kind of religious politics declines as ethnocultural communities are assimilated into modern society.

And modernization did eventually have a significant impact on such communities. The initial conditions of American society were strikingly "modern" by European standards, and the pace of social and economic change was even quicker. Massive population movements, steady economic growth, dramatic technological developments, and rapid urbanization, with the accompanying upward mobility, social integration, and expanded education of the population, all put stress on the traditional religiosity of ethnocultural communities.

By the late nineteenth century, the plausibility of orthodox beliefs was challenged by rationalist alternatives, derived from science, technology, and higher learning (Moseley 1981). Likewise, ascriptive ethnic and religious identifications were weakened and replaced by individual choice (Roof and McKinney 1987). And a truly dazzling array of religious organizations gave individuals an ever-widening range of options to choose from, including no religious affiliation at all (Stark and Bainbridge 1985). Indeed, Americans increasingly confronted the "heretical imperative" common to all modern societies: religion is no longer "given" and all are forced to choose (Berger 1979).

Ethnocultural communities responded to these stresses in many different ways. One response was to vigorously reassert "the old time religion," rejecting modernity where possible. The most obvious results of such "traditionalism" were numerous attempts to preserve orthodoxy, producing beliefs capable of combating modern skepticism. Another effect was to develop a large and multi-faceted "carapace" of church and parachurch organizations to protect the faithful from a hostile world (Marty 1986:208). And for individual traditionalists, renewed orthodoxy became a source of intense personal commitment and the central feature of their lives.

There have been several waves of traditionalism in the twentieth century, the best known being the fundamentalist and Pentecostal movements among evangelical Protestants, but including the more recent charismatic movement and other "renewal" efforts among mainline Protestants, Catholics, and even Jews (Wuthnow 1986). These movements also influenced many deeply religious people to whom rigorous traditionalism was appealing but ultimately unsatisfying. All told, traditionalism appealed most to less "modern" people: those still attached to ethnocultural communities, and those characterized by relatively low levels of affluence, mobility, and education (Berger 1981).

A second and opposite response was to "translate" the old faiths into contemporary categories of thought, to "bargain with modernity" (Berger 1979:100). Again, the most obvious results of such "modernism" were numerous attempts to rationalize traditional creeds, producing beliefs plausible to the modern mind. A related phenomenon was the construction of large, bureaucratic organizations to stretch the "canopy" of religion over a broad and diverse body of believers (Marty 1986:150). And for individual modernists, rationalized religion de-emphasized the spiritual and thus occupied a less central place in their lives.

Mainline Protestants, the dominant American ethnocultural community, were the first to follow this path, but other groups, including many Jews, Roman Catholics, and even some evangelical Protestants, followed along eventually, making different concessions to modernity (Wuthnow 1986). In its various guises, modernism also influences many conventionally religious people, to whom religious institutions were no longer fully satisfying and yet still important. All told, this option appealed most to more "modern" people: those less attached to ethnocultural communities, and those characterized by relatively high levels of affluence, mobility, and education (Hargrove 1986).

A third response, closely related to modernism but novel in the American experience, was acceptance of the full implications of modernity: increasing numbers of Americans became secular, abandoning religious beliefs, affiliations, or identifications all together (Roof and McKinney 1987). For these people, religious beliefs were replaced by a variety of rationalist perspectives, many of them openly hostile to religion. A related phenomenon was the emergence and growth of non-religious organizations fulfilling many of the roles once performed by religion. And at the individual level, questions of belief became an entirely private matter, devoid of public consequences and implications (Wilson 1982:ch.6).

Although diverse in views and backgrounds, secularists were especially numerous in the most modern segments of society: those fully assimilated and cosmopolitan, and those characterized by very high levels of affluence, mobility, and education. Secularism also appealed to many people with only nominal religious attachments, to whom such matters were of little consequence except as impediments to their other interests. Indeed, the absence of religion and associated cultural values allowed other concerns, such as economic matters, to have much greater influence.

Despite their apparent differences, these three responses to modernization -- traditionalism, modernism, and secularism -- had a common effect: they diminished the importance of ethnocultural religious communities. By the 1970s, these older formations were being replaced by new divisions, as traditionalists and modernists (often urged on by secularists) were restructuring American religion into rival "conservative" and "liberal" camps (Wuthnow 1988). Extensive mobilization and counter-mobilization by these camps generated intense conflict across the religious landscape (Wuthnow 1989). These disputes, and the responses of individuals to them, concentrated theological, moral, and political "conservatives" in some places within and across religious communities, and their "liberal" counterparts in others (Roof and McKinney 1987). The organizational and social differences between traditionalists and modernists gave these divisions depth and staying power.

This religious restructuring is having important effects on political alignments, first fragmenting and then reorganizing them. The initial effect is the division of religious politics along functional lines: community leaders, activists, and believers often have different concerns, creating a veritable mosaic of political activities (Jorstad 1990). At one extreme, communities suffer from political disjuncture, with leaders and some activists offering comprehensive programs that are opposed or ignored by other activists and the people in the pews. At the other extreme, leaders and activists are demobilized politically because of the costs of controversy or the poor match of political options with their concerns, leaving activists and believers to their own devices. And in between is limited political engagement, where leaders and activists pursue narrow objectives consistent with a fragile consensus within their communities. All told, this mosaic reflects the decline of religious solidarity, undermining old alignments and perhaps setting the stage for new ones.

The next effect of this restructuring is the realignment of religious politics along ideological lines. Across the religious landscape, traditionalists and modernists are gravitating towards different political parties, with the Republicans becoming the home of "traditional values" and the Democrats harboring religious and secular "progressives." Taken to its logical conclusion, the GOP could increasingly become "God's own party," an alliance of religious traditionalists from many backgrounds, while the Democrats could become a "party of modernity," a coalition of secularists, modernists, and the otherwise heterodox. Such a realignment could well revive religious solidarity in politics.

Traditional religiosity *itself* could become an important basis for conservative attitudes and Republican identification, while more modernist or secular beliefs could generate liberal views and Democratic identification. And mutually-reinforcing connections between religion and politics, similar to those found in ethnocultural communities, could be re-established: religious and secular leaders would articulate distinctive theological or philosophical bases for politics, mobilizing activists in religious and secular organizations for ideological combat, and evoking religious and secular identifications to mobilize voters. This would set the stage for a new kind of electoral conflict in America, strikingly reminiscent of European politics: religious supporters of "order and tradition" struggling with secular forces of "rights and reform" over the role of religion in public life, control of schools and curricula, sexual morality, and traditional social arrangements.

Religion and Political Alignments in 1988

In the 1988 election we find a mosaic of connections between religion and electoral politics, but with a clear trend towards ideological divisions. We will organize our discussion around the components of the old ethnocultural alliances, moving from traditional Democratic to traditional Republican groups, and ending with the newest group, the secular.

The Politics of Ethnic Community: Black Protestants. By the late 1980s, the black community was the most reliable element of the Democratic coalition and perhaps the most dynamic force on the left. The special history of blacks notwithstanding, black politics resembles that of earlier ethnocultural communities, particularly in group solidarity. And the church plays a central role both in fostering that solidarity and in mobilizing a political bloc, overcoming numerous hurdles to black participation.

The black clergy is crucial to this process, articulating an "ideology of liberation" that encourages political participation and maintains a distinctive black identity (Lincoln and Mamiya 1990:212-214). These values and the institutional independence of the black church generate a corps of activists who pursue a distinctive liberalism in a variety of forums, from protest marches to community building. The black church was *the* critical resource in the Jackson campaign (Chapters 1 and 6), and also provides key support for other black candidates and for the Democratic Party (Lincoln and Mamiya 1990:215-227). Religious commitment is associated with higher turnout among blacks, reflecting the consistent vision of religious leaders and the cohesion of community activists (Chapter 9).

Nevertheless, religion may be emerging as a source of political division. Black clergy face serious criticism from black intellectuals, often militantly secularist in orientation (cf. Reed 1986), and their churches encounter competition from secular civil rights organizations (Hadley 1985). Furthermore, religious blacks are often quite conservative on social issues, differing substantially from secular blacks, who are more liberal across the board. Such differences help explain variations in black voters' enthusiasm for Jackson, the attraction of many to Pat Robertson's candidacy, and the appearance of a small but vocal cadre of black conservatives and Republicans. Although such incipient divisions are still obscured by the common experience of racial discrimination, they may eventually undermine black solidarity. Ironically, the economic and social integration sought by black church leaders would contribute to the demise of such solidarity and reduce their own influence, much as occurred in other ethnocultural communities.

This possibility is brought into sharp relief by the Jackson campaign. Reverend Jackson's white backers, at least among party activists, were among the most secular groups in American politics (Chapter 6 and 7), and even his support among the white clergy was confined to modernists (Chapter 5). Jackson's attack on established economic elites was a beacon to disadvantaged groups and liberal activists alike, drawing them into the Democratic Party, even in the South, but it also threatened the influence of black religion. The growing importance of secular elements in the black community and the emerging alliance with secular white activists may eventually compromise the unique role of the black church. If this secular versus religious division grows, it would deprive the left -- and blacks -- of a powerful political organization, and perhaps cause the decline of a key Democratic voting bloc as well (Lincoln and Mamiya 1990:233-235).

Old Ethnic Communities: Jews and Catholics. Alternatives for the future of black politics can be seen in older Democratic ethnic groups, such as Jews and Catholics. As Jews climbed the socioeconomic ladder, they became less religious, but remained strongly liberal and Democratic, while "modern" Catholics have become less religious and more liberal on many issues, but also much less Democratic. Unlike blacks, both groups display increasing disjuncture among their religious leadership, activists, and laity, discontinuities that help account for their current political alignments.

Jewish politics shows the influence of religious beliefs as well as their absence. By ethnocultural tradition and specific religious values, Jews were long among the sturdiest elements of the Democratic coalition. Modernity has reinforced, rather than undercut, this position. For many highly educated, upwardly mobile, professional Jews, living in the nation's most cosmopolitan areas, secular worldviews have replaced traditional religiosity with the Jewish "lay religion" of liberalism (Chapter 11). And high status has replaced community connections in fostering political involvement. Such Jews may well provide a preview for apostates from other faiths. As Steven M. Cohen has pointed out, Jewish liberalism still has distinctively Jewish elements, but "other Americans with the same education, with the same religiosity (or lack thereof), and with parents of the same political stripe would be almost as liberal as comparable Jews" (1989:36).

Religious orthodoxy and high commitment are rarer among Jews than in other faiths, but they do, in fact, produce political conservatism and Republican voting, as evident among the Orthodox (Chapter 11). Although Jewish activists in Republican Party circles are not particularly numerous, they are also more likely to be observant than their Democratic counterparts. Thus, modernity has changed the character, if not always the direction, of Jewish alignments: secular

Jews are more liberal and the religious more conservative. Growth of the traditionalist wings of Judaism may eventually reduce Democratic margins among Jews, but by how much is difficult to say. And such sources of new GOP strength may be augmented by other factors, such as economic conservatism, that appeal to the most secular and assimilated Jews, particularly in younger cohorts.

On the whole, Jewish community leaders were remarkably quiet in 1988, displaying a pattern common to many contemporary religious institutions: demobilization. Inaction reflected the social diversity, special sensitivities, and multiple goals of Jews, including both support for Israel and social reform (Chapter 4). What little data exists on rabbinical politics suggests that rabbis may be similarly divided, much like the Catholic and Protestant clergy (Heilman and Cohen 1989). Jewish community leaders and political activists were on balance liberal and Democratic, providing a lion's share of Democratic resources, but not pursuing any one program. And a modicum of involvement also appeared on the Republican side and in a few conservative organizations, particularly on the question of Israel. The net result is that Jewish elites produced no consistent political message, and in the absence of any clear direction to the contrary, most Jewish voters followed their past inclinations, and voted Democratic.

Compared to Jews, Catholics are a much larger, more diverse, but more tightly-organized community. Once firmly embedded in the Democratic coalition due to lower class and minority religious status, many Catholics have moved rapidly up the socioeconomic ladder and into the cultural mainstream (Greeley 1990). Although the "new ethnic" Catholics, such as blacks and Hispanics, still resemble old ethnocultural communities, such as the Irish and Italians, and vote heavily Democratic, white Catholics now closely resemble other Americans, and have consequently drifted away from the Democrats, particularly at the presidential level (Chapter 10).

Religiosity plays a rather complex role in this movement, however. Although Catholics increasingly resemble Protestants in religious observance, they show a different political pattern: those less religious, and more liberal on social issues, are most likely to vote Republican, while the more religious and socially conservative still vote Democratic (Chapter 10). Careful controls for ethnicity and demography might help sort out this situation (Leege and Welch 1989). In the 1988 National Election Study, for example, the majority of very observant Catholics have "ethnic" traits and vote Democratic. But there is also a large minority of highly-observant and assimilated Catholics who vote Republican in presidential elections, and these may provide a core for a traditionalist and Republican faction similar to those appearing among Protestants and Jews. On the other hand, there are also a large number of nominal Catholics, some attracted to the Democrats on social issues and others to the GOP on economic matters.

In any case, modernity moves Catholics away from their traditional religious *and* partisan identifications simultaneously, creating a strong potential for realignment. Traditionalist Catholics could well shift to the GOP, much as evangelical Protestants have done, and other Catholics could remain Democratic on non-religious grounds, like many Jews. Something along these lines seems to be happening among political activists, where Catholics involved in the Republican Party are more observant than their Democratic counterparts. Still, Catholic activists among Democrats range from those who are quite religious and often find themselves discomfited by the party's secularist drift, to a great many nominal activists, who are very liberal and often the most active in the party.

These complex divisions in the Catholic laity surely reflect the mixed cues emanating from church leaders. In recent times, the Catholic bishops have formulated a distinctive Catholic schema to judge parties and candidates, rejecting contemporary ideological choices (Chapter 3). But the bishops' pastorals on nuclear arms and the economy, as well as their efforts on abortion, have met with mixed success. All three campaigns created dissension among knowledgeable laity, with individuals responding according to their own political and social views (D'Antonio et al. 1989:ch. 8). In 1988, the bishops showed much more limited political involvement, attempting to engage *both* sides of prevailing political alignments with little success.

The bishops' attempts to grapple with the emerging ideological divide is immensely complicated by polarization within the national and international Catholic communities. Everywhere organizations of Catholic clergy and laity have lined up along a traditionalist and "liberal" divide. In the United States, the dominant "liberal" faction faces a renewed conservative challenge, not only from domestic traditionalists but also from the Vatican, as John Paul II remolds the American hierarchy in what Penny Lernoux (1989:ch.10) called "the Roman Restoration." As Richard Gelm (1990) has shown, recent papal appointees have been much more traditionalist on religious issues and Republican in their politics, contrasting with the liberal Democratic appointees of the Vatican II era and 1970s. Conservative forces may also be bolstered by clerical recruitment: there is some evidence that the declining number of men entering the priesthood are also disproportionately traditionalist and conservative (Hudson 1986).

If these trends persist, more traditionalist policies may appear in the Catholic Church, and consequently, more defections among liberal clergy, lay activists, and parishioners. Such a pattern would probably increase GOP inroads among Catholic traditionalists, although it is unclear what the effect would be on upscale, marginally-identified Catholics who now vote Republican, or the "new ethnic" Catholics who are solidly Democratic.

The New Guard: Evangelical Protestants. Until very recently, white evangelical Protestants were a Democratic constituency, at least in their primary homeland, the South. However, these evangelicals have substantially shifted their allegiance to the GOP in recent times, joining Northern evangelicals who have been part of the party since its inception. Religion has played an important role in this striking realignment, influencing clergy, lay activists, and voters alike. Although they have not quite achieved the solidarity of black Protestants, evangelicals have voted massively for recent Republican presidential candidates (Himmelstein 1990).

Evangelical leaders played an important role in legitimizing this new political activity. For most of this century, evangelicals were apolitical, concentrating on otherworldly matters. After War II, however, evangelical churches gradually returned to public life, reflecting the rapid upward mobility of their members and their increasingly frequent conflicts with the state (Wald 1990). This trend culminated in the late 1970s and early 1980s, when "born-again" Christians helped elect Presidents from both parties. And although some evangelical groups, such as the Pentecostal and Holiness churches, are not fully politicized, increased activism among their clergy and laity in 1988 foretells more complete mobilization.

Leaders of the more "modern" evangelical institutions, such as the National Association of Evangelicals, practiced limited political engagement in 1988, as in the recent past, pursuing a few issues directly arising from commonly held evangelical beliefs (Chapter 2). They consistently espoused a program of "traditional values," focusing on social issues such as gender roles and sexual practices, but on occasion extending to such American "traditions" as a free-market economy and a strong defense. While ostensibly nonpartisan, this program clearly indicated that, as the party of social conservatism, the GOP was the appropriate choice for evangelicals. This strategy was realistic and has met with considerable success, in stark contrast to the activities of the more militantly traditionalist leaders of parachurch groups, who offered a similar message, but imbedded in a broader right-wing agenda. This agenda proved to be too ambitious even for many traditionalists, let alone the larger evangelical public. Such a disjuncture helps explain the failure of the traditionalist assault on the Republican nominating process in 1988.

It is in this context that the Robertson campaign and the broader Christian Right is best understood. To staff his "invisible" army, Pat Robertson drew heavily on the resources connected with evangelical traditionalists, especially television ministries and related charismatic and Pentecostal churches. These activists were very effective at grassroots politics, much to the surprise of regular Republicans (Chapters 1 and 6). However, the very circumstances that allowed Robertson to mobilize these intensely committed activists precluded formation of electoral majorities: it proved difficult to mobilize even traditionalist voters by religious zeal alone, given their religious particularism and social diversity. Robertson's attack on established cultural elites did have long-term effects, however, bringing new activists into the Republican Party, where they joined other evangelicals and mainline Protestant conservatives.

In fact, evangelicals were broadly successful in mobilizing activists, from campaign workers to ministers. The activation of the clergy was important because of the expanding church resources under their influence. Indeed, church attendance and religious commitment served to increase turnout among evangelical voters as well as to bolster Republican identification and votes (Chapter 8). While evangelical clergy are not yet as active politically as their mainline colleagues, they are rapidly approaching that level (Chapter 5). And the striking convergence of theological orthodoxy and political conservatism gives a broad intellectual underpinning to the new Republican coalition. Thus, the combination of orthodox values, church context, and religious commitment has brought the party preferences of evangelicals into line with their long-standing social conservatism.

The realignment of evangelicals was not without its tensions, however, spawning ideological divisions. For example, the Southern Baptist Convention, the largest Protestant denomination, has witnessed conflict between "fundamentalist" and "moderate" Baptists that threatens to split the denomination (Ammerman 1990). In other sectors of evangelicalism, "conservatives" and "liberals" have formed parachurch institutions, such as Focus on the Family and Evangelicals for Social Action, and these divisions are spreading to the clergy, lay activists, and parishioners (Marsden 1989). Since only a few evangelical activists identify with the Democrats, the effects of this split will be felt primarily within the GOP, as a "hard right," more conservative than Republican, competes for influence with a "moderate right," more Republican than conservative. Indeed, this latter group is made up of the most "modern" evangelicals, and they have much in common with mainline Republicanism.

The Old Guard: Mainline Protestants. Mainline Protestants have long been the backbone of the GOP and still are, changing only slightly over the past fifty years (Kellstedt and Noll 1990). Although mainline Protestants still comprise an important upper-status group, their political importance is diminished by their declining numbers and religious commitment, trends that reflect their "modern" characteristics. Indeed, nominal membership in these churches is very common, and many of their highly educated and affluent offspring have become secular. These trends have caused a great deal of internal dissension, contributing further to the decline of mainline influence (Sweet 1989).

Mainline Protestant religious leaders and parish clergy have moved sharply to the left in recent times and toward the Democratic Party, reprising the liberal activism of the "social gospel" and "New Breed" eras. Deeply influenced by modernist theology and higher education, these church leaders have adopted a "prophetic" posture critical of many aspects of American society, including race and gender relations, the regulation of sexual behavior, the distribution of wealth, international policies, and often as not, traditional religious beliefs and practices (Chapter 2). Despite the religious source of these complaints, the positions taken and the rationales offered usually coincide with those of the secular left (Neuhaus 1984).

The modernist drift of the mainline leadership is far from complete, however, and it has spawned intense conflicts within all of the major denominations. A host of "renewal" and "revitalizing" organizations have sprung up, hoping to steer their churches in a more traditional direction, and they routinely confront "progressive" or "liberation" caucuses dedicated to further modernizing Protestantism (Jorstad 1990). The most common political result is disjuncture: leaders, clergy, and activists operate from different values and on opposing agendas. And the people in the pews hear mixed messages, and often as not, politically unpalatable ones. This pattern stands in sharp contrast to the greater consistency of political cues in evangelical churches, white and black, but resembles the experience of Catholics.

These divisions are vividly apparent among the mainline clergy (Chapter 5). Modernist ministers, especially where they are dominant, are highly mobilized to work for liberal causes. But their orthodox counterparts are increasingly active as well, working for conservative causes and candidates. Where the factions are evenly matched, as in the United Methodist Church, ministers on both sides are effectively demobilized, at least in electoral politics (Chapter 5). These divisions have spread to lay activists as well, whose religious concerns have infiltrated the broader political process (Chapter 7). Mainline traditionalists and modernists are found in both political parties, where they find compatible allies among other traditionalists and the secular. Despite this diversity, mainline Protestant activism still heavily favors the GOP, reinforcing the historic connection of Protestants with the Republican coalition.

Although mainline religious leaders and clergy are overwhelmingly liberal and Democratic, they apparently have only modest influence on their flocks: mainline Protestants vote Republican (Chapter 8). As with their evangelical brethren, religious commitment increases turnout, intensifies Republican identification, bolsters the GOP's share of the vote, and enhances social issue conservatism. Indeed, mainline traditionalists often have more in common with new evangelical Republicans than with less-committed fellow parishioners. And this latter group is quite numerous, evincing less enthusiasm for social issues and offering some modest support for liberal and Democratic causes. For these Protestants, declining religious commitments are often replaced by other sources of party allegiance, such as economic conservatism, as with "modern" Jews and Catholics.

The cleavages between traditionalists and modernists are most fully advanced among mainline Protestants. Indeed, some analysts predict massive conservative split-offs from some mainline denominations, and others note that individual membership defections may have the same effect, creating theologically -- and politically -- homogeneous churches. The creation of ideologically pure, "liberal" Protestant institutions might alleviate factionalism, but only at the cost of membership and resources. And few entirely modernist churches have prospered. The Unitarian-Universalists are a good example. Although this group is far from inconsequential in elite politics (see Chapter 7), it elicits only weak organizational commitment from members and is far less influential than mainline Protestants aspire to be (Tapp 1973). Indeed, the biggest problem facing mainline and other modernists is the lack of committed followers.

An Advanced Guard? The Secular. Mainline Protestants have been challenged not only by resurgent traditionalists, but by the growing number of secular people as well. While relatively little is known about this highly diverse and modern group (Hadaway 1989), their political tendencies are fairly clear: they tend to be quite liberal, more supportive of the Democratic party (though not strongly attached), and hostile to religion and traditional social values. Although some are "libertarians" rather than "liberals," attracted to economic conservatism, they usually unite with liberals when social issues arise on the public agenda (Guth and Green 1990). The numbers, rate of growth, political resources, and social location of the secular give them considerable political influence.

Indeed, secular perspectives are endemic among the "New Class" of knowledge professionals, including journalists, artists, college professors, and lawyers (Hargrove 1986). For some, secularity is neutral and passive, but for others it involves a vigorous rejection of traditional religion, and active hostility to its public influence (Wills 1990:15-25). The membership of many liberal groups, such as the ACLU, NOW, NARAL, Public Citizen, and National Committee for an Effective Congress, is dominated by secular individuals, and thus it is not surprising that these organizations routinely oppose the encroachment of religious values on public life. The secular bulk very large among Democratic party activists at both state and national level (Chapters 6 and 7), and to a lesser extent among Democratic voters (Erikson, Lancaster, and Romero 1989), but are quite rare in Republican circles.

The secular may have serious electoral disadvantages, however. Although they are represented far out of proportion to their numbers in the media and other strategic leadership cadres, their organizations are far smaller than most religious institutions, and generally lack a large grassroots following (cf. Foundation for Public Affairs 1990). Secular activists are less embedded in community organizations, and thus far less active and influential than more religious activists (Guth and Green 1990). And secular citizens are much less likely to participate in politics, including voting, than their social status would suggest (Ornstein et al. 1988). All these liabilities may hamper the Democratic Party, where religious change is both sapping its organizational strength and engendering serious disputes.

Religion and Future Political Alignments

"What is clear," concludes Martin Marty, "is that nothing lasts in American religious politics" (1990:332). Nonetheless, there is much evidence to suggest that a new religious component is appearing in American party alignments: an ideological division between religious conservatives on the one hand, and religious and secular liberals on the other, reminiscent of European politics. While it is unclear how fully and quickly this new alignment will emerge, the prospects are strong enough to warrant speculation about the shape of the resulting party coalitions.

If present trends continue, the Republican Party is likely to solidify its position as the party of traditionalists, drawing strength from the well-springs of traditional religious commitment. The GOP is already the party of Protestantism, with the reunion of its evangelical and mainline wings, and has a special appeal to Protestant traditionalists. To attract Catholic and Jewish traditionalists, however, the GOP must avoid a narrow Protestant image. And the rewards of such appeals would be substantial: a realignment of conservative Catholics toward the GOP could produce a solid electoral majority.

Of course, the addition of conservative Catholics and perhaps Orthodox Jews to the Republican coalition would create new tensions requiring great political skill to manage. Much more problematic, however, is the fate of other groups. If the GOP plays too much attention to traditionalists, more "modern" mainline Protestants and secular identifiers, conservative on economic issues but more liberal on social questions, may well defect. Maintaining a coalition of religious and secular conservatives may be much more difficult than sustaining an alliance of traditionalists, particularly if the Democrats offer palatable alternatives to the secular.

If the Democrats solidify their position as the party of the secular and modernist, the already difficult task of managing a coalition of cultural minorities may become impossible -- and not only at the presidential level. The defection of white evangelicals and erosion of Catholic support have been serious blows to the Democrats, and such defections may well continue, extending eventually to Jews and blacks, albeit on a smaller scale. Although the influx of religious modernists and secularists may augment Democratic ranks in the future, they have not as yet compensated for the loss of older religious constituencies.

Thus, the loyalty of blacks, Hispanics and other new ethnocultural minorities is of particular importance to Democrats, and may be relatively easier to maintain, at least on economic, if not cultural grounds. However, even this prospect is not without its problems: many secularists are not economic liberals, and furthermore, even liberal secularists may threaten the religious institutions crucial to mobilizing minority groups in large numbers. Indeed, managing voting blocs may be less of a problem than replacing the political resources historically provided by religious activists and institutions. New organizational underpinnings will be needed to make a secular party an effective one. Thus, the Democrats may not only become a party of minorities, but a minority party as well.

Of course, many factors will affect the emergence of such alignments. The relative salience of social issues compared to other matters, such as the economy, will hasten or retard the working out of these forces in routine politics. And both the growth of various groups, and the continued effects of modernization on their religious character, will expand or contract their role in party coalitions. If present trends continue, however, this new connection between the Bible and the ballot box will characterize politics in the next century.

References

Ammerman, Nancy 1990. *Baptist Battles*. New Brunswick, NJ: Rutgers University Press.

Berger, Peter L. 1979. *The Heretical Imperative*. Garden City, NY: Anchor Press Doubleday.

Berger, Peter L. 1981. "The Class Struggle in American Religion." *The Christian Century*, February:194-199.

Berger, Suzanne. ed. 1982. *Religion in West European Politics*. London: Frank Cass.

Cohen, Steven M. 1989. *The Dimensions of American Jewish Liberalism*. New York: American Jewish Committee.

D'Antonio, William V., James D. Davidson, Dean R. Hoge, and Ruth A. Wallace. 1989. *American Catholic Laity in a Changing Church*. Kansas City, MO: Sheed & Ward.

Erikson, R.S., T.D. Lancaster, and D. Romero. 1989. "Group Components of the Presidential Vote, 1952-1984." *Journal of Politics*, 51:337-346.

Foundation for Public Affairs. 1990. *Public Interest Profiles 1988-89*. Washington DC: CQ Press.

Gelm, Richard. 1990. "The United States Catholic Bishops: A Survey Research Perspective." Presented at the annual meeting of the American Political Science Association, San Francisco.

Greeley, Andrew M. 1990. *The Catholic Myth: The Behavior and Beliefs of American Catholics*. New York: Charles Scribner.

Guth, James L., and John C. Green. 1990. "Politics in a New Key: Religiosity and Participation Among Political Activists." *Western Political Quarterly*, 43:153-179.

Hadaway, C. Kirk. 1989. "Identifying American Apostates: A Cluster Analysis." *Journal for the Scientific Study of Religion*, 28:201-215.

Hadley, Charles D. 1985. "Black Ministers, Black Political Organizations and the Coming Transformation of their Role in Louisiana Politics." Presented at the annual meeting of the Southern Political Science Association, Nashville, Tennessee.

Hargrove, Barbara. 1986. *The Emerging New Class*. New York: Pilgrim Press.

Hartz, Louis, ed. 1964. *The Founding of New Societies*. New York: Harcourt, Brace.

Hatch, Nathan O. 1989. *The Democratization of American Christianity*. New Haven: Yale University Pres.

Heilman, Samuel C., and Steven M. Cohen. 1989. *Cosmopolitans & Parochials: Modern Orthodox Jews in America*. Chicago: University of Chicago Press.

Himmelstein, Jerome L. 1990. *To the Right: The Transformation of American Conservatism*. Berkeley, CA: The University of California Press.

Hudson, William. 1986. "Parish Reaction to the Roman Catholic Bishops' Pastoral Letter." Presented at the annual meeting of the American Political Science Association, Washington, DC.

Jorstad, Erling. 1990. *Holding Fast, Pressing On.* New York: Praeger Press.

Kelley, Robert. 1979. *The Cultural Pattern in American Politics.* New York: Alfred Knopf.

Kellstedt, Lyman A., and Mark A. Noll. 1990. "Religion, Voting for President, and Party Identification 1948-1984," in Mark A. Noll, ed., *Religion and American Politics.* Pp. 355-379. New York: Oxford University Press.

Leege, David C., and Michael R. Welch. 1989. "Religious Roots of Political Orientations: Variations Among American Catholic Parishioners." *Journal of Politics,* 51:137-162.

Lernoux, Penny. 1989. *The People of God.* New York: Viking.

Lincoln, C. Eric, and Lawrence H. Mamiya. 1990. *The Black Church in the African American Experience.* Durham, NC: Duke University Press.

Marsden, George M. 1989. "Unity and Diversity in Evangelical Resurgence," in David W. Lotz, ed., *Altered Landscapes: Christianity in America 1935-1985.* Pp. 61-76. Grand Rapids, MI: Eerdmans.

Marty, Martin E. 1986. *Modern American Religion.* Volume I. Chicago: The University of Chicago Press.

Marty, Martin E. 1990. "The Twentieth Century: Protestants and Others," in Mark A. Noll, ed., *Religion and American Politics.* Pp. 322-336. New York: Oxford University Press.

McCormick, Richard L. 1986. *Party, Period and Public Policy.* New York: Oxford University Press.

Moseley, James G. 1981. *A Cultural History of Religion in America.* Westport, CT: Greenwood Press.

Murrin, John M. 1990. "Religion and Politics in America from the First Settlement to the Civil War," in Mark A. Noll, ed., *Religion and American Politics.* Pp. 19-44. New York: Oxford University Press.

Neuhaus, Richard John. 1984. *The Naked Public Square.* Grand Rapids, MI: Eerdmans.

Ornstein, Norman, A. Kohut, and L. McCarthy. 1988. *The People, the Press, and the Public.* Reading, MA: Addison-Wesley.

Petrocik, John R. 1981. *Party Coalitions.* Chicago: University of Chicago Press.

Reed, Adolf, Jr. 1986. *The Jesse Jackson Phenomenon.* New Haven: Yale University Press.

Roof, Clark Wade, and William McKinney. 1987. *American Mainline Religion.* New Brunswick, NJ: Rutgers University Press.

Stark, Rodney, and William S. Bainbridge. 1985. *The Future of American Religion: Secularization, Revival, and Cult Formation.* Los Angeles: University of California Press.

Sweet, Leonard I. 1989. "The Modernization of Protestant Religion in America," in David W. Lotz, ed., *Altered Landscapes: Christianity in America 1935-1985.* Pp. 19-41. Grand Rapids, MI: Eerdmans.

Swierenga, Robert P. 1990. "Ethnocultural Political Behavior in the Mid-Nineteenth Century: Voting, Values, Culture," in Mark A. Noll, ed., *Religion and American Politics.* Pp. 146-171. New York: Oxford University Press.

Tapp. Robert B. 1973. *Religion Among the Unitarian-Universalists.* New York: Seminar Press.

Wald, Kenneth D. 1987. *Religion and Politics in the United States.* New York: St. Martins.

Wald, Kenneth D. 1990. "The New Christian Right in America: Mobilization Amid Modernization," in Emile Sahliyeh, ed., *Religious Resurgence in the Contemporary World.* Pp. 49-66. Albany, NY: State University of New York Press.

Wald, Kenneth D., Dennis E. Owen, and Samuel S. Hill. 1988. "Churches as Political Communities." *American Political Science Review,* 82:531-548.

Wills, Garry. 1990. *Under God: Religion and American Politics.* New York: Simon and Schuster.

Wilson, Bryan. 1982. *Religion in Sociological Perspective.* New York: Oxford University Press.

Wuthnow, Robert. 1986. "Religious Movements and Counter-Movements in North America," in James A. Beckford, ed., *New Religious Movements and Rapid Social Change.* Pp. 1-28. Beverly Hills, CA: Sage Publication.

Wuthnow, Robert. 1988. *The Restructuring of American Religion.* Princeton, NJ: Princeton University Press.

Wuthnow, Robert. 1989. *The Struggle for America's Soul.* Grand Rapids, MI: Eerdmans.

About the Book and Editors

The 1988 elections abruptly brought the importance of religion in American politics into sharp focus. Two ministers, Pat Robertson and Jesse Jackson, sought their party's presidential nominations by mobilizing key religious constituencies. In addition, a host of other religious groups, from the Catholic bishops to the Jewish community, sought to influence the election outcome. More than ever, religion was a critical factor in the ballots cast by millions of Americans. As the twentieth century draws to a close, it is clear that religion will continue to be a powerful factor in electoral politics.

This volume investigates the many ways religion influenced electoral politics in 1988, tracing the links between elites, activists, and voters in the major religious traditions. Special attention is paid to the leaders of Protestant, Catholic, and Jewish organizations; to important sets of activists, such as ministers, party leaders, and campaign contributors; and to the behavior of key voting blocs, including white evangelical and mainline Protestants, black Protestants, Catholics, and Jews.

James L. Guth is professor of political science at Furman University, where he chairs the Department of Political Science. He has published extensively on interest groups, campaign finance, and religion and politics and is best known for his research on the politics of the Southern Baptist clergy. **John C. Green** is associate professor of political science and director of the Ray C. Bliss Institute of Applied Politics at the University of Akron. His research interests include campaign finance and religion and politics.

Index